B 29 P4633   Philosophical subjects: essays presented to P.F. Strawson.

81-406

JUL 2000

JUN 2004

JUN 09

JUL X X 2015

WITHDRAWN

PHILOSOPHICAL SUBJECTS:
ESSAYS PRESENTED TO P. F. STRAWSON

PHILOSOPHICAL SUBJECTS

Essays Presented to P. F. Strawson

EDITED BY

ZAK VAN STRAATEN

CLARENDON PRESS · OXFORD

1980

Oxford University Press, Walton Street, Oxford OX2 6DP

OXFORD LONDON GLASGOW
NEW YORK TORONTO MELBOURNE WELLINGTON
IBADAN NAIROBI DAR ES SALAAM LUSAKA CAPE TOWN
KUALA LUMPUR SINGAPORE JAKARTA HONG KONG TOKYO
DELHI BOMBAY CALCUTTA MADRAS KARACHI

© *The several contributors listed on pages v and vi, and, so far as the residual copyright in the whole work is concerned, Oxford University Press 1980*

All rights reserved. No part of this publication may be reproduced, stored in a retrieval system, or transmitted, in any form or by any means, electronic, mechanical, photocopying, recording, or otherwise, without the prior permission of Oxford University Press

Published in the United States by
Oxford University Press, New York

British Library Cataloguing in Publication Data
Philosophical subjects.
   1. Philosophy—Addresses, essays, lectures
  I. Strawson, Peter Frederick
  II. Van Straaten, Zak
  100   B29   80–40185

ISBN 0–19–824603–X

Set, printed and bound in Great Britain by Fakenham Press Limited, Fakenham, Norfolk

Preface

Professor Strawson is a philosopher's philosopher. The philosophical literature of the last twenty-five years exhibits the considerable influence which his work has had on professional philosophers. The wealth of ideas which occur in his works in such fields as the philosophy of logic, logic, the philosophy of language, the philosophy of mind, Kant scholarship, aesthetics, and moral philosophy have produced a lively secondary literature. Two prominent instances are his debates with Russell on the theory of descriptions, and with Quine on aspects of philosophical logic.

In the present volume twelve philosophers present essays to P. F. Strawson on the occasion of his sixtieth birthday. All of the essays are original and occur here for the first time. The great variety of topics canvassed in the essays reflects the broad sweep of Professor Strawson's philosophical interests.

Professor Strawson has replied to all the contributors, and it is his replies, taken as a whole, which give a valuable and unique insight into his philosophical beliefs.

Peter Frederick Strawson was born on 23 November 1919. He was educated at Christ's College, Finchley, and St. John's College, Oxford, where he read Philosophy, Politics, and Economics, graduating with a BA in 1940. His career was interrupted by war service (1940–6) in the Royal Artillery, and the Royal Electrical and Mechanical Engineers. Professor Strawson's first teaching position was as Assistant Lecturer in Philosophy at the University College of North Wales (1946–7). In 1947 he was appointed to a Lectureship at University College, Oxford, becoming a fellow of University College in 1948, where he remained for the next twenty years (1948–68). He was promoted to Reader in 1966 and when Gilbert Ryle retired in 1968 Strawson succeeded him as Waynflete Professor of Metaphysical Philosophy. His appointment to one of the four chairs of philosophy in the University of Oxford meant that

Strawson had to move from University to Magdalen College, the traditional home of the Waynflete professor.

Professor Strawson was Visiting Professor at Duke University (1955–6), and Visiting Professor at Princeton University (1960–1: 1972). He has also lectured or read papers at universities or institutions in the United States of America, Canada, Mexico, Argentina, India, Israel, and a number of European countries.

Numerous Honours have been bestowed on Professor Strawson through the years. These include being created a Fellow of the British Academy in 1960; a Foreign Honorary Member of the American Academy of Arts and Sciences in 1971; and an Honorary Fellow of St. John's College, Oxford in 1973. In the Queen's Jubilee year, 1977, Professor Strawson was knighted in recognition of his philosophical work and academic leadership.

My hope is that the present volume, in addition to paying homage to Professor Strawson on the occasion of his sixtieth birthday, will stimulate the continuing debates on, and discussions of, Professor Strawson's philosophical works.

Zak Van Straaten

Contents

FREE-WILL AND RATIONALITY *A. J. Ayer*	1
ACCOUNTABILITY *Jonathan Bennett*	14
THE TRANSCENDENTAL 'I' *J. L. Mackie*	48
THE PRIMITIVENESS OF THE CONCEPT OF A PERSON *Hidé Ishiguro*	62
THINGS WITHOUT THE MIND—A COMMENTARY UPON CHAPTER TWO OF STRAWSON'S *INDIVIDUALS* *Gareth Evans*	76
MEANING, COMMUNICATION, AND KNOWLEDGE *John McDowell*	117
THE INDIVIDUATION OF PROPER NAMES *L. Jonathan Cohen*	140
THE VARIABLE AND ITS PLACE IN REFERENCE *W. V. Quine*	164
STRAWSON ON SUBJECT AND PREDICATE *P. T. Geach*	174
WHAT WOULD BE A SUBSTANTIAL THEORY OF TRUTH? *David Wiggins*	189
INTENTIONS AS JUDGEMENTS *David Pears*	222
PRIMA FACIE OBLIGATIONS *John R. Searle*	238
P. F. STRAWSON REPLIES	260
SELECT BIBLIOGRAPHY OF P. F. STRAWSON'S PRINCIPAL PUBLICATIONS	297
INDEX OF NAMES	301

Free-will and Rationality

A. J. Ayer

In his most interesting and influential essay on 'Freedom and Resentment'[1] Professor Strawson has done us a great service in drawing our attention to the very wide range of attitudes and judgements in which the notion of responsibility plays an essential part. Discussions of the perennial issue of Free-will and Determinism have tended to concentrate far too narrowly on the question of punishment. The result is that those who have sought to argue that we do not need to be free in order to be responsible, or that if we do it is not in any sense that is inconsistent with determinism, have had things made easier for them by the fact that the idea of retributive punishment has fallen rather into disrepute. This has helped to secure a more favourable reception for their contention that nothing of value will be lost if the notion of responsibility is analysed or revised in such a way that agents are held responsible, and therefore liable to be rewarded or punished, for their actions, only in cases where there is good reason to believe that the prospect and bestowal of rewards and punishments will so affect them and others as to increase the likelihood of their behaving in future in ways that are considered socially beneficial and decrease the likelihood of their behaving in ways that are considered socially harmful.

Even in this relatively narrow area, I think that there has been a tendency to underrate the extent to which this purely utilitarian approach is at variance with our ordinary ways of thinking. Even those who are emotionally repelled by the association of punishment with the idea of revenge, or those who regard the notion of expiation as intellectually or morally indefensible, will still be found adhering to two principles which do not fit into the utilitarian pattern. These principles

[1] *Proceedings of the British Academy*, 1962. Reprinted in Sir Peter Strawson's *Freedom and Resentment and Other Essays*.

are first that persons ought not to be punished for offences which they have not committed; and secondly that they ought not to be punished for actions which it was not in their power to avoid. The second principle is subject to some elasticity. For instance, it may be that someone has reached a state in which it is not in his power to avoid acting as he does, but he is still held liable to punishment because his being in that state is thought to be the result of previous actions which it was in his power to avoid: or it may be that someone is exonerated for an action which he was thought capable of avoiding, but only at a price, such as the probable loss of his life, which it was not in the circumstances thought reasonable for him to pay.

I know that utilitarians have made an effort to accommodate at least the first of these principles within their theory. To my mind, this effort has not been successful. I think that their theory will still be found to authorize the taking of punitive action, as a purely preventive or deterrent measure, in circumstances where it would not, in the general view, be morally justified and would, indeed, do violence to their own moral sentiments, if these were not wholly subjugated to their theory. This is not, however, a question that I wish to argue here. I am not concerned to criticize our utilitarians for depriving us of our concept of justice or for their failure, if indeed it is a failure, to make the loss good. I want only to stress the fact that they do deprive us of it and the reasons for which they do so. They deprive us of it by severing the historical connection, which there undoubtedly has been and indeed continues to be for most minds, between the concept of justice and the concept of desert, and the reason why they do so is that, while wishing to preserve as much of the idea of justice as is capable of rescue, they believe that the concept of desert is empty, if not meaningless, in the light of the possibility that all human actions are determined.

The service which Strawson has rendered us is to draw out the full implications of this rejection of the concept of desert. As he rightly points out, it is not only the concept of justice that is affected but almost all the concepts that enter into our estimations of one's own and other people's worth. We do indeed feel admiration or distaste for people's natural endowments, their good or bad looks, their native intelligence or stupidity, the good or bad dispositions which seem to form part of their genetic inheritance. To a very much greater extent, however, our judgements of their merits and demerits, and the feelings with which these judgements are allied, relate to qualities and dispositions which we imply that the agent need not have developed and to behaviour which it was, or at least once had been, in his power to avoid. Strawson reminds us how often in our relations with one another we display and think that we have good reason to display such feelings as gratitude and resentment, how we take pride in our achievements and feel remorse for our misdeeds, how actions to which we are not a party can evoke our moral approval or indignation. In all these cases there is a tacit or explicit reference to the concept of desert. A person who does me a benefit deserves my gratitude because he could have withheld the favour. I feel remorse for my neglect of my friends, because I could have taken more trouble to please them. In my hatred of tyranny, wherever it is displayed, the idea is implicit that the tyrant could have restrained himself, or even if this is no longer possible, that he himself is at least partly to blame for having become the monster that he is. But how can any of these attitudes be justified if there is even any probability that determinism reigns over all actions, and if one of the consequences of determinism is that no one could ever have acted otherwise than as he did?

Strawson himself does not put the issue quite so sharply, partly no doubt because he begins by allying himself with those who say that they do not know what the thesis of determinism is. He can afford to adopt this standpoint because his ignorance of the exact content of determinism is not such as to preclude his knowing that it is a general thesis about the springs of human conduct, and the main point which his essay is intended to establish is that no thesis which applies to human conduct indiscriminately can pose such a threat as I have been describing. More concretely, if we follow him in speaking of the feelings and judgements, which carry the implication of desert, as entering into 'ordinary inter-personal relationships'[2] as well as into our assessments of moral worth, and if we follow him also in speaking of someone who judges or responds to human behaviour only from the point of view of its causes and effects as taking an 'objective attitude'[3] towards it, then his contention is

[2] Op. cit., p. 11.   [3] Ibid., p. 12.

first that 'it is practically inconceivable'[4] that the acceptance of the thesis of determinism, whatever it may turn out to be, would lead to a thoroughgoing substitution of 'objective attitudes' for those that currently figure in our moral assessments and our interpersonal relationships, and secondly that even if this substitution could actually be made, it would not be rational to make it.

So far as I can see, the only argument which Strawson advances in favour of the first of these contentions is that whenever we do adopt an objective attitude towards some agent, either in respect of some or all of his actions, it is always for a special reason. Our resentment of what we should otherwise regard as an injury is inhibited, even when it is the work of one whom we take to be a responsible agent, because we have reason to believe that in this particular case he did not intend it or was subject to some pressure which it would not have been reasonable to expect him to resist. In such circumstances his action does not qualify as an injury. In other cases the disqualification may attach to the agent, if we judge that through no fault of his own he wasn't fully in command of himself. These cases are episodic, but there is also an important sub-class of cases in which an agent is persistently absolved from responsibility, because we view him 'as psychologically abnormal – or as morally undeveloped'.[5] It is only in cases such as these that we tend to treat the person in question not as an appropriate object of our ordinary interpersonal attitudes, but 'as an object of social policy'; someone 'to be managed or handled or cured or trained'.[6] And the same considerations apply to what Strawson calls our vicarious moral judgements. It is only when for some special reason the agent is seen in an 'abnormal light' that we think it inappropriate to react to his behaviour in the ways that are characteristic of our regarding him as 'a member of the moral community'.[7]

The reason, then, why Strawson thinks it unnecessary for his purpose to explore the general thesis of determinism is that on the comparatively rare occasions on which we do adopt a purely objective attitude towards our fellow human beings, it is always the result of our detecting some special sort of abnormality in their natures or in the conditions under which they have

[4] Ibid., p. 11.   [5] Ibid., p. 8.   [6] Ibid., p. 9.   [7] Ibid., p. 17.

acted, and that for the rest 'the human commitment to participation in ordinary interpersonal relationships is too thoroughgoing and too deeply rooted for us to take seriously the thought that a general theoretical conviction might so change our world that, in it, there were no longer any such things as interpersonal relationships as we normally understand them'.[8] Consequently, no matter what the general thesis of determinism turns out to be, and however strong the arguments in its favour, we can rely on the fact that 'a sustained objectivity of interpersonal attitudes, and the human isolation which this would entail, does not seem to be something of which human beings would be capable'.[9]

Now Strawson may very well be right in making this empirical conjecture. Many philosophers and scientists have accepted or believed that they accepted a general thesis of determinism, and no doubt many laymen have followed their lead, but I do not think that any scientific enquiry has yet been made into the effect that this has had upon their social outlook. There is indeed the example of Professor Skinner who has written of the general adoption of the objective attitude not only as a future possibility but as a condition of his picture of Utopia, but I do not know whether he consistently adheres to this position in his own private life. It would cast no deep shadow on his sincerity if he did not, since from his point of view it would prove no more than that his own conditioning had been imperfect. So far as my own observation goes, professing determinists are not the less likely to feel gratitude or resentment, or pride or remorse or moral indignation, or to avoid any of the other commitments which their theory might be expected to deny them. If this is generally true, it is a point in Strawson's favour. Even so, I think that he reaches his conclusion too easily, and my ground for this charge lies in his avoidance of any discussion of the general thesis of determinism. I hope to show that the content which it is reasonable to attach to the thesis is not so irrelevant to his argument as he supposes it to be.

Let me say at once that I do not myself propose to examine the thesis in depth. There are just two points about it that seem to me to have an important bearing upon the present question. The first of them is that the thesis is vacuous if it claims no more

[8] Ibid., p. 11.   [9] Ibid.

than that every human action is subject to law; for any collection of phenomena whatsoever can be made to fit some set of generalizations, if no restrictions are placed on the character of these generalizations or their complexity. The thesis is worth discussing only if it is interpreted as claiming that all human actions are subject to what I call manageable laws; that is to say, the generalizations have to be such that we could actually use them to explain every facet of human behaviour, and that not merely *ex post facto*; they would have to enable us to make consistently successful predictions. In this form, the thesis has surely not been proved to be true. On the other hand, I do not think that we have any *a priori* reason for rejecting it.

The second and more important point is linked to the first. The thesis owes its force in this context to its being taken to entail that no one could ever have acted otherwise than as he did. We need, therefore, to examine what this conclusion comes to. I think it useless to begin with the suggestion that 'he could have acted otherwise' means 'he would have acted otherwise, if he had chosen'. Not only is the equivalence open to doubt, but at best it only leads to the question whether he could have chosen otherwise, on which we gain no foothold with this approach. A more profitable course, as I see it, is to ask under what conditions we actually judge that a man could not have acted otherwise, or conversely that he could. And here the answer does not seem to me far to seek. The cases in which we judge that the man could not have acted otherwise are those in which our beliefs encompass a set of particular facts and a set of well-established hypotheses which together entail or at least make it highly probable that he acted as he did. I ignore for the sake of simplicity the class of cases in which we judge that an action was avoidable but that it would not have been reasonable in the circumstances to expect the agent to avoid it. Conversely, the cases in which we judge that the man could have acted otherwise are those in which we are not in a position to draw the inference that he acted as he did, whether the shortage lies in our command of the requisite facts or the well-established hypotheses, or both. Obviously, to escape making it trivially true that all actions which are known to have occurred were unavoidable, it has to be stipulated that the stock of particular facts to which appeal can be made does not include the fact that the action in question took place, or any fact which entails it without the assistance of some available hypothesis.

The consequence of this analysis is that the question whether or not a person could on some particular occasion have acted otherwise than as he did is made relative to the state of our knowledge. There might be thought to be a problem as to whose knowledge is at issue, but I think that this can be circumvented. We can regard the claim that a person could have acted otherwise in a given instance as an open challenge to produce the information which would meet the conditions laid down for judging that he could not, and so long as this information is not forthcoming the claim remains acceptable.

Now it is noteworthy that the exceptional cases in which, as Strawson recognizes, we tend to adopt an 'objective' rather than a 'personal' attitude towards a particular action, or towards the over-all behaviour of a particular type of agent, are those in which we do think that we command a set of scientific hypotheses from which, in conjunction with facts which are practically ascertainable if not already ascertained, the conclusion that the behaviour takes place can be derived with at least a high degree of probability and in quite a specific form, even if it does not reach down to every detail. It is indeed true that the actions of those whom we do include in the moral community, with all that Strawson takes this to imply, are not always or even very often such as greatly surprise us. Our friends and acquaintances form habits with which we become familiar. There are social norms with which we can usually trust them to comply. Our treating them as responsible agents is not just dependent on the greater difficulty that we have in predicting what they will say and do. The difference lies rather in the way that we arrive at these conclusions. Whatever justification we may have for attributing to them the personal character, and the particular beliefs and intentions, in terms of which we account for their behaviour, the generalizations involved are not accorded the status of scientific laws. They are statements of tendency which are not thought to be sufficiently strong or far-reaching to make the actions which they govern unavoidable. They do not sustain the verdict that the agent could not have acted otherwise.

This does not mean that the actions which we are accustomed to view in this fashion are thought to be incapable of being explained scientifically. There have indeed been 'libertarians',[10] as Strawson calls them, who have regarded the ascription of free will to human beings as requiring that if the actions which they freely perform are caused, their causes must include as a necessary condition an exercise of the will which is itself spontaneous; and faced with this difficulty have opted for free will. One of the weaknesses of their position, as Strawson remarks, is that this notion of the spontaneous exercise of the will is very obscure. If what is meant is that there is a random factor in what we choose to do, then it does not seem that the libertarians will have gained their objective, even if they are right. For why should the extent to which our actions occur by chance make us any more responsible for them than we would be if they were causally determined?

The more common view nowadays is, however, one that sets no *a priori* limit in this domain to the extension of the empire of science. For instance, many philosophers hold that what we normally classify as mental events are factually identical with events in the subject's brain, and they think it likely that events in the brain are subject to causal laws. Even so, this belief does not appear to inhibit them from making moral judgements, of a not purely utilitarian kind or from entering, as Strawson puts it, into 'ordinary interpersonal'[11] relationships. Are we to infer from this that they are inconsistent, or that their materialistic beliefs are not entirely sincere? Is it simply a vindication of Strawson's thesis that the thoroughgoing adoption of an 'objective attitude' is practically inconceivable?

It is tempting just to say 'Yes' to all three of these questions, but I think that it would be wrong. I suggest that what saves these philosophers from inconsistency is that their theory of the physical determination of mental events is not a working theory. They may sincerely believe that some specific theory of this sort is true, but they do not in fact know how it operates. They are not in a position to put any such theory to any widespread practical use. Physiology does not yet provide us with a complete explanation of the transition from one particular brain-state to another, or with the means of identifying or even uniquely correlating particular mental with cerebral

[10] Ibid., p. 25.   [11] Ibid., p. 17.

events. Possibly these theoretical advances will be made, but even if they are, there will still be some way to go before the theory can be put to much practical use. To make only one simple point, it is not easy to see how we are going to be furnished with the requisite information about the current states of people's brains. Consequently, if my analysis is correct, a philosopher who believes that a given action was physically determined can still truly say that the agent could have acted otherwise. He can say so because we do not have the detailed scientific knowledge from which to derive the conclusion that the agent acted as he did.

But now suppose that this were altered. Suppose that the requisite physiological or psycho-physical theories were developed and that we could use them in everyday life to make mainly accurate predictions. Or if this be thought too fanciful, let us suppose that the theory of conditioning were developed to a point where it became possible to implant desires and beliefs and traits of character in human beings, to an extent that it could be deduced, at least in fairly general terms, how any person who had been treated in this way would most probably behave in a given situation, and that we lived under a regime in which these powers were exercised upon us, let us say from early childhood. It may be remarked that there have been, and are, regimes in which a very large measure of such control has been seriously attempted; and that the historical evidence tends to show that its effects are not so overwhelming as some behavioural psychologists would have us believe. This is not, however, the point at issue. We are once again postulating a scientific advance to which, so far as I can see, there is no objection of logical principle. We are supposing that the methods of conditioning, to whatever ends they may be directed, are both universally employed and almost totally effective, and the question is whether our interpersonal attitudes would be likely to withstand them.

My own view is that they most probably would not, unless, what is also conceivable, the conditioning itself were directed towards their preservation. Otherwise, I think that if it were a matter of common knowledge that these methods were practised, and if we understood the ways in which they operated, or even just the nature of their effects, sufficiently well to be able to account by their means for almost everything that anybody said or did, we should be most strongly disposed to assume an objective attitude not only towards our fellow human beings but even towards ourselves. It would be as if we were spectators of a play in which we also participated with no other option than to enact the roles allotted to us. Even those who were charged with writing and directing the play would see themselves as guided to frame it along certain specific lines. We could still attach moral and aesthetic values to the ways in which the various characters performed, but the judgements and attitudes which depend on our seeing people as responsible agents would be missing.

Would such a point of view be rational? It might be argued that the question does not arise. If we have come to a point where we see everything as decided for us, we shall hardly be troubled with the question what decisions we ought to take. 'Things and actions are what they are and the consequences of them will be what they will be.'[12] We should no longer have the inclination to 'desire to be deceived'.[13] Once again, however, the position may not be quite so simple. For instance, if the general belief that we cannot act otherwise than as we do were derived not from the prevalence of conditioning but from the general acceptance of a working physiological theory, then the fact of our believing that a causal explanation of each of our choices was readily available might not preclude our seeing the choices as needing to be made. I think that it would make some difference here whether we knew that the result of our deliberation had actually been predicted, and one need not assume that this would always be the case. It is anyhow worth noting that our ability to explain such things as the drawing of inferences does not dispense them from their subjection to normative standards. However detailed our knowledge of the way in which a calculating machine works, we can still coherently raise the question whether its calculations are correct.

An easier course of argument, which will have the advantage of giving the question of rationality a keener point, is to suppose that we are at a stage where the development of efficient processes of over-all conditioning is admitted to be practically feasible, and the question which we have to decide is whether we

[12] Bishop Butler, *Fifteen Sermons*, No. 7, para. 16.   [13] Ibid.

should favour or oppose it. The possibility of there being a causal explanation for our coming to whatever decision we do is not a factor in this argument since we are still in a position in which, if I am right in my analysis, either decision is open to us. Let us suppose also that we are taking for granted the truth of the very dubious proposition that the policy to which the conditioning was adapted would be and remain beneficent, and that we see it as leading to the prevalence of objective attitudes. Would it be rational for us in this case to favour 'the march of mind'?[14]

Strawson's answer is that it would not. He views rational choice 'in the light of an assessment of the gains and losses to human life, its enrichment or impoverishment'[15] and considers that from this point of view a state of affairs in which objective attitudes were generally prevalent would be of less value than one in which our present commitments to interpersonal relations were maintained. So far as I can see, he offers no argument in favour of this conclusion, and indeed I think that we should not expect him to. He had taken the issue to a point where it becomes a matter of moral sentiment, and we have only, as William James once put it, 'to confess to each other the motives for our several faiths'.[16]

For my part, I am strongly inclined to side with Strawson on this matter, but I have a qualm which he does not seem to share. As he hints in a footnote,[17] there is another sense of 'rational' in which the rationality of an attitude is measured not by the probable consequences of adopting it but by the standing of the beliefs which enter into it. In this sense, an attitude is irrational if it rests on a belief which we have no good reason for accepting: more seriously so, if it rests on a belief which we have good reason to reject. Such reasons may be various: but one of them surely is that the belief requires the satisfaction of a concept which dissolves on analysis, where what I mean by its dissolving is that a dissection of it reveals no possible circumstances in which its application would be justified.

Now my trouble is that I believe this to be true of the concept of desert. I do not deny that the extension with which this concept is unwarrantably credited could be roughly covered by

---

[14] See T. L. Peacock, *Crotchet Castle*.   [15] Op. cit., p. 13.
[16] William James, *Essays in Radical Empiricism, p.* 276.   [17] Op. cit., p. 13.

a different concept of a utilitarian character; but that is beside the point. I am speaking of the concept that we actually employ, the one that sustains our actual attributions of moral responsibility and the whole range of attitudes into which they enter. Even in our present state of knowledge, without any forecast of further scientific developments and their probable consequences, I cannot discover any circumstances in which the application of *this* concept would be justified. Whether we conceive of human actions as subject to causal or statistical laws, or whether we explain them in terms of motives the emergence of which leaves room for the play of chance, there is, as Lord Melbourne said of the award of the Garter 'no damned merit about it'; and no demerit either. Our actual attributes of merit and demerit depend upon the use of a metaphysical idea of self-determination, which Strawson himself dismisses as inane.[18]

But if the concept of desert is empty, so is the concept of responsibility which is founded on it. The moral judgements, in which persons are credited with such responsibility, are consequently irrational, in the sense of the term with which we are now concerned, and so are all the attitudes that either involve such moral judgements or commit us to the same ascriptions of responsibility; in effect, all the attitudes that Strawson prizes.

I find myself, therefore, in a dilemma. I attach a strong value to being rational in this second sense. I am dismayed when any belief that I hold appears to me irrational, in the way that I have just defined irrational belief, and in such a case I think that I ought to discard the belief, so far as this seems to be within my power. Correspondingly, I see it as an objection to an attitude that it rests on any such irrational belief, and again I think that I ought to try to refrain from adhering to it, so far as I can. From this it appears to follow that I should set myself to cultivate an objective attitude towards myself and others, and to welcome an ordering of society in which it was generally prevalent. What should concern me morally would be just the beneficence of the conditioning. At the same time I have to confess that the prospect of any such Brave New World repels me. Why it should do so is not clear to me. I see no harm, but

[18] Ibid., p. 24.
[19] Op. cit., p. 13 fn.

rather goodness, in the attempt to influence people by argument and precept. This too is a form of conditioning, though not in many cases as effective as one would like it to be. Why then should I recoil from the idea of our all being subject to forms of conditioning that really would be effective and beneficent? If I were pressed for an answer, I should probably be reduced to saying something to the effect that it seemed to me an infringement of liberty or an affront to the dignity of man. But what would this mean? It looks as if I half-consciously hold the metaphysical belief in self-determination which my reason repudiates.

This shows, it may be said, that I just am not able to be rational, in the way I think I ought to be, which should not prevent my looking forward hopefully to scientific advances that will cause such disabilities to be overcome. But there is more to it than that. The fact is that I hold strong moral convictions, and strong personal attachments and antipathies, in which the unredeemed concepts of merit and demerit play an essential part; and that the idea of replacing these feelings and convictions by objective attitudes is not, on balance, attractive to me, not only as applying to myself, but also as a matter of general policy. Like Strawson, I am disposed to see the outcome as an impoverishment of 'human life'.

I am inclined therefore to endorse Strawson's epigram that 'if such a choice were possible', as unlike him I think it quite easily might be, 'it would not necessarily be rational to choose to be more purely rational than we are'.[19] I wish only that I could accept it as blithely as he does; without my present feeling of intellectual discomfort.

Accountability

Jonathan Bennett

I shall present a problem about accountability, and its solution by Strawson's 'Freedom and Resentment'.[1] Some readers of the latter don't see it as a profound contribution to moral philosophy, and I want to help them. It may be helpful to follow up Strawson's gracefully written discussion with a more staccato presentation. My treatment will also be angled somewhat differently from his, so that its lights and shadows will fall with a certain difference, which may make it serviceable even to the converted. Thirdly—rounding out my apologia—I shall point to some disputable things in 'Freedom and Resentment', and to problems arising from it, which must be worthwhile if it is the masterpiece I take it to be and perhaps even if it isn't.

1. ACCOUNTABILITY

We welcome some events, and regret some. Among the kinds of events which may be welcomed or regretted are human actions. When we regret an action, we may blame the agent for it, resent his doing it, hold it against him, find fault with him, speak of or to him in a manner which is censorious or vilifying or abusive, seek revenge, demand punishment. These responses are all related to *blame*—not as a faulty compass may be blamed for an accident, but in the stronger sense in which the object of blame must be believed to be personal, and the attribution of blame is a censure or reproach, which could naturally carry with it thoughts about moral unworthiness. When we welcome an action, we may respond with praise, admiration, gratitude, thoughts of reward, or the like. These responses can be thought of as praise-related—not as one might praise a fine physique or

---

[1] P. F. Strawson, 'Freedom and Resentment', first published in 1962 and reprinted in *Freedom and Resentment and Other Essays* (London, 1974), pp. 1–25. My page references will be to the reprint.

beautiful hair, but rather as one might accompany praise with thoughts of moral worth.

I shall assume that blame-related and praise-related responses to actions constitute two classes of responses, each of which is unified enough for philosophy to be done about it. (If they do not, this essay will collapse; but so also will much of the literature.) Any unclarity about the borderlines of the two classes will be harmless, because my main points can be made in terms of responses which are well in from the boundaries.

Certain discoveries about why a regretted action was performed will lead any civilized person to regard blame-related responses as inappropriate. Suppose someone commits a murder, and it turns out that he had a brain tumour which had a crucial role in the causation of the murderous act: every victim of such a tumour would be virtually certain to commit hostile and violent acts, and this man will become a mild and reliably law-abiding citizen once his tumour is removed. In that case, it would be inappropriate to respond to the murder with reproaches etc., or to seek revenge or demand punishment. In such a case, the man is not blameworthy.

Similarly, if a welcome action is explicable in a certain way, praise-related responses are inappropriate. If a benefactor was manifesting an insane compulsion to give things away, the beneficiary may welcome the gift but should not be grateful for it. In such cases, the agent is not praiseworthy.

It is widely believed, I think rightly, that what stops the performer of a regretted action from being blameworthy is just what stops the performer of a welcomed action from being praiseworthy. Anyway, the two sets of conditions have a large overlap, and that overlap is my topic in this essay.

I stipulate that by 'accountable' I shall mean 'blameworthy or praiseworthy': someone is 'accountable' for an action, in my usage, if a blame- or praise-related response to the action would not be inappropriate. And my concern is with a problem about the conditions for 'accountability' in this sense. Since appropriateness can be a matter of degree, so can accountability; but I shall mainly use all-or-nothing formulations, to keep things simple.

2. A PROBLEM

I cannot pretend to tell, even abstractly, the whole story about the conditions for accountability; but two conditions cover enough of the ground for my purposes. For someone to be accountable for an action, (i) the action must relate in a certain way to his decisions, and (ii) his decision-making capacities must satisfy a certain condition. More specifically: he is accountable for doing A only if (i) he would not have done A if he had decided (or chosen or willed or wanted, etc.) not to do A; and (ii) he could have decided not to do A. There is no special problem about (i): if it is not satisfied, then something prevents him from not doing A, or makes him do A; and it is unproblematic to accept that the agent is then not accountable for doing A. But condition (ii), and especially its use of 'could have', raises a problem which I shall now present as abstractly as possible.

If determinism is true, then for any event E at time t_2 there obtained at time t_1 a state of affairs which was causally sufficient for E's occurrence at t_2 and which therefore causally ruled out the non-occurrence of E at t_2. Now, it is not obviously absurd to think that 'A state of affairs obtained which causally ruled out the non-occurrence of E' entails 'E could not have not occurred'; and so it is not obviously absurd to think that determinism implies that nothing which did happen could have not happened, and thus implies that there is no accountability.

There are two ways of meeting this difficulty.

3. THE LIBERTARIAN ANSWER

One is to suppose that determinism is false. So it probably is, in which case some events 'could have' not happened, in the sense of not being preceded by causally sufficient conditions for their occurrence. But this does not help to rescue accountability; for a chance event, whose occurrence is a matter of absolutely brute, inexplicable fact, is one for which obviously nobody is accountable. I am assuming that accountability requires intelligibility, and that something which is not caused cannot be rendered intelligible or removed from the 'brute fact' category. Causal explanation is not the only kind; but no explanation is possible for an event for which there is no causal explanation. For arguments directly in support of this, see Hobart's classic paper.[2] Indirect support comes from the plausibility of current philosophical theories which give the concept of cause a primary place in memory, personhood, action, and so on.[3]

It is also instructive to look at actual attempts to base accountability on the falsity of determinism. For example, C. A. Campbell says that accountability belongs only to actions which arise partly from 'effort of will': causes may limit what a man can do, but he is accountable only if causes leave open the question of whether the man will follow his baser desires or rather the call of 'duty', and *that* depends upon how much 'effort of will' he exerts towards doing what he conceives to be 'his duty'.[4] But Campbellian 'effort of will' cannot be what we ordinarily describe in terms of 'effort' or 'trying' or 'struggling to do one's best' or the like; for those expressions designate phenomena which have thick causal roots running back into the past. For instance, the extent to which someone tries to do his best can be affected by parental and other influences, and by his having resolved to do his best, meditated on the importance of morality, and so on. But such influences cannot bear upon Campbellian 'effort of will', which is a pure repository of uncaused determinants of action. So we don't know what Campbellian 'effort of will' is, and hence can have no reason to connect it in any way with accountability. I predict the same fate for any attempt to base accountability on uncaused inputs into action.

4. THE RECONCILING ANSWER

The other way of trying to rescue accountability is by arguing that any sense of 'could have' which makes it true that

---

[2] R. E. Hobart, 'Free Will as Involving Determination and Inconceivable Without It', *Mind*, vol. 43 (1934), pp. 1–27.

[3] On memory, see C. B. Martin and M. Deutscher, 'Remembering', *The Philosophical Review*, vol. 75 (1966), pp. 161–96. On personhood, see John Perry, 'Personal Identity, Memory, and the Problem of Circularity', in J. Perry (ed.), *Personal Identity* (Berkeley, 1975), pp. 135–55. On action, see, for instance, Donald Davidson, 'Actions, Reasons, and Causes', *The Journal of Philosophy*, vol. 60 (1963), pp. 685–700; and D. G. Brown, *Action* (Toronto, 1968), ch. 4.

[4] C. A. Campbell, 'In Defence of Free Will', published in 1938 and reprinted in *In Defence of Free Will with Other Philosophical Essays* (London, 1967), pp. 35–55; see especially pp. 42–5.

(1) If determinism is true, then only what did happen could have happened

is stronger than any sense of 'could have' which makes it true that

(2) An agent is accountable for an action only if he could have decided not to perform it.

I accept that there is this ambiguity, and that the non-existence of accountability therefore does not follow from determinism; and this is the currently most popular view of the matter. But it needs to be stiffened by an account of *what* the sense of 'could have' is which renders (2) true. The various attempts to explain this sense have in common something like this: An agent 'could have' decided differently if there was no impediment or obstacle to his doing so; the idea being that just as there are outer obstacles to *executing* one's will, there are also inner obstacles or impediments to the *exercise* of one's will. (It would be easy to restate this whole discussion in terms of 'compulsion' or 'coercion' of the will.) Now, of course, the problem has been relocated, and we must explain what an 'obstacle' is. There is no special problem about (outer) obstacles to the executing of one's will: they are just states of affairs which bring it about that one does not refrain from performing an A even if one chooses, decides, wants, etc. not to perform an A; and it is not puzzling that accountability should require the absence of such obstacles, for the blame- and praise-related responses are essentially directed to what agents *willingly* do. But there is a double problem about obstacles to the exercise of the will: in these cases, the item's status as an 'obstacle' is not secured by its standing in opposition to the agent's will; nor is its relevance to accountability secured by the action's not being done willingly.

The first half of the problem might be solved by an exhibition of linguistic facts – a demonstration of the principles according to which a brain tumour may count as an 'obstacle' while certain other causally sufficient conditions do not. But that will leave untouched the harder, deeper half of the problem: if tumours are impediments whereas some brain-structures are not—or if brainwashing is coercive whereas normal education is not – then why does accountability depend upon facts about impediments or about coercion?

5. THE SCHLICKIAN RATIONALE

Until 'Freedom and Resentment' appeared, the only answer to this question that the literature contained was the one offered by theories of accountability like Moritz Schlick's.[5] These focus on the notion of moral pressure, considered as a means for changing the likelihood that the person concerned (or others who know of the 'pressure') will act similarly on later comparable occasions. Moral pressures extend from faint expressions of (dis)approval through to dire punishments and munificent rewards—a mixed bag, but all capable of generating *threats or inducements*, i.e. of equipping someone with a thought of the form 'If I perform an A, the upshot is likely to be U', which may affect his decision whether to perform an A. (For brevity, I shall concentrate on deterrence, ignoring encouragement; and on deterrence of the protagonist, ignoring onlookers.) Now, if someone performs an A and would not have been deterred by threats, then on future closely similar occasions he will again be undeterred by them; and so it is not useful to apply them to him by morally pressuring him in respect of the A which he has performed. That, according to Schlickian theories, explains the *extent* of the concept of accountability: the man with the brain tumour, for example, is not accountable for what he did because it is so unlikely that the exerting of moral pressures would have deterred him from doing it. Similarly with the person who has been brainwashed. Quite generally—say the Schlickian theories—we do not hold babies, the insane, the intellectually handicapped, the tortured, accountable for the bad things they do, because it is not useful to apply moral pressures to someone who is too young, too ill, too stupid, too hard-pressed, to be affected by them.

Accountability is strongly correlated with susceptibility to moral pressures, and so Schlickian theories draw the line—or locate the continuum—in about the right place. And they do

---

[5] Moritz Schlick, *The Problems of Ethics* (trans. D. Rynin, New York, 1939), ch. 7. See also Hobart, op. cit., pp. 24–7; P. H. Nowell-Smith, *Ethics* (London, 1954), pp. 300–6; and John Hospers, 'What Means this Freedom?' in Sidney Hook (ed.), *Determinism and Freedom in the Age of Modern Science* (New York, 1958), pp. 113–30, at pp. 115–19.

not employ an unexplained 'could have', but only the relatively plain 'would have' which occurs in the form 'If he had thought ..., he would have decided ...'. Furthermore, they describe accountability in a way which explains why the concept's limits lie where they do. Without that explanatory component, Schlickian theories would not be seriously interesting.

6. WHY SCHLICKIAN THEORIES ARE UNACCEPTABLE

With it, however, they are in trouble: the Schlickian description of what accountability is—or of what the concept is *for*—strikes everyone as incomplete and strikes most people as wrong. The latter will say that although a distinction based on the utility of a certain sort of therapy or behaviour-control might *coincide* with accountability/non-accountability, it cannot give the latter's essence, and that the Schlickian account of what the line is *for* does nothing like justice to the real nature of our praise- and blame-related responses. When we express indignation for someone's cruelty, or admiration for his unselfishness, we usually are not engaged in any sort of therapy: blame-related responses all involve something like hostility towards the subject; whereas a moral-pressure therapist, though he may have to feign ill-feeling for therapeutic purposes, can in fact be in a perfectly sunlit frame of mind. And—to move briefly to the 'welcome' side of the fence—one may apply moral pressures to encourage a welcomed kind of behaviour while remaining in an ice-cold frame of mind, with no feelings of gratitude, admiration or the like.

Schlickians defend their omission, arguing that we ought to jettison blame-related responses and handle ill-doers purely with a view to producing the best possible outcome. But what about the praise-related responses? Schlickians never say that we should give up admiration and gratitude and settle for 'therapies' aimed at encouraging recurrences of the welcomed kind of behaviour; but shouldn't they say just that? If blame-related responses are condemned just because we cannot explain the extent of accountability except by relating it to the relevance of a certain kind of 'therapy', then there is a strictly analogous case against the praise-related responses; but obviously we ought not to give up admiration and gratitude. So something has gone wrong.

Accountability 21

We need to make room for at least part of what Schlickian theories omit, doing so in a manner which is not embarrassed by renewed difficulties over explaining why the line falls where it does. This double need is, in my view, satisfied by 'Freedom and Resentment'.

7. REACTIVE FEELINGS

According to Strawson, all that is omitted by Schlickian theories is the element of what he calls *reactive attitudes*, from which I shall at first lift out the component notion of a *reactive feeling*. Reactive feelings are ones which are prominent in blame, reproach, vilification, resentment, admiration, gratitude, praise, and so on. (If I could define 'reactive' I would do so, rather than resorting to examples. The problem of definition will be discussed in §§13–15, below.) Clearly, Schlickian theories offer us a way of handling accountability, or some notion coextensive with it, in a manner which does not demand reactive feelings. It is a manner which does demand the objective attitude towards the person concerned. The phrase 'the objective attitude' is Strawson's, and the core of its meaning seems to be this: To adopt the objective attitude towards something is to inquire into how it is structured and/or how it functions. The notion of objectivity will be further discussed in §15, below.

Many people find that feelings such as those of resentment and gratitude, indignation and admiration, do not easily occupy the mind along with a thoroughgoing concern to study the subject's behaviour patterns. Strawson mentions one familiar manifestation of this conflict between reactive feelings and objectivity of attitude—namely the common ability to dispel a hostile reactive feeling *by* cultivating objectivity of attitude towards the offender, e.g. dispelling indignation by viewing him as 'a case'.

In so far as reactive feelings won't mix with thorough objectivity, to that extent we must choose: we cannot always proceed as Schlick would have us do and throw in reactiveness for good measure. Now, really, all that Schlickian theory advocates is that we let our response to each welcomed or regretted action be guided by a concern for achieving the best over-all outcome. So if reactive feelings are to have a place in our lives, we cannot always ask ourselves 'What response to that action will be for the best in the long run?' Displays of indignation or of gratitude often produce good results; but such feelings cannot be motivated by the desire to produce good results, nor, it seems, are we able closely to control them by thoughts of what will bring the best results. So apparently reactive feelings can have a considerable place in our lives only at the risk of our sometimes not acting in the most fortunate manner; and that fact might be used in a Schlickian counter-attack. Strawson's defence is to maintain that it would be unfortunate if we were always guided by the thought of what would be most fortunate: the prospect of human life with continual Schlickian preoccupations and no reactive feelings, he says, is barely conceivable and wholly repellent. And so the practical question 'Should we try to rid ourselves of reactive feelings?' is given a suitably practical answer.

8. THE EXTENT OF ACCOUNTABILITY: STRAWSON'S RATIONALE

When should reactive feelings occur? Well, to start with, Strawson marks off the area in which they would be just inappropriate, as fear is in the absence of danger. We could call this the area of non-accountability. Strawson gives a non-Schlickian rationale for that line's falling where it does, i.e. for the extent of the concept of accountability (pp. 7–9). It has two parts, corresponding to the two main things Strawson says about the role of reactive feelings in our lives. (1) They get their value from their role in normal, adult, interpersonal relations; and so it is inappropriate to have such feelings towards someone whose youth, mental ill-health, etc. incapacitates him—whether temporarily or permanently—for such relations. (2) They are essentially expressions of one's caring about the attitudes of other people; and so they can be inappropriate because 'he didn't realize...', 'they couldn't help...', 'she didn't mean...' etc., where behaviour does not really manifest attitudes which it superficially seems to manifest. Under both (1) and (2), incidentally, there is plenty of room for accountability to be a matter of degree.

Without denying that this is a therapeutically useful place to draw the line, therefore, Strawson can still maintain that utility is not the whole story since he has also a non-Schlickian explanation for the line's falling where it does.

9. THE TOPOLOGY OF BLAME

Within the area where reactive feelings are never simply inappropriate, there may be sub-areas where they would predictably be so harmful that they should be systematically excluded from them: Strawson gives the example of the feelings of a psycho-analyst towards a patient. (Another plausible candidate is the constructing and applying of the penal code—a topic I have discussed in a separate paper.[6]) However, to try *always* to keep reactive feelings within the bounds of prudence—avoiding every counter-productive fit of pique or surge of love—would involve keeping them continuously under objective–teleological control; and that seems to be impossible. If our lives are to have a measure of warmth and *engagement* and spontaneity, we must pay the price of sometimes not acting in the most prudent or fortunate way. This throws a new light on the conspicuous unruliness of our emotional lives. It is not merely true, but inevitable and acceptable, that the detailed facts about when a given person has feelings of indignation, admiration, resentment, gratitude etc. is partly a matter of individual temperament, personal style, the mood of the moment, perhaps physiological accident.

A picture might help. There is a large 'accountability' circle within which reactive feelings are confined: it roughly coincides with the circle within which moral-pressure therapies have some chance of success. Inside that, there are smaller circles marking areas from which it is prudent to exclude reactive feelings because they are so counter-productive there. Their range, then, consists of the area which lies inside the large circle and outside the smaller ones. They are free to roam through that area without further confinement: one cannot mark off further sub-areas within which reactive feelings are mandatory, or establish any rules of the form: if . . ., then it is *wrong not to* be indignant (grateful, resentful, etc.). In speaking of the ability to dispel a reactive feeling on a given occasion by cultivating thorough objectivity towards the person in question, Strawson says that we 'sometimes' have this option (p. 9); but I think that

[6] J. Bennett, 'Towards a Theory of Punishment', *Philosophic Exchange* (1980).

he would and should allow that that option is always theoretically open, i.e. that it is never just wrong—though it is sometimes psychologically impossible—to dispel one's reactive feelings by retreating into objectivity. We can regard someone as 'a case' without believing or pretending that he is mentally ill etc.; for it is just a matter of thoroughly viewing him, in a spirit of inquiry, as a natural object, and this can never be 'wrong in the nature of the case'.

This has an important upshot, which for brevity's sake I shall state only in terms of blame. Consider the proposition that someone 'is blameworthy'. Strawson has a sense for this if it means that it *would not be wrong to* blame the person, but not if it means that it *would be wrong not to* blame him. There is a way of thinking about accountability according to which a person's being 'to blame' implies that blame ought not to be withheld from him (though he may be spared its consequences because of forgiveness); but Strawson's account has nothing like this—no imperatives demanding indignation or any other reactive feeling, but only imperatives forbidding them in certain areas, and permissions to have them in the remaining areas.

This is one mark of the non-propositional nature of blaming, praising etc. in Strawson's account: feelings are made central, and are not tied systematically to any propositions about their objects. My feeling of indignation at what you have done is not a perception of your objective blameworthiness, nor is it demanded of me by such a perception. It expresses my emotional make-up, rather than reflecting my ability to recognize a blame-meriting person when I see one. The gap left by the Schlickian account is not to be filled by facts about desert or about the meriting of blame, facts which are acknowledged by the adoption of reactive attitudes; rather, in Strawson's words, 'it is just these attitudes themselves which fill the gap' (p. 23).

In this respect, Strawson's account makes no provision for an element which is present in some people's notion of accountability. Yet he says that it provides a basis for an understanding 'of what we mean, i.e. of *all* we mean, when, speaking the language of morals, we speak of desert, responsibility, guilt, condemnation, and justice' (p. 23). I believe that his theory is more revisionary—or, to coin a needed word, excisionary—than that implies. Perhaps Strawson means to claim only to have provided for every *coherent* element in 'what we mean', so that what is offered is not a fully conservative theory but rather a maximal salvage. I think that that claim would be correct, but I cannot prove it is. I don't anticipate anyone's denying that Strawson's account is all right as far as it goes, but some may maintain that it is not the whole story. We can evaluate that claim when they tell us what the rest of the story is supposed to be.

10. WHY THE SPINOZIST ATTACK IS PERSUASIVE

There is a strength in Strawson's position which he does not point out. Consider the way in which many careful and intelligent people are influenced by what I shall call 'Spinozism', by which I mean lines of thought in which a person is presented as a natural object whose structure and behaviour ultimately results from nothing but the behaviour of parts of the universe other than himself; in which his behaviour is presented as wholly predictable; and so on. Faced with these Spinozist lines of thought, many people are led to say that the person is not really accountable for what he does—that his behaviour results from his structure and his environment, both of which are ultimately hands that were dealt to him by God or Nature, so that neither they nor anything resulting purely from them should be blamed upon the person himself.

It is usual to say that when someone is swayed by Spinozism he is succumbing to conceptual muddle, failing to grasp *which* sufficient conditions count as 'compelling', *which* relations to the universe count as 'victimhood', *which* sort of predictability defeats accountability, and so on. No doubt these charges are often justified; but to suggest that they completely explain why people regard Spinozism as a challenge to accountability is not just insulting but plainly wrong; for many people, even after the muddles have been sorted out, remain strongly inclined to say that if a person is as God or Nature made him, and if how he is determines what he does, then it is 'in some ultimate sense hideously unfair' that he should be blamed for what he does. That phrase comes from Bernard Williams.[7] In the course of giving a perspective on Kant's theory of freedom, Williams

---

[7] Bernard Williams, 'Morality and the Emotions', reprinted in his *Problems of the Self* (Cambridge, 1973), pp. 207–29, at p. 228.

offers something which could explain the power of Spinozism to create doubts about accountability. It is that one element in 'moral ideas influenced by Christianity' is the thought 'that moral worth must be separated from any natural advantage whatsoever', a thought which led Kant 'to the conclusion that the source of moral thought and action must be located outside the empirically conditioned self'.

Anyone who thinks that moral worth cannot depend upon natural advantage is bound to see Spinozism as ruling out accountability. For Spinozism shows how all the facts about a man can be viewed as natural (dis)advantages which he has. (Even his existence. My very existence could be my bad luck, although there is no separate I who *has* the bad luck to *have* the existence.[8] To see this, consider that under certain genetic circumstances a person's very existence could be regarded as an injury or wrong done to him by his parents, although there is no separable *he* on whom the existence, and thus the injury, were inflicted.) I am sure that the Christian–Kantian thought does explain why Spinozism is thought to abolish accountability. And in representing the source of the phenomenon as positive, unitary, and deep-rooted, it is much truer to the observed facts than is the explanation which traces it to a scatter of conceptual failures.

I am not defending the Christian–Kantian thought. On the contrary, I agree with Williams: 'No human characteristic which is relevant to degrees of moral esteem can escape being an empirical characteristic, subject to empirical conditions, psychological history, and individual variation'; which is why Kant's treatment of moral worth, moral desert, accountability etc. is 'a shattering failure'. In fact, the Christian–Kantian thought generates a logically unsatisfiable concept of accountability—one which will not let a person count as blameworthy unless he is 'free' or 'autonomous' or 'self-made' in a sense in which it is logically impossible to be free or autonomous or self-made.

The familiar question of whether 'the ordinary concept of accountability' is logically incoherent is, presumably, the question of what role the Christian–Kantian thought plays in com-

---

[8] See Richard G. Henson, 'Responsibility for Character and Responsibility for Conduct', *Australasian Journal of Philosophy*, vol. 43 (1965), pp. 311–20; at pp. 319–20.

mon thinking about accountability. How widespread is it throughout the populace? In the minds of those who have it, is it sufficiently dominant to be constitutive of their 'concept of accountability'? I suspect that it is very widespread, but not very dominant; so I hesitate to say that the 'the ordinary concept of accountability' is logically unsatisfiable. On the other hand, Strawson's claim to have provided for '*all* we mean, when ... we speak of desert' (p. 23), and his blunt dismissal of the sceptical view that 'blame is metaphysical' (p. 24), do perhaps underestimate the strength of the Christian–Kantian thought. In particular, they do not do justice to the fact that although the plain man's moral thinking is not dominated by that thought, it is not informed either by any coherent alternative to it. But the point is not worth pursuing. We all know what happens when ordinary thoughtful people are pressed to get clear about accountability; and it doesn't matter how, if at all, the facts can be expressed as a thesis about 'the ordinary concept of accountability'.

What *is* interesting is the question of why the Christian–Kantian thought should have any acceptance at all. The explanation must lie partly in Christianity itself. If God is ultimately responsible for every fact about the natural realm, and is also the arbiter and punisher of wrongdoing, then there is something perfectly repellent about the idea of someone's being blameworthy for an action which is a truly natural event, whether fully caused or not. The God of Christianity cannot justly blame us for anything, it seems, unless he has given us some ultimate kind of agency which takes our actions right out of his field of operations, so that they cannot be fully explained by any combination of natural causes and of random events of the sort that would count as disorderly conduct on God's part. Thus, Christianity puts pressure upon its adherents to base accountability on some ultimate, not-of-this-world kind of autonomy, a kind which I—with Williams and others—believe to be logically impossible.

But the Christian–Kantian thought extends more widely than does any considered theology of God as creator and judge; and although that may be partly due to inertia, there is also a different explanation for the Christian–Kantian thought, which I now present. It is mine, I think, rather than Strawson's;

but it rests squarely on the fundamental tenets of 'Freedom and Resentment'.

Spinozism makes us look at a person in a strenuously objective manner. The concept of accountability has primarily to do with reactive feelings such as those of indignation and resentment, gratitude, and admiration. Many people are unable to have these feelings towards someone *while* regarding him in a thoroughly objective manner. If those three propositions are all true, then it is to be expected that many people who entertain Spinozist thoughts about a malefactor will have their indignation drained out of them. They are not discovering something about the malefactor which disqualifies indignation, renders it wrong or inappropriate; they are merely adopting an attitude of mind towards him which makes it hard or impossible for them to maintain their feelings of indignation, resentment, etc. But they may fail to realize that that is what is happening. Usually when a kind of intellectual operation dispels a kind of feeling, it does so by disqualifying it, showing it to be inappropriate—as when fear ebbs upon the discovery that there is no danger, and pride evaporates when one realizes that the applause was ironical—and so it would not be surprising if someone who found that Spinozist thoughts dispelled his indignation should think he was discovering that where Spinozism is true indignation is inappropriate. Furthermore, most people when they are swayed by Spinozism don't think of blameworthiness, etc. in terms of *feelings* at all, and so they will tend to construe their loss of indignation, etc. as the loss of the judgement that the subject is 'to blame'; and when a judgement is sent packing by an intellectual operation one naturally thinks that it has been refuted or at least discredited.

That could directly explain the success of the Spinozist attack on the belief in accountability. But it might also explain it indirectly, by helping to explain the persistence of the Christian–Kantian thought, which in turn supports the Spinozist attack.

11. DISPELLING AND DISQUALIFYING

The foregoing explanation requires (1) that when someone is drawn by Spinozism towards the conclusion that the subject is not to blame for his actions, he is losing his feelings of indignation, etc.; and (2) that in such cases the feelings are being dispelled without being disqualified or shown to be inappropriate. Of these (1) seems clearly to be true: it fits what happens when people are swayed by Hospers's eloquent and persuasive Spinozist attack on accountability;[9] and I really cannot imagine anyone being moved by Spinozism while continuing to boil with rage against the malefactor. As for (2): well, it would be absurd to accept *that* the feelings are being disqualified, in the absence of any account of *how* or *why*. Admittedly, I cannot explain how an intellectual operation can dispel a feeling without disqualifying it; but that gap in my position still leaves me with a reason for saying that Spinozist thoughts do not disqualify indignation, etc. If they did, the conclusion must be that if men are explicable natural objects we oughtn't to have reactive feelings towards them. But they *are* natural objects; yet if we try to imagine our lives without reactive feelings we find ourselves (here I follow Strawson) confronted by a bleak desolation. We cannot be obliged to give up something whose loss would gravely worsen the human condition, and so reactive feelings cannot be made impermissible by any facts, e.g. the fact that men are natural objects.

That argument presupposes that the question 'Ought we to give up reactive feelings?' is a basically practical one. Anyone who construes it in that way will agree with Strawson that it is to be answered 'in the light of an assessment of the gains and losses to human life' (p. 13). The serious controversy concerns the nature of the question, for it has usually been assumed that the decision about whether to permit ourselves indignation etc. must depend strictly upon whether our fellow humans are objectively (un)meritorious in some way which calls down blame or praise upon them. Even on the Strawsonian position which I am adopting, a theoretical question is involved: reactive feelings would be inappropriate if men couldn't enter into relations of love, hate, etc. But given that men do lie within the large circle, the remaining question is a practical one which does not strictly depend upon the establishing of any further kind of fact about the present.

Strawson does not prove this; nor can I. But the literature contains no coherent account of any relevant 'further kind of

[9] Hospers, op. cit., pp. 119–27.

fact', and Strawson offers a liberating hypothesis which suggests a way of dispensing with this elusive theoretical item. It is reasonable to adopt his hypothesis if it stands up and every rival to it falls flat.

The greatest single achievement of 'Freedom and Resentment', in my view, is its showing how the question 'Ought we to retain praise, blame, etc.?' could be a fundamentally practical one rather than having a strict dependence upon a perpetually troublesome theoretical question. Given that construal of the question, answering it is a straightforward matter.

Strawson emphasizes—more than I would want to—that we could not possibly relinquish all reactive feelings. Still, ought we to try? Ought we to strive in that direction? We do have a live question about what course we should steer, and I have been expounding Strawson's answer to it.

12. HARMFUL KINDS OF REACTIVE FEELINGS

Even if we should not set ourselves against all kinds of reactive feelings, perhaps some should not be retained. Some people think it would be better if we lacked resentment and anger, etc., while retaining gratitude and every sort of love, etc. Strawson would not agree, I believe. He characterizes reactive attitudes as essentially 'participant', and associates 'sustained objectivity' with 'isolation'; and this suggests that the semi-Spinozist ideal which is now in question would involve our participating in personal relations only while they please us, and withdrawing into 'isolation' whenever others behave in ways we regret. Put like that, it sounds unattractive; but I am dubious about this formulation of the semi-Spinozist ideal, because I am not sure just what the truth is in the description of reactive attitudes as 'participant'. I shall explore that matter in §14 and §18 below.

I have heard it argued that the semi-Spinozist ideal is self-defeating, because the non-adverse reactive feelings require the adverse ones. For instance: 'You can't really love someone with whom you never get angry.' Clearly, some people hold that view of love, but the mere existence of such certainties does not count for much: it used to be thought that you can't really love a woman whom you never beat. I don't advocate the semi-Spinozist ideal, but I offer it as needing discussion even if one follows Strawson in rejecting the wholly Spinozist ideal of relinquishing all reactive feelings.

Others think that we ought at least to try to relinquish adverse reactive feelings about ourselves, especially guilt and remorse. This could be called the Yeatsian ideal:

> I am content to follow to its source
> Every event in action or in thought;
> Measure the lot; forgive myself the lot!
> When such as I cast out remorse
> So great a sweetness flows into the breast
> We must laugh and we must sing,
> We are blest by everything,
> And everything we look upon is blest.[10]

What is in question in the third line is not the 'reactive' kind of forgiveness which Strawson talks about (p. 6), but rather the kind which consists in opting out of blame and into objectivity of attitude, into 'measuring the lot'—the sort which supplies whatever truth there is in *Tout comprendre, c'est tout pardonner*. Yeats's rejection of remorse was part of his fight against 'emotions... in which there is not an athletic joy'; this was not a rejection of all adverse reactive feelings, for 'indignation is a kind of joy'. Remorse, he rightly thought, isn't.

The Yeatsian ideal need not make us complacent about our past wrongdoings and failures: complacency can be warded off by self-criticism, which is consistent with perfect objectivity of attitude. To be self-critical and self-corrective, we need standards by which to judge our behaviour; but neither the Yeatsian nor the all-in Spinozist ideal contains the slightest threat to the value-system according to which we judge some actions to be good or right or successful and others to be bad or wrong or failures. Without having any tendency to remorse or guilt, I may resolve not to exhibit contempt towards other people, and when I do contemn someone I may regret this very much, and be concerned to find out what went wrong—'measure the lot'—and correct it.

I don't endorse the Yeatsian ideal either; but like the semi-Spinozist one it is worth thinking about.

[10] W. B. Yeats, 'A Dialogue of Self and Soul', in his *Collected Poems* (London, 1952) at p. 267. I am indebted to Michael Goldberg for my other two brief quotations from Yeats.

13. DEFINING 'REACTIVE': SOME FAILURES

It is time to look at the problem of explaining what 'reactive' means. As a start with this, I should belatedly emphasize that Strawson's key term is not 'feeling' but 'attitude', though it seems clear that in his view reactive attitudes are to a large extent matters of feeling. I have abstracted 'feeling' from the fuller and more complex notion, so as to give maximum prominence to what I see as most original in Strawson's treatment; but now I must put reactive feelings back into their context of reactive attitudes.

The OED says that an attitude of mind is a 'mode of regarding the object of thought'. That seems right so far as it goes, but it doesn't go far. There are two basically different construals for 'mode of regarding'. To adopt a certain 'mode of regarding' something may be (1) to regard it in a certain manner, e.g. carefully or upside down or through a glass darkly or analytically; or (2) to regard it as a certain kind of thing, e.g. as a good friend or as a fiend incarnate or as a potential meal. Let us see whether either of these helps us with 'reactive attitude', given that reactive attitudes must be especially associated with praise- and blame-related responses, and must stand in contrast—I do not say conflict—with an objectively inquiring attitude.

(1) I cannot find any adverbs of *psychological* manner which are special to reactive attitudes. It might be thought that the objective attitude is essentially cool whereas reactive attitudes are essentially warm (gratitude) or hot (indignation); but those metaphors fail us without even being unpacked. All we need do is to lay some others alongside them—burning curiosity on the one hand, and icy contempt on the other.

We should also examine adverbs of *conceptual* manner, as they might be called: perhaps what is special to reactive attitudes is that they involve bringing their object under some special concept(s). Well, they *do* involve bringing into play the concepts of person, action, and intention; but that cannot help us to define 'reactive', for those concepts can also be involved when reactiveness is entirely absent. In approaching someone with clinical objectivity, one need not confine oneself to the concepts of physical object, animal, bodily movement, cause, etc.; on the contrary, one may regard him as a *person* who *acts* in certain ways for certain *reasons*, without one's attitude being any less clinical or more censorious.

Another approach through 'conceptual manner' which I once tried was this: 'Viewing someone as a natural object involves seeing him as an analysed complex, whereas taking a reactive attitude to him involves seeing him as a unitary whole.'[11] In that I was following Hobart: 'It is in the whole act and the whole trait and the whole being that excellence and preciousness inhere; analysis must needs show us elements which, taken severally, are without moral expressiveness.'[12] I still think that to regard someone as a natural object one must conceptually dismantle him into sub-systems (things that can be studied objectively without much dismantling must be simpler than any person is), whereas reactive attitudes are directed towards people viewed as 'morally expressive' and thus taken as wholes. And that could help to explain the difficulty of combining thorough objectivity with reactive attitudes. But it cannot define 'reactive' for us, for it is not only when one is engaged in praise- or blame-related responses to people that one regards them in a non-analysing manner.

I have no other suggestions under the heading of 'adverbs of manner'.

(2) Let us then try the other construal of 'mode of regarding': to adopt a reactive attitude towards someone is to *regard him as an F*, for some special value of F, this being construed as something stronger than merely bringing the concept of F to bear on him somehow, since that falls within the 'adverb of conceptual manner' category which I have just finished with. One possibility is that to regard someone as an F is to bring one's mind to bear upon him *in the belief that* he is an F. Let us explore this a little. I think that Strawson will have to say that if reactive attitudes essentially involve some belief about their objects, it must be a true belief. He does allow that reactive attitudes stand in the way of pure rationality (p. 13 n.), and he apparently sees some truth—though also some distortion—in the idea that in reactive feelings one's 'humanity' battles one's 'intelligence' (p. 10). This is strong stuff, but it stops short of

---

[11] J. Bennett, *Kant's Dialectic* (Cambridge, 1974), p. 207.
[12] Hobart, op. cit., p. 14.

allowing that reactiveness as such involves untruth, and I am sure that Strawson would not want to go so far. So he cannot explain 'reactive attitude' in terms of 'believing that the person is an F' unless in general the person *is* indeed an F. But then the contrast with the objective attitude has been obliterated, for presumably every *fact* about a person—e.g. the fact that he is within the reach of normal personal relationships—has a place in a thoroughly objective view of him. *Some* cases of objectivity are marked off by their 'belief' component: Strawson speaks of 'viewing the deranged person simply as something to be understood and controlled [and] as outside the reach of personal relationships' (p. 12); but that is not intended to distinguish 'reactive' from 'objective', for Strawson does not equate 'adopting the objective attitude towards *x*' with 'believing that *x* is deranged'.

14. INTERPERSONAL RELATIONS

All we are left with is a construal of 'regarding him as an F' which likens it to 'regarding it as something to eat' or '... as something to swim in' or the like, where the crux is what one regards the object (not as *being* but) as *being good for*. It is not a matter of the concepts or beliefs that one has, but rather of the behaviour that one envisages engaging in with regard to the object. (This connects directly with the notion of a *physical* attitude; a hostile bodily *att*itude is a posture which is *apt* for combat, 'att' and 'apt' having the same source.) Perhaps, then, a reactive attitude is essentially a posture of the mind which is *apt for inter-action of a certain kind.*

There is evidence that Strawson *would* want to explain what a 'reactive attitude' is in some such terms as those. He speaks of reactive attitudes as the 'non-detached attitudes and reactions of people directly involved in transactions with each other' (p. 4), links them essentially with 'involvement or participation in a human relationship' (p. 9), and their absence with 'human isolation' (p. 11), and repeatedly characterizes them as 'participant' and as 'involved'. It seems, then, that we are to understand 'reactive' by grasping an associated notion of a kind of involved, participating, interpersonal transaction.

Strictly, those characterizations are offered only for what Strawson calls 'personal' reactive attitudes—ones which involve reactive feelings which one has on one's own behalf, e.g. resentment and gratitude. Strawson has two other categories of reactive attitudes. There are impersonal or moral reactive attitudes: these are the 'vicarious analogues' of the former, the idea being that moral indignation is something like resentment on behalf of another (or perhaps on behalf of oneself, but not merely because it is oneself). And there are self-reactive attitudes, including remorse and shame and, I suppose, self-congratulation. Now, we might hope to define 'reactive' by first explaining 'personal reactive attitude' in terms of the relevant kinds of interpersonal involvement, and then relating the other two categories of reactive attitude to the personal ones. Each step in this procedure, however, involves difficulties. I start with the one concerning personal reactive attitudes.

In §18 below I shall discuss *how* reactive attitudes relate to the relevant kinds of interpersonal relation; but my present problem concerns not the relation but the second relatum. The problem starts with the fact that the terms 'interpersonal relation', 'participation', etc. do not, unaided, mark off the territory which Strawson wants to delimit. A therapist and his patient can be closely *involved* with one another, in a therapeutic programme in which they both *participate*; but that involvement might be quite untouched by anything Strawson would call 'reactive', at least on the therapist's side. Obviously, that is not the sort of involvement he has in mind: he lists such relations as those between siblings and between lovers, and speaks of 'inter-personal human relationships', once adding 'as we normally understand them'. The intention to exclude therapist–patient working relations is clear, but they are not being excluded by means of anything with which one could build theory. And their mere absence from Strawson's list doesn't help, because the whole point of trying to define 'reactive' is to escape from dependence on lists. As for 'interpersonal relationships': well, the therapist is one person and his patient is another; and if they do not have what 'we normally understand' by an interpersonal relationship then what we normally understand must be narrow. The narrowing may be well founded, but until we can say what it rests on we cannot avail ourselves of it. The job cannot be done with any formula about a relation in which each party treats the other as a person; for the therapist does treat his patient as a person—a person who needs help.

One might try the idea that reactive attitudes involve relationships which are not just interpersonal but *essentially* so (see Strawson, p. 10): the relation of therapist to patient is of a kind that *could* obtain between veterinarian and cat, or between mechanic and motor-car; whereas reactivity-involving relations *cannot* obtain except between items which are viewed as personal (either persons or anthropomorphized dogs or theologized weather, etc.). Attractive as this approach is, I cannot make it work. For a relationship to be of the sort characteristic of reactive attitudes, we cannot require that *every* kind to which it belongs is essentially interpersonal: my resentment of you is intense, intermittent, embarrassing, damaging, incurable, and so on—each of these features marks off a 'kind' of relation which is not essentially interpersonal. Well, then, perhaps a relation is of the reactive sort if it is of *some* essentially interpersonal kind? But that lets in too much. My unaccusing regret at my brother's selling his farm, though not essentially interpersonal *qua* regret, is essentially interpersonal *qua* regret-over-someone's-action; and yet there is nothing reactive about it.

To rescue the foregoing approach we need some unarbitrary and uncircular constraint(s) on what is to count as 'a kind'. I cannot find any that will do the job.

15. TELEOLOGICAL INQUIRY

Some light can be thrown on what reactiveness is by a more careful contrast with objectivity. In §7 above I explained 'the objective attitude' as the *inquiring* frame of mind; but really all we are concerned with here is *teleological inquiry*, by which I mean, provisionally, inquiry which aims at achieving some practical end, not the mere acquisition of knowledge and understanding. Purely theoretical inquiry also manifests 'the objective attitude', naturally so-called, but it lies beyond the range of our present concerns.

This is because our central problem concerns praise- and blame-related responses to welcomed and regretted actions: we want to understand how they differ from responses which don't involve praise or blame *but which do still embody welcomes and regrets*. Purely theoretical inquiry, aiming at no practical end, lies outside the range of our interests simply because it expresses no pro or con attitude, no welcome or regret, with respect to the item inquired into.

That is pretty clearly Strawson's view of the matter. His principal account of 'the objective attitude' is in a passage where, after sketching how we handle 'the extreme case of the mentally deranged', Strawson says: 'We may have occasion ... to adopt a fundamentally similar attitude to a "normal" human being; to concentrate, that is, on understanding "how he works", with a view [1] to determining our policy accordingly or [2] to finding in that very understanding a relief from the strains of involvement' (p. 12). These two purposes are very different. Most teleological inquiry is like (1): truths are sought so that they may be applied in the pursuit of an end. In (2) also they are to be a means to a further end, but not by being applied. Still, the two can harmlessly be grouped as 'teleological inquiry'.

I submit that reactive attitudes never generate teleological inquiry. Objection: 'Vengefulness is reactive if anything is; yet it may involve inquiries into "how he works", aimed at establishing truths which will help one to get revenge. On your definition, this is teleological inquiry.' To counter this, I strengthen the definition: teleological inquiry seeks truths which can be applied in the pursuit of ends which are viewed as desirable either inherently or as means to some subsequent inherent good. That rules out those 'ends'—the revenges and rewards—which essentially look to the past, while retaining all those which look to the present or the future. This, I submit, is not just an *ad hoc* repair, but marks an important difference between two kinds of goal-pursuing activity. And I contend that it is a mark of reactive attitudes that they do not involve teleological inquiry, in my present sense of that phrase.

I don't say that a reactive attitude towards *x* cannot coexist with teleological inquiries about *x*: that evokes the 'conflict' thesis, which is not now in question. My present contention is just that teleological inquiry is never caused or implied or supported by a reactive attitude: if my teleologically inquiring into 'how he works' can be explained by my having attitude A towards him, then A cannot be a reactive attitude. For instance, my endeavour to learn how to get him to repeat a certain kind of behaviour cannot be explained by my gratitude to him. Even if I am grateful to him, what explains my teleological inquiry must be something else—presumably my desire for a repetition of the welcomed kind of behaviour. Or so I maintain.

I now add a further suggestion. The attitude of x towards y is reactive *if and only if* it is a pro or con attitude which could not explain x's engaging in teleological inquiry into how y works. I cannot find any convincing counter-examples to this biconditional.

It does not make 'reactive' and 'objective' complementary within the class of pro and con attitudes. What I propose is this: if x's attitude to y *does* generate teleological inquiry, to that extent it is objective; if it *could not* do so, it is reactive; it is *could but does not*, it is neither.

Consider the attitude of Dives towards Lazarus when he passes him on the street and feels fastidious disgust at his stink, his sores, his cringing whine. He hurries on: so far from inquiring, he tries to shut out the facts by shutting out the sensory intake; and so it would be an abuse of language to call his attitude towards Lazarus 'objective'. But it does not belong with the attitudes which Strawson calls 'reactive': it is too far removed from resentment, indignation, and blame, and is too close to what Lazarus might feel about a dead animal in the gutter. These intuitions about Dives' disgust are nicely confirmed by my suggested criteria. The disgust is not reactive because it *could* explain teleological inquiries: if Dives studied Lazarus's condition with a view to ameliorating it or having him arrested, etc. this could be because he found Lazarus disgusting. But this episode of disgust is not objective because it does not, in fact, lead Dives to teleological inquiries.

However, my proposed necessary and sufficient condition for an attitude to be 'reactive' is not useful or satisfying. It says only that reactiveness is incompatible with a certain causal or explanatory power—i.e. that x's attitude cannot both be reactive and be the cause or explanation of x's engaging in teleological inquiry. This doesn't tell us what reactiveness is, but only names one of its properties—and a negative, modal, relational property to boot.

So I have failed to say in general terms what reactiveness is,

Accountability 39

or what the kind of interpersonal relationship is which defines the home ground of personal reactive attitudes. But I still think that Strawson has made a profound contribution to the understanding of accountability; for his account could do its principal work without using 'reactive' or any substitute for it, and merely speaking separately of 'resentment', 'gratitude', 'indignation' and a few others.

16. THE OBJECTIVE-REACTIVE CONFLICT

Still, it is regrettable that we still have no satisfactory theoretic unification of these matters. If we had one, it might help us to understand the tendency of reactive attitudes to be in conflict or in tension with thorough objectivity. What is the source of this conflict or tension, and how strong is it?

As regards the latter question: it is trivially true that an *exclusively* objective frame of mind must absolutely exclude everything non-objective; but the question is whether a *thoroughly* objective frame of mind can be combined with reactive attitudes. Not in me, it seems; and many of my acquaintances say the same. So would Dostoyevsky:

> But what can I do if I don't even feel resentment? ... My anger, in consequence of the damned laws of consciousness, is subject to chemical decomposition. As you look, its object vanishes into thin air, its reasons evaporate, the offender is nowhere to be found, the affront ceases to be an offence and becomes destiny, something like toothache, for which nobody is to blame.[13]

Perhaps there is a 'law of consciousness' by which thorough objectivity casts out reactive attitudes. Some people deny that this dependably happens when *they* 'look' with Dostoyevsky or 'measure the lot' with Yeats; but this conflict of testimony could reflect our unclarity as to what the issue is. On the other hand, the phenomenon may be subject to real interpersonal variation.

Strawson seems undecided about the strength of the conflict. He makes it absolute when he says that the objective attitude 'cannot' be emotionally toned with resentment, gratitude, etc. (p. 9), and when he alludes to the 'human isolation' which 'a sustained objectivity of interpersonal attitude ... would entail' (p. 11). But his reference to 'the tension there is, in us'

---

[13] F. Dostoyevsky, *Notes from Underground* (Penguin Books, 1972, trans. J. Coulson), p. 27 (Ch. 1, §5).

between the two sorts of attitude (p. 10) suggests something weaker.

As for the question of why there should be any conflict or tension: Strawson merely emphasizes how *different* the objective attitude is from reactive ones; but more explanation is needed of why that should set them against one another. Perhaps it is just a matter of the limits on how much mental variety one can manage at a single time—limits which a virtuoso of the inner life might transcend through practice. Or perhaps reactive attitudes essentially prepare for personal interaction while the objective attitude prepares for inquiry, these two sorts of *activity* being somehow incompatible. In that case, the two sorts of attitude would be derivatively in conflict, like simultaneously readying oneself for a sexual encounter and for giving an after-dinner speech. But, to revert to the theme of §14 above, this suggestion cannot be evaluated until we know just what sort of personal involvement or interaction, if any, is definitive of 'reactive attitudes'.

On the question of the strength, and the source, of the objective–reactive conflict I am also defeated.

17. THE OTHER TWO CATEGORIES

I mentioned that Strawson's account starts with 'personal' reactive attitudes and then adds to them self-reactive attitudes and impersonal or moral ones. As part of a general evaluation, and no longer in pursuit of a definition of 'reactive', I want to examine these two extensions of the account.

First, I should say more about how personal reactive attitudes are introduced. Having instanced some of 'the many different kinds of relationship which we can have with other people', Strawson remarks that 'in general, we demand some degree of goodwill or regard on the part of those who stand in these relationships to us' (p. 6); and he represents personal reactive attitudes as essentially a person's responses to the goodwill, indifference, etc. of those with whom he is suitably interrelated. These two elements—kinds of relationship, and demands for goodwill within them—generate the two parts of Strawson's line around accountability: the agent is not to blame because *he* is incapable of entering into relationships of the relevant kind, or because *his action* did not really manifest a lack of goodwill. That collaboration between the two elements is a smoothly efficient affair, increasing one's confidence that Strawson has them right.

Confidence wanes, however, when one looks at the extension of the account from personal reactive attitudes to impersonal and self-directed ones (pp. 14–16). Here, Strawson makes one of the two elements do all the work. He connects personal reactive attitudes with the demand that others show goodwill towards oneself, impersonal ones with the demand that others show goodwill towards men in general, and self-directed ones with the demand upon oneself that one show goodwill towards others. Nothing is said about any interpersonal relations within which such demands arise; and indeed Strawson says explicitly that the moral reactive attitudes 'permit ... a certain detachment' (p. 4) and remarks on their not needing to include 'antecedent personal involvement' (p. 17). The impression is conveyed that to have impersonal or self-directed reactive attitudes is *just* to 'acknowledge the claims' of men upon men or of others upon oneself. Strawson does not quite say this, but it is suggested by his silence regarding what else is involved in these two kinds of reactive attitude.

But there must be more to them than that. I might 'acknowledge' your 'claim' to my goodwill, and thus regret my failures to give it to you, yet handle these lapses through self-criticism and self-amendment with no tincture of guilt or remorse; in which case I acknowledge the claims but do not have the corresponding kind of reactive attitude (unless Strawson counts self-criticism as 'reactive', in which case I am lost). Analogously, I might hold strongly that people should show goodwill towards one another, yet not be indignant when they fail to do so; for I may adopt a non-reactive, clinical, corrective, objective attitude to every instance I encounter of man's inhumanity to man. I submit that the answers to the questions 'Why does he regret [welcome] that action?' and 'Is his response reactive?' are logically independent of one another. If they are, then impersonal and self-directed reactive attitudes cannot be fully explained in terms of the acknowledging of claims: those 'acknowledgements' explain welcomes and regrets, but cannot explain the reactiveness.

Objection: 'If you respond non-reactively to John's failure to show goodwill towards James, then you cannot have acknowledged James's *claim* to goodwill from John or endorsed his *demand* for it.' The words 'claim' and 'demand' occur frequently in Strawson's discussion; and I concede that it is plausible to link '*demand* for x' with the idea of indignation at x's not being given. But this link cannot be used to explain what 'indignation' is. If it has any explanatory value, it runs the other way, enabling us to explain 'demand' by reference to indignation, as Strawson does: 'The making of the demand *is* the proneness to such attitudes' as those of 'disapprobation and indignation' (p. 22). Anyway, I doubt if 'demand' really covers all the ground: I can find no place for it in describing such undisappointed reactive feelings as those of gratitude and reciprocating love.

Perhaps we should try to fill out the treatment of impersonal and self-directed reactive attitudes by restoring the interpersonal-relation element. But Strawson doesn't want us to do this, and one can see why: if my indignation at your treatment of him is essentially to involve an interpersonal relationship, who are its relata—you and I? or you and he? Each answer seems peculiar. Yet I wish to defend the answer 'You and I'; but first I must return to the home ground of *personal* reactive attitudes, for Strawson's treatment of them contains a small defect whose consequences are now plaguing us.

18. RELOCATING ONE ELEMENT

Personal reactive attitudes are introduced, as I have noted, through the notions of claim-to-goodwill and interpersonal relation. Now, Strawson speaks of the goodwill which is demanded *in* certain relations; but isn't it also demanded outside of them? And cannot the latter demands also generate reactive attitudes? And, to take in some of the territory not covered by 'demand' and 'claim', cannot gratitude, for instance, occur without any antecedent personal involvement? 'But in all these cases there is the "involvement" created by the very behaviour to which the reactive attitude is a response.' That is true, but I am sure that Strawson is not thinking of kinds of involvement or 'interpersonal relation' which could be created just by kicking somebody or throwing him a coin. A large theme in 'Freedom and Resentment' is the contrast between the involvements which go with reactive attitudes and

Accountability 43

the 'isolation' which would be entailed by their absence, as well as the 'relief from the strains of involvement' (p. 12) which can be brought about by a temporary replacement of reactive by objective attitudes; and all of that is reduced to nonsense if one construes 'involvement' etc. so as to include mere helpings and harmings.

As for the converse: Strawson himself clearly implies that the fact that ill-will occurs within a relationship of the emphasized sort does not guarantee that the response to it will be reactive.

One might conclude that the notion of interpersonal relation is not supposed to help explain what a personal reactive attitude is, and is offered only as part of the natural history of reactive attitudes—a mere description of their place in our lives. But that is hard to reconcile with the amount of weight Strawson seems to lay upon such expressions as 'participant' and 'non-detached'. Fortunately, there is another way out.

It is to give the notion of an interpersonal relation (of the relevant kind) a role in the analytic or explanatory part of the account, but not quite the role initially allotted to it by Strawson. What should be emphasized, I suggest, is not the relations *within which* reactive attitudes arise, but rather the relations *towards which* they point. If I resent someone's treatment of me, there may have been antecedently no special kind of relation between us; but my very resentment creates one, or sets the stage for one. I cannot say what the 'special kind' is: that is the problem which I could not solve when trying to define 'reactive' in §14 above. But still I submit that it helps if those participations and involvements which Strawson emphasizes are seen not primarily as the ground in which reactive attitudes grow but rather as embodied in or consequential upon them; not as required in the past or present, but as implied or suggested or invited for the future.

This idea is implicit throughout most of 'Freedom and Resentment', which is why I could quietly adopt it in my section on interpersonal relations. But it needs to be made more emphatic and explicit than Strawson makes it. It could lead to a tightening of the curiously loose and structureless paragraph in which 'reactive attitudes' are first introduced (p. 6). It could also let us strengthen a soft spot in Strawson's rationale for the line around the concept of accountability. The reason why 'seeing someone [as] deranged or compulsive' tends to 'set him apart from normal participant reactive attitudes' (p. 9) is that those attitudes connect with normal interpersonal relations. Connect *how*? If reactive attitudes essentially embody or point towards or prepare for interpersonal relations, then it is clear how someone's incapacity for the latter makes it inappropriate to have reactive attitudes towards him. But if the connection is just that reactive attitudes (should?) arise out of events between people who are interrelated, it is not clear how the argument runs. It would apparently have to put 'He is deranged' on a par in with 'He is a stranger to me': in each case there *is* no significant relationship between us, and so (for some still unclear reason) it would be inappropriate for me to have a reactive attitude towards him. I can find no basis here for attaching importance to the difference between a person's being unrelated to me and his being incapable of relating to me; whereas that difference becomes paramount if reactive attitudes are seen as pointing towards possible or imagined future interpersonal relations rather than as growing out of past ones.

The proposed relocation of the notion of interpersonal relation could also greatly help the extension of the account to cover the other two categories of reactive attitudes. A self-reactive attitude does involve an important 'interpersonal' relation: remorse, for instance, can be represented as a confrontation—with an accusing glare on one side and downcast eyes on the other—between one's present self and some past self. I offer this as a realistic view of what self-reactive attitudes are like, though admittedly a still incomplete one; and as better than an account which focuses on the acknowledging of claims.

Similarly with impersonal reactive attitudes: moral indignation—we can now say—involves actually or imaginatively putting oneself into, or readying oneself for, a special kind of relation with the person towards whom the indignation is directed.

This in turn throws light on Strawson's view that 'moral' reactive attitudes are significantly more 'detached' than personal ones are. In my revised version, the important kind of 'interpersonal relation' is equally present in both categories. In many moral cases, the attitude is only an entertaining of an imagined relation, but the same is true in many personal cases, e.g. gratitude to a now-dead benefactor, anger at a still-unidentified thief, resentment towards an oppressor whom one hopes never to see again. There is this much in Strawson's thesis: a reactive attitude of the kind he calls 'personal' is a response to someone's attitude towards *oneself*, and so personal reactive attitudes must be in that sense self-involving. But I see no reason to think that they must pertain to the important kinds of interpersonal relation to a greater degree than the 'moral' ones do.

This presumably connects with Strawson's suggestion that 'the tension between objectivity of view and the moral reactive attitudes is perhaps less than the tension between objectivity of view and the personal reactive attitudes' (p. 17). I can find no reason to agree with this. (Indeed, severe objectivity seems *more* apt to banish a blaming attitude than a resentful one; but the evidence for this might be reinterpreted as showing that objectivity is harder to achieve where one's own interests are concerned. So that is a stand-off.) I can only conjecture that Strawson was guided here by the idea that moral reactive attitudes are significantly more 'detached' than personal ones are; so this is another burden which is lifted from our shoulders if the notion of interpersonal relations is relocated in the manner I have advocated.

19. GENERALIZING THE OTHER ELEMENT

The relocation of the notion of interpersonal relation frees us to reconsider the demand-for-goodwill element in the account. It is salutary to be reminded of how much we care about the attitudes of others towards ourselves and towards one another; but I contend that this 'caring' belongs to the natural history of reactive attitudes rather than to the elucidation of 'reactive attitude'. We can understand the idea of someone's being genuinely morally indignant over someone else's attitude to natural beauty, for instance; and so moral indignation does not have to be a response to someone's attitude *towards people*. If nothing else really merits moral indignation, that is a substantive moral truth rather than a fact about the concept of moral indignation.

Essentially the same point holds for non-moral reactive attitudes, but here there is a terminological snag. Strawson assumes—rightly, in my view—that an attitude counts as 'moral' only if it rests on a general principle, or anyway on something which does not essentially refer to any particular item. So an attitude of mine is not moral if its basis essentially involves myself: I am *morally indignant* at your contemptuous attitude towards a benefactor, but I *resent* your contemptuous attitude towards *me*. But the basis for an attitude might lack generality—thus depriving the attitude of the status of 'moral'—in some quite different way. For a bit of behaviour might enrage me on a particular occasion, although it neither infringes any general principle which I hold nor essentially involves myself. For instance, I take no general stand on attitudes to natural beauty, but on this one occasion it just makes me angry to see a man walk unheedingly past the masses of Alpine Lilies and Indian Paintbrush. Or I have an unreasoned 'thing' about Bruckner, which leads me to feel something like gratitude towards anyone who loves his music. That anger and that 'gratitude' are both reactive, I suppose; but they are not 'moral', since one concerns a particular occasion and the other a particular person, and neither rests on general principles. But neither of them fits comfortably under Strawson's label '*personal* reactive attitude', since that label so naturally suggests an attitude which responds to someone's attitude *to oneself*.

I suggest, therefore, that the two basic categories of reactive attitudes are 'non-principled' and 'principled' (or 'moral'), with 'personal' as an important species within the former.

As for self-reactive attitudes: some of them are principled and some are not; for an attitude of self-censure or self-congratulation may, but need not, rest upon some principle which one holds. Strawson focuses primarily on the principled ones—which rest on one's acknowledgement of others' claims on one's goodwill—and perhaps they matter most. But there are others, such as self-reproach for having made a fool of oneself in public. Incidentally, Strawson's use of the word 'moral' is unsatisfactory on any showing, for his 'moral' category positively excludes self-reactive attitudes. Admittedly, what is 'moral' must have a general basis; but that is no obstacle to allowing that self-reactive attitudes can be moral. My remorse over my cruelty is as principled as my indignation over yours.

So much for taxonomy and terminology. Returning now to the substantive point: I suggest that although it is all right to tie reactive attitudes to responses to *somebody's attitude*, it is unduly narrowing to tie them to responses to *somebody's attitude towards somebody*. The '... towards somebody' bit must loom large in the natural history—and perhaps also in the ethics—of reactive attitudes, but not in the account of what reactiveness is.

When the account is thus generalized, it covers cases which are untouched by Strawson's treatment. Also, as I have shown, it forces us to make independently worthwhile revisions in the taxonomy and terminology. And, finally, it makes no difference to the relevant part of Strawson's rationale for the line around accountability. For that concerns cases where, despite appearances to the contrary, 'the agent's attitude and intentions [are] what we demand they should be' (p. 7); and this need not draw on the idea that the relevant 'attitude' must be towards one or more people.[14]

[14] An earlier version of this paper was the subject of extremely helpful comments by Peter Remnant, Richard Sikora, Earl Winkler, and, especially, Donald G. Brown.

The Transcendental 'I'

J. L. Mackie

What theme unites the images of Zeno Vendler mounted on a horse and watching, through Hannibal's eyes, the battle of Cannae, of Peter Strawson blazing a trail through a jungle of phenomena, and of Elizabeth Anscombe floating in a tepid bath? It is, of course, the transcendental 'I'.[1]

Vendler's argument is best stated from his own point of view. For reasons that Kripke and others have stressed, Zeno Vendler, this man that I am, could not have been born at any other period, or of parents other than those who actually generated me. Yet I can imagine living at a different period, I can imagine my being Hannibal or Claudius. But the impossible cannot be imagined; so it must be possible that I should be Hannibal or Claudius. But Claudius has one individual essence, and Vendler has another, so Vendler could not be Claudius and cannot be imagined to be Claudius. The 'I' that is the subject of such a transference 'has no content and no essence; it is a mere frame in which any picture fits; it is the bare form of consciousness' (p. 117). 'The transcendental "I" is not a thing ... The transcendental aspect of my being consists in nothing else but in the realization that I, as a subject of experience, am only contingently tied to the senses of this body, ... in one word, it consists in my ability to perform feats of transference' (p. 118).

Anscombe's argument turns upon a contrast between the use of 'I' and what would be the use of a proper name '*A*', which everyone used of himself (a human being, a person with a body), though each person also had another name which others used of him. A hint of the contrast is given by the term 'self-

---

[1] See Zeno Vendler, 'A Note to the Paralogisms', in *Contemporary Aspects of Philosphy*, edited by Gilbert Ryle (Stocksfield, 1977), pp. 111–21; P. F. Strawson, *The Bounds of Sense* (London, 1966), pp. 162–70; and G. E. M. Anscombe, 'The First Person', in *Mind and Language*, edited by Samuel Guttenplan (Oxford, 1975), pp. 45–65.

consciousness', which 'is something real ... which "I"-users have and which would be lacking to "*A*"-users, if their use of "*A*" was an adequate tool for their consciousness of themselves' (p. 51). But the crucial question is whether 'I' is or is not a referring term of some kind or other. If so, it is 'secure against reference-failure. Just thinking "I ..." guarantees not only the existence but the presence of its referent' (p. 55). The 'conception' through which 'I', if it is a referring term, either a name or a demonstrative, attaches to its object can only be 'the thinking of the I-thought, which secures this guarantee against reference-failure' (p. 55). Though '*A*', in use, would also be guaranteed to have a reference, it would not be guaranteed to have the right reference, since what I take to be part of my own body may not be so. Consequently, '*if* "I" is a referring expression, then Descartes was right about what the referent was' (p. 58). Its referent can be nothing but a (stretch of a) Cartesian Ego. But Descartes's position 'has ... the intolerable difficulty of requiring an identification of the same referent in different I-thoughts' (p. 58). 'How do I know that "I" is not ten thinkers thinking in unison?' (p. 58).

Anscombe therefore takes the difficulties of the Cartesian position as completing a *reductio ad absurdum* of the suggestion that 'I' is a referring expression of any kind. 'Getting hold of the wrong object *is* excluded, and that makes us think that getting hold of the right object is guaranteed. But the reason is that there is no getting hold of an object at all. With names, or denoting expressions (in Russell's sense) there are two things to grasp: the kind of use, and what to apply them to from time to time. With "I" there is only the use' (p. 59).

Anscombe's negative conclusion, then, is similar to Vendler's. There is nothing to which 'I' refers; 'I am E.A.' (or 'Z.V.') is not an identity proposition. But their positive accounts diverge. Whereas Vendler stresses feats of transference, Anscombe at least centres the use of 'I' in such thoughts as 'I am sitting', 'examples of reflective consciousness of states, actions, motions, etc. ... of this body. These I-thoughts ... are unmediated conceptions (knowledge or belief, true or false) of states, motions, etc. of this object here' (p. 62). She sets aside such typically Cartesian thoughts as 'I am thinking about thinking', 'I hope, fear, love, etc.', and even 'I have a headache' and 'I see a variety of colours'. It is a corollary of her view that 'No problem of the continuity or reidentification of "the I" can arise' (p. 62); it is merely that the same human being has different I-thoughts at different times. A 'lapse of self-consciousness' is just a lack of 'unmediated agent-or-patient conceptions of actions, happenings, and states'. But these conceptions, she maintains, 'do not involve the connection of what is understood by a predicate with a distinctly conceived subject'. The notion of such a subject is just a '(deeply rooted) grammatical illusion' (p. 65).

Strawson, too, speaks of an illusion, though not a grammatical one. He argues that Kant exposed and, less completely, explained 'a natural and powerful illusion' by which 'we mistake the necessary unity of consciousness for ... an awareness of a unitary subject' (p. 163). Reconstructing and completing Kant's account, he says that while 'a certain character of connectedness and unity' in a temporally extended series of experiences, yielding 'experience of a unified objective world', 'makes room for the idea of *one* subjective or experiential route through the world', and so provides 'as it were, the basic ground for the possibility of an empirical use for the concept of the subject of such an autobiography, the concept of the self', this is not in itself enough. It is also vital that 'our ordinary concept of personal identity does carry with it empirically applicable criteria for the numerical identity through time of a subject of experiences (a man or human being) ... which involve an essential reference to the human body'. This 'supplies an absolutely firm basis for a genuinely object-referring use of names and personal pronouns, in sentences in which states of consciousness, inner, experiences, are ascribed to the objects referred to by the names or pronouns' (pp. 163–4). But 'the fact that lies at the root of the Cartesian illusion' is that 'When a man (a subject of experience) ascribes a current or directly remembered state of consciousness to himself, no use whatever of any criteria of personal identity is required to justify his use of the pronoun "I" to refer to the subject of that experience' (pp. 164–5). Yet Strawson insists that when 'I' is thus used in 'criterionless self-ascription', it does not 'lose its role of referring to a subject'. He suggests that it can still refer to a subject because either it issues from the mouth of an empirically identifiable person or, if used in soliloquy, it is used by a person who would acknowledge the applicability of ordinary empirical criteria to the question of his own identity with someone who performed some earlier action. ' "I" can be used without criteria of subject-identity and yet refer to a subject because, even in such a use, the links with those criteria are not in practice severed'(p. 165).

Strawson, then, is partly in agreement but partly in disagreement with Anscombe and Vendler. Like them he holds that 'a purely inner and yet subject-referring use for "I" ' is an illusion. Consequently 'If we try to abstract this use, to shake off the connection with ordinary criteria of personal identity ... what we really do is simply to deprive our use of "I" of any referential force whatever. It will simply express, as Kant would say, "consciousness in general"' (p. 166). But what Strawson here says that we may try to do, Anscombe and Vendler think we have done. They say that the central use of 'I' is this non-referring one, whereas Strawson says that the ordinary use remains referential, because the links with empirical criteria of identity are not in practice severed. (Also, unlike Anscombe, Strawson does not shy away from the characteristically Cartesian thoughts: for him it is especially states of consciousness, inner experiences, that are self-ascribed immediately and without criteria.)

We have, then, two issues. Are Strawson, Anscombe, and Vendler all in the right in their general support of a Kantian against a Cartesian view? And, where they differ, is Strawson right against the others in saying that 'I' remains a referring term?

On this second question, the view of Anscombe and Vendler is paradoxical. Surely ordinary speakers commonly at least intend to use 'I' as a referring term. On first learning the jargon they would say confidently that it is one. If this is a grammatical illusion, it is one nearly all of us share. Also, as Anscombe admits, the rule for the truth of propositions with 'I' as subject is

> If X makes assertions with 'I' as subject, then those assertions will be true if and only if the predicates thus used assertively are true of X.

—for example, 'I am sitting' said by E.A. will be true if and only if E.A.—that human being—is then sitting. It is hard to see how 'I', so used, can be failing to refer to X (or E.A.) if that is how it helps to determine the truth or falsity of the assertion. Again, Anscombe admits that children sometimes use their own names instead of 'I', and that this could conceivably be the standard practice. But, she says, what is semantically a name in other people's mouths will not be so in one's own: 'it will not signify like a name' in one's own utterances (p. 64). This is what consistency requires her to say; but it underlines the paradox.

However, Anscombe and Vendler have arguments to support their initially surprising claims. Anscombe's main argument is that no reference other than the Cartesian one (to which there are, she believes, decisive objections) could be guaranteed against the two kinds of reference-failure, the lack of a referent and the risk of a wrong reference, the risk that what I take to be I might not be I. This is how 'I' differs from 'A', the hypothetical second name that every human being uses of himself. But what does this show? Surely only that the *sense* of 'I' differs from that of 'A'. If 'I' has a reference, then the way in which it gets its reference differs from the way in which 'A' gets its; but 'I' might still have a reference, and might even happen always to have the same reference as 'A'. But how could there be a sense which guaranteed 'I' against both kinds of reference-failure?

As Locke saw, the basic fact, which also gives a clue to the answer to this question, is the occurrence (in each of us), both at the same time and in temporal succession, of co-conscious experiences, of both the Cartesian and the Anscombian varieties – awareness of feelings, bodily positions, intentional movements, and so on. These, as they occur, joining on to a pre-existing co-conscious system (from which components are also constantly dropping off) are ascribed to a single supposed subject. Why, or even how, we do this is for the moment irrelevant, though I shall revert to it later; it may well be a sophisticated, learned, performance; but it is enough that it occurs. Built on this occurrence is a linguistic rule for the use of 'I': each item that enters this co-conscious system as I-ascribed, that is, it is appropriately reported by such sentences as 'I am writing', 'I have a headache', 'I wonder whether . . .' Thus it is linguistically, and therefore trivially, guaranteed that whatever

I take as 'I' *in this way* is I; but the reality on which this linguistic procedure is based is just the serial co-consciousness of experiences and thoughts. But if 'I' is then used with the intention of referring, must it either refer to a Cartesian Ego or, if there is no such thing, and yet it is intended to refer to such, *always* involve a failure of reference? No, because there is something which in all normal cases really will be writing, or having a headache, or wondering, and so on: the human being who uses such sentences assertively either in conversation or in soliloquy. And even in abnormal cases, where the asserted predicate is not true of this human being – I have a delusion that I am writing – it is still about this human being that I am mistaken. So in fact, though not by the above-mentioned linguistic rule alone, reference to this human being will be secured.

However, this is not the only linguistic rule for the use of 'I'. Another is that if someone says to X 'You are ...', X can agree by saying 'Yes, I am...' or disagree by saying 'No, I'm not...' That is, 'I' is located partly as a counterpart to 'you' (and to 'he' and 'she' in certain uses). And this tends to fix its reference as being to the human being who uses it. (But of course this works both ways: the meanings of 'you' and 'he' and 'she' are also affected by the fact that they are counterparts of 'I'.) 'I', therefore, is governed by at least two meaning rules: one which makes it refer to whatever it is whose self-consciousness it expresses, which is at best factually and contingently this human being, and one which binds it directly, linguistically, as Anscombe's 'A' is bound, to the human being who uses it. The over-determination of meaning by such initially divergent rules might conceivably cause trouble; but since the rules contingently converge in the end, it does not.

I want to say that when the first rule is implemented—the one linked with self-consciousness—we have a guarantee against the second kind of reference-failure: there is no danger that what I thus take to be I might not be I. And only then. The second rule, like that for 'A', secures us only against the first kind of reference-failure: it ensures that there is a referent somewhere around. But it might be objected that even the first rule does not achieve this. The reference of the 'I' that expresses self-consciousness to this human being could conceivably fail, and it can be deliberately abandoned. It would fail if I were to become disembodied, which is conceivable though it may well be physically impossible, and it is abandoned when, with Vendler, we engage in feats of transference. And in these marginal cases the over-determination of meaning by the two rules does cause trouble: in employing one rule we have to ignore the other.

This brings us to Vendler's argument, which seems straightforward and, given its assumptions, conclusive. It is necessary that Z.V. is not Claudius. But I can imagine my being Claudius, so it is not necessary that I am not Claudius. From this it does not, indeed, follow that I am not Z.V. But it does follow that I am not necessarily Z.V., and hence that 'I am Z.V.' cannot be a true identity statement if both 'I' and 'Z.V.' are rigid designators. 'I' cannot be used as a rigid designator, as a name or a definite description used referentially, both in 'I am Z.V.' and in 'I might have been Claudius'.

Once it is thus set out explicitly, we can see that the argument does not show that 'I' is never used to refer to a thing (or person or human being), but only that there are some uses in which it does not rigidly designate a human being, and hence that if it does then rigidly designate anything, this will have to be a Cartesian Ego. It follows that if there is another use in which it does rigidly designate the human being who uses it, 'I' must be ambiguous. But this is only to put in other words what was suggested above, that 'I' is governed by two meaning rules which initially diverge, though they converge again in ordinary circumstances. Vendler's examples of transference stress that there are special kinds of thinking in which the divergence is unresolved. I as a subject of consciousness, or perhaps as a mere pseudo-subject in a series of co-conscious experiences, might have been Claudius, though I, this human being, could not.

But should we speak here of a subject or of a pseudo-subject? Vendler is wrong to say that the 'I' which is the subject of transference is 'the bare form of consciousness', though he is right to say that it is a frame in which any picture fits. When I imagine being at Cannae, it is *my* being at Cannae that I imagine, not that of a bare form of consciousness. (After all, a good many thousand 'forms of consciousness' were there, but this is not the central part of what I imagine.) Yet it is not, in general, that I imagine there being experiences linked by co-

consciousness to my actual ones: I do not have to think of myself, at Cannae, remembering the twentieth century. I ascribe the imagined experiences to a subject. I need not imagine them as linked by co-consciousness to the present series, and *a fortiori* I do not merely do this. (Nor is it merely that I am joining them to this series just by imagining them: for that would be true of anything I imagined, and so cannot explain the distinctive element of my imagining *my* being there.) But still we have the nagging question, is it to a real subject or to a pseudo-subject that I ascribe them? As we noted, there is a real subject of my actual experiences—these imaginings among them—namely this human being. So when I imagine whatever is the subject of my actual experiences as being at Cannae, it is to this human being that I in effect ascribe the imagined experiences; but not directly, not explicitly, and that is how I avoid the contradiction of supposing this human being to have lived at a different time.

The two premisses of Vendler's main argument—'Z.V. could not have lived at a different period' and 'I could have lived at a different period'—both call for fuller interpretation. As I have argued elsewhere about such Kripkean modal theses, the first really means only that we have a way of thinking and speaking about the same individual with respect to counterfactual possibilities that precludes this. We think of the same individual, even in counterfactual possibilities, as being whatever persistent thing of that kind has the same origin.[2] Possibilities for this individual (human or non-human) are possible divergences from its actual history. But the second premiss brings out another way in which I can think, with respect to counterfactual possibilities, of this special individual, myself. I hold on to myself merely as the subject, whatever it may be, of these present experiences. The counterfactually imagined experiences are made its simply by direct fiat. I do not construct an apparently objective course of events and then have to identify myself with some item already in it: rather I tell a story about myself as centre.

It may be objected that if the subject of these present experiences happens to be this human being, then it could not

[2] Cf my '*De* What *Re* is *De Re* Modality?', in *The Journal of Philosophy*, Vol. 71 (1974), pp. 551–61, and my *Problems from Locke* (Oxford, 1976), pp. 152–9.

have been at Cannae. This is true in the sense that (unless we allow travelling backwards in time) there is no objectively describable possibility which we would count as this human being's being at Cannae. But that does not conflict with the fact that in constructing a subjective, egocentric, story I can think of 'I' simply as the subject, whatever it may be, of these present experiences and not include any features of any individual essence which would prevent me from coherently imagining this subject's being at Cannae.

In this, as with many similar puzzles, some vagueness or equivocation about the scope of a definite description is a source of trouble, and care about such scope is the formal treatment required for clarity. Since the subject of my present experiences is in fact this human being, we can say truly, giving the description large scope, 'As for the subject of my present experiences, it is not possible that it should have been at Cannae', but also, giving it small scope, 'It is coherently imaginable that the subject of my present experiences should have been at Cannae'. And 'I' may well have one sense, though perhaps not its only one, in which it is equivalent to this definite description.

The conceivability of disembodiment is no more of a problem. I can conceive that the subject, whatever it may be, of my present experiences is not and has not a body; yet if that subject is in fact this human being, which would cease to exist if this body ceased to function, there is no objectively describable possible state of affairs which would count as this subject's being disembodied.

We can cope, then, both with Anscombe's argument and with Vendler's. They fail to disprove what indeed seems to be the case, that 'I' not only is regularly a referring term, but also regularly refers to the human being who uses it. But this reference is secured by two different rules which constitute different senses for 'I'. One rule links it, like Anscombe's 'A', directly to this human being. The other rule links it directly only to the subject, whatever it may be, of these experiences, and therefore only indirectly and contingently to this human being. In feats of transference and in the conceiving of one's own disembodiment the latter sense only is employed: the former would yield a contradiction and is in practice ignored.

On one central issue, then, I am agreeing with Strawson against Anscombe and Vendler. But I doubt whether Strawson would accept this talk of two senses for 'I'. He insists that even in the uses which correspond to what I have just called the latter sense the links with empirical criteria of personal identity are vital. '"I" can be used without criteria of subject-identity and yet refer to a subject. It can do so because—perhaps—it issues publicly from the mouth of a man who is recognizable and identifiable as the person he is by the application of empirical criteria of personal identity; or, even if used in soliloquy, is used by a person who would acknowledge the applicability of those criteria in settling questions as to whether he, the very man who now ascribes to himself this experience, was or was not the person who, say, performed such-and-such an action in the past' (p. 165). But this seems wrong. There have been philosophers, from Joseph Butler to Richard Swinburne, who have denied that anything empirical constitutes decisive criteria for personal identity, and I think that about the analysis of our present ordinary concept of personal identity they are right.[3] If so, not only they but also those whom they correctly report do not 'acknowledge the applicability of those criteria'. Nor is it only by issuing publicly from the mouth of an identifiable man that 'I' refers to a subject. Anscombe remarks that our imagination makes something of the idea of mediums and possession, arguing that the following communication is conceivable (and presumably also understandable): 'Try to believe this: when I say "I", that does not mean this human being who is making the noise. I am someone else who has borrowed this human being to speak through him' (p. 60). Such considerations as these show that the use of 'I' to refer to a subject is not contemporaneously parasitic upon any links with empirical criteria of the identity of a human being. (But the example is also a difficulty for Anscombe herself. To explain how our imagination makes something of this idea, she compares the notion of possession with that of an interpreter who quotes his principal's words, including 'I', in direct speech. But this is different: the principal is normally another human being who is being *quoted*, but if there were a case of possession, it would be some other 'spirit' speaking directly, then if not there.)

[3] See *Problems from Locke*, pp. 192–5.

Strawson also says: 'It is not easy to become intensely aware of the immediate character, of the purely inner basis, of such self-ascription while both retaining the sense of ascription to a subject and forgetting that immediate reports of experience have this character of ascriptions to a subject only because of the links I have mentioned with ordinary criteria of personal identity' (p. 166). What he speaks of forgetting is what I would deny. Since, as he says, such self-ascription is immediate and has a purely inner basis—what I have called being joined on to a series of co-conscious experiences—what *present* role can the alleged links with ordinary criteria play? Strawson does not explain this, and it is hard to see how they can be playing any role, in view of ways in which they can be broken or dispensed with, for example in thought about mediums and possession or in a Butler–Swinburne–everyday concept of the absolute identity of a person.

On the other hand, taking up a theme that was set aside earlier, we can allow that these empirical criteria are historically important: they will have contributed to the development of the concept of a unitary subject to which experiences (etc.) are ascribed. In what he calls 'the coup de grâce to Cartesianism', Strawson, following Kant, argues that Descartes's rational psychology is powerless to defend its conclusions against alternative but equally empty theories. Perhaps there are a thousand souls simultaneously thinking the thoughts that one man's utterance expresses. 'How could the—or each—soul persuade itself of its uniqueness?' (p. 168). Anscombe echoes this: 'How do I know that "I" is not ten thinkers thinking in unison? Or perhaps not quite succeeding. That might account for the confusion of thought which I sometimes feel' (p. 53). But these intendedly rhetorical questions themselves hint at an answer. The approximation to harmony that my thoughts display is some evidence, though not conclusive evidence, of a single thinker, of a source whose parts, if it has parts, are closely interconnected. As jam sessions go, my mental performances are fairly successful. If there were a thousand, or even ten, souls thinking in near unison, this would call for some explanation of how it was achieved. Nevertheless, it is obvious that historically the notion of a single subject of experiences is borrowed from that of a single human being: in particular, it is other people's view of me as one person that has consolidated my unitary view of myself. Again, it is no accident that what I have called the two senses of 'I' converge. They grew up together: they developed in virtue of their convergence in the ordinary central uses. Each of us learned to use 'I' to refer to the subject, whatever it may be, of his co-conscious experiences because he was having those experiences in circumstances in which the corresponding predicates were true, and many of them observably true, of this human being. So when Strawson says that 'immediate reports of experience have this character of ascriptions to a subject only because of the links ... with ordinary criteria of personal identity', we can accept this if 'because' has a causal, historical, sense; what I deny is that we should accept it if 'because' stands for a contemporaneous linguistic constraint.

We finally return, then, to the other major issue, that between Kant and Descartes. Am I now rejecting what Strawson takes as Kant's insight and opening the way for the acceptance of a Cartesian Ego after all? Not quite. I am conceding to Descartes that whatever sophistication and learning may lie behind our present competence, we do now have a way of ascribing experiences, states, and actions to a supposed single subject, independently of any criteria for its unity and identity through time and without any contemporaneous reliance on the equation of this subject with a body or a human being, and we can therefore coherently engage in feats of transference or speculations about disembodiment which would conflict with such an equation. My essence is thinking and nothing but thinking in the sense that thinking alone is contemporaneously involved in this ascription. But I agree with Kant and Strawson and Anscombe and Vendler, against Descartes, that such a method of ascription does not suffice to introduce a thing to which these items belong and whose existence involves thinking alone, which is ontologically distinct from the body and of which we know, just in virtue of this method of ascription, that this thing can continue to exist whether there is a body or not. Descartes's mistake was to suppose that something whose style of introduction into our thought and speech involved nothing but thinking was thereby shown to be such that its existence involved nothing but thinking. The truth of the matter is that 'I' in one sense—as we may call it, the transcendental 'I'—genuinely refers to something which is introduced in the style of a Cartesian Ego, and yet what makes this a successful reference to an actual persisting thing is the fact that there is a human being, a body alive and functioning, which is not only the user of this 'I' but also the subject of the thoughts by way of which it refers.

There is, however, a further question: is the ordinary concept of *I* itself Cartesian? That is, is *I* not merely introduced in the style of a Cartesian Ego but also conceived as having an individuality independent of anything physical? Two considerations point in this direction.

First, can I still perform feats of transference once I know that I am in fact a human being, for whose existence and persistence the existence and persistence of this body—or at the very least this central nervous system—are needed? I should have to put this knowledge aside. I cannot include it within my transference imaginings without making them internally incoherent. But it will not be easy to put this knowledge aside if I am thinking of *I* just as the subject, whatever it may be, of these experiences, and thereby leaving the door wide open for its identification with this human being. It will be easier to do so if I have a positively Cartesian concept of myself and firmly deny my ontological dependence on my body.

Secondly, can I perform feats of transference with regard to you? If so, how? We ordinarily recognize, of course, that every *he* is an *I* to himself, but this recognition enables me only to understand that *you* can imagine your being at Cannae; it does not give *me* a way of imagining your being at Cannae. Yet I seem able to do this (for example, to imagine your being at Cannae with me). This would be a further difficulty not only for Ascombe and Vendler but also for Strawson, since I cannot regard it as possible that you, that particular human being, should have been at Cannae. I already believe that you have experiences, act intentionally, and so on, and I known something of what these experiences and actions are. So I can think of you, in one sense, as the subject, whatever it may be, of those experiences and actions, and I just might be able to ignore the fact that it was by way of my identification of you as that human being that I came by such knowledge as I have of your thoughts and actions, and so coherently imagine that that same subject, whatever it may be, existed at an earlier period. But again it will be much easier to think of something identical with you as existing at an earlier period if I have some category available, so that I can think of you, at Cannae, as the same so-and-so as you are now, and the appropriate category will be that of a Cartesian Ego, something which exists simply as a subject of thoughts and actions and which has, and can be thought of even in fantastically counterfactual imaginings as having, an absolute identity sustained neither by bodily continuity nor by chains of co-consciousness.

I am inclined to think, then, in view of our readiness to engage not only in first person but also in second and third person transferences, that our present ordinary concept of *I* (and of *you* and *he* and *she*) is partly Cartesian, and that in whittling down the meaning of the transcendental 'I' to 'the subject, *whatever it may be*. . .' and thereby allowing it to have a genuine reference to this human being, I am proposing a conceptual reform. A mere analysis of this part of our concept would equate 'I' rather with 'the subject, which exists in and by being a subject. . .', and therefore would compel us to say that though this is intendedly a referring term, it always fails of reference. For the arguments which suggest that our ordinary concept is (partly) that of a Cartesian Ego have no tendency to show that there really are any such things.

The Primitiveness of the Concept of a Person[1]

Hidé Ishiguro

1. Professor Strawson said in his book *Individuals* that the concept of a person was primitive. He made this claim in order to show up certain conceptual difficulties involved in two different theories which still leave their traces in philosophy. One is the Cartesian view, and the other is what Strawson calls the no-ownership view of experiences. But Strawson's positive view of the concept of a person has been criticized even by those who neither hold Cartesian views nor are tempted by any no-ownership view of experiences. For example, it has been suggested that what Strawson himself says about m-predicates (material predicates) and p-predicates (person predicates) entails that the concept of a person is not primitive.

I think that there is something very important in the claim that the concept of a person is primitive. Strawson's claims will enable us to develop a theory which tells us why the question whether certain beings are persons and others are not admits of an objective answer (rather than an answer based on our arbitrary decision). And as the answer does not involve reference to other kinds of entity besides persons, it does not require us to believe in the existence of souls as entities within us. Nor do we need to have a way of distinguishing persons in terms of purely physical characteristics.

Suppose, for example, that the concept of a person were like that of a friend. The application of 'friend' is based on a mutual decision to treat one another in a special way. If 'person' were similar, one would be mistaken about who was to count as persons only if one was mistaken about their attitude towards oneself. (Just as one may be mistaken about another being a friend if the other is actually quite indifferent to one.) In this case one could never say that it was wrong for someone not to

---

[1] In writing this paper I profited from comments by Cora Diamond, Barry Stroud, David Wiggins, Peter Winch, and Richard Wollheim.

regard blacks as persons, or that a particular society was mistaken in not treating madmen as persons. But we want to say this. It seems not to depend on our personal decision or even group decisions that some beings are persons—that they belong to a particular sort of thing to which we belong. It is something which we can make mistakes about and come to discover that we have done so. (The fact that there are borderline cases and the fact that differences between kinds of things are continuous do not tell against their being questions with objective answers.) Nevertheless I want to argue that, when one realizes that one was mistaken in not treating a being as a person, the basis of the realization is very different in kind from the basis upon which we come to realize, for example, that we were mistaken in treating whales as fish and not mammals. It is not like discovering a hitherto unnoticed morphological feature which the being shares with other human beings (as it was in the case of whales).

Certain points made in the last decade by Hilary Putnam and Saul Kripke and others on the relation of reference and meaning of certain words, will illuminate in an unexpected way what was so interesting in Strawson's claim. But Strawson's view of persons will actually take us further than have recent arguments about the referential theory of meaning. It suggests that such supposed dilemmas as 'Does one understand what a concept is by indexical means *or* by giving a defining property?' are just as misleading as was Russell's division of knowledge into knowledge by acquaintance and knowledge by description. These are not exhaustive alternatives. How one comes to understand what sort of things fall under a concept usually involves much more than either pointing, defining, or describing.

I will not at this point try to specify completely what is meant by a concept being primitive in the interesting sense Strawson requires. I hope it will become clearer during this paper. Nevertheless I will begin by saying a few things about it. First, to say that a concept is primitive is not to say that it is simple. Many complex concepts are primitive in a sense we will explain later. We shall see that primitiveness has more to do with the indispensability of a concept than with its simplicity. In the second place, primitiveness is not a feature of concepts in any absolute sense. A concept is primitive relative to another concept. In Strawson's argument, the important point is that the concept of a person is primitive relative to the concept of a mind and to the concept of a body. What we have to establish is the utility, for the understanding of the concept *person*, of the sense of "primitive" in which one concept can be said to be primitive relative to another concept.

2. My aim is to throw light on what is peculiar to the concept of a person rather than to attempt to exegesis of Strawson's argument, but it will throw light on the nature of the problem itself to bring to light and examine some of the assumptions inherent in Strawson's argument.

(a) A concept can be primitive even if the extension of the concept is a part (a proper subset) of the extension of another concept. It is not enough to point out, as some have done, that the class of persons is a subclass of animals, in order to prove that the concept of a person cannot be primitive. Strawson admits that we find it natural to indicate as persons the members of a certain class of moving material objects (*Individuals*, p. 113). But people are not identified as things of a specific kind of moving material object. To consider something as falling under the concept of a person, we need not first identify that thing as falling under the concept of moving material object. (Strawson at least believes that we do not. For when we ascribe p-predicates to ourselves—as when we say we are thinking hard or trying to catch the bus—we consider ourselves as persons, without first identifying ourselves as a specific kind of moving material object.) This is so even if we are as a matter of fact all moving material objects. Primitiveness then is an epistemic notion. The mere fact that f's are a subset of g's is not sufficient for the denial of the concept f's being primitive. Conversely a concept is not primitive just because an instantiation of it is not made up of other entities. Even if an electron were not made up further of elementary particles, the concept of an electron would not necessarily be primitive relative to that of an electric charge, if we had to use the concept of an electric charge in identifying an electron.

(b) We must remember the distinction between what Strawson calls 'sortal universals' and 'characterizing universals'. The ascription to a thing of a concept that expresses a characterizing universal presupposes that the thing has been identified as an individual falling under *some* sortal universal, and 'A sortal universal supplies a principle for distinguishing and counting individual particulars which it collects. It presupposes no antecedent principle or method of individuating the particular it collects. Characterizing universals, on the other hand, whilst they supply principles of grouping, even of counting particulars, supply such principles only for particulars already distinguished or distinguishable in accordance with some other antecedent principle method' (*Individuals*, p. 16). (It follows from this that an assertion about a number is an assertion about a sortal concept not about just any first-order concept. One can count three animals, or four boxes, but not three reds of four pales. Is the red box one instantiation of red, and are each of its six surfaces instantiation? How about half of each surface? Are they instantiations of red as well? Then there would be twelve of them...) Unlike *red* or *pale*, the concept *person* represents a sortal universal. Thus it supplies a principle of distinguishing and counting individual particulars. Notice that one and the same thing can be an instantiation of many different sortal universals; but, in order to individuate the thing, it is only necessary to take note of one of the sortal universals that it instantiates. Thus it *may* not be necessary to have the concept of a person, in order to individuate what are in fact persons. Departing perhaps from Strawson, I believe that the sortal 'animal' will do the same job. The reason why I think the sortal concept person is important is not so much for purposes of the individuation of persons as for the purpose of the differentiation of the individuals who are persons from those who are not.

(c) Concepts that correspond to sortal universals are intimately linked, according to Strawson, with *how* we ascribe the predicates which characterize them. What is important is not merely the fact that a person is a thing to which both m-predicates and p-predicates are said to be ascribable. It is the manner in which p-predicates are ascribed that matters. According to Strawson p-predicates have a unique logical character.

It is essential that p-predicates should have both first and third (or second) person ascriptive uses. Thus a thing falling under the sortal concept *person* must 'both [be] a self-ascriber and an other-ascriber of such predicates [p-predicates], and must see every other [person] as a self-ascriber' (*Individuals*, p. 108). I take this feature of p-predicates seriously and shall ignore here the other explanation of the distinction between p-predicates and m-predicates given by Strawson.[2]

In the case of the self-ascription of p-predicates (or at least some p-predicates) Strawson apparently believes that I do not have to identify myself as a kind of material body. That I have these feelings and thoughts is something I know without identifying my body (even if the use of these predicates themselves could not have been acquired without understanding myself as a material body observable to others). I know which actions I am intentionally carrying out without observation of my body. On this basis I can see movements of others as actions, interpreting them in terms of their intentions—as movements of individuals of the type to which I also belong (*Individuals*, p. 112). It is true that if I necessarily have to identify other people as material bodies, then in so far as I understand myself as being the same type of thing that other people are, I am identifying myself as a material thing. But because I can ascribe a p-predicate to the individual which is myself, *without identifying a particular kind of material body*, the sortal concept 'person' is said to be primitive relative to the concept of a body.

(d) In so far as Strawson believes that an ascription of a characterizating universal presupposes the ascription of a sortal universal, we can see that Strawson holds to what may be called a category theory. That is to say that for Strawson (contrast Frege), the domain over which a predicate is defined is restricted. For Strawson, p-predicates are 'not ascribable' to things which do not possess consciousness. 'Ascribable' here does not mean 'truly ascribable' (as some readers have hypothesized) but obviously means 'such that it makes sense to ascribe them'. In a footnote (*Individuals*. p. 99) Strawson writes 'The idea of a predicate is correlative with that of a range of

[2] Strawson writes that m-predicates do not involve any assumptions of consciousness on the part of the thing to which they are ascribed. But I find this explanation very unsatisfactory, for in whatever manner we define consciousness, it seems to me clear that the extension of the property of having consciousness is far bigger than the extension of the concept of being a person. Whereas self-ascription of certain predicates seem to distinguish persons as we know them from other sentient beings.

distinguishable individuals of which the predicate can be significantly though not necessarily truly affirmed.'

Many influential philosophers who have written on logical theory in recent years have assumed that for the sake of clarity, as well as for convenience in formal calculi, we should treat predicates as defined over unrestricted domains. One of the most forceful critics of the category theory has probably been W. V. Quine. He has attacked it for the obscurity of the notion of the category involved as well as for the restrictions that it imposes on negation and complement. (These restrictions are thought to be foreign to formal logic. Let us not here discuss this point. For we know that e.g. Van Fraassen's super-valuation Theory will enable us to close truth-value gaps. And we also know that Frege's formal system with predicates defined over unrestricted domains generated paradoxes. So that something has to be done, even if it is not necessary to impose a theory of categories.)

Let us consider the obscurity that Quine and others have ascribed to the notion of category. Many people have attacked category theorists for being dogmatic or obscure. How do they know, it is asked, that certain statements make no sense? If a category theorist believes that colour predicates like 'is green' are restricted to material things, say, then he can always spell out the presupposed restriction into the predicate itself and consider the predicate 'is a material object and is green' and this will satisfy a believer in unrestricted domains. Not much hangs on whether we call the sentence in which the predicate is ascribed to an object which lies outside the predicate's restricted domain senseless or false (or necessarily false). What is important is to see that our understanding of *what* it is that the predicate ascribes depends on our understanding of such ascriptions to objects in the relevant restricted domain. In other words our understanding of the meaning of the predicate does depend on our understanding of what it is for objects of certain types to satisfy the predicate.

In his critical commentary on Strawson's notion of p-predicates Professor Bernard Williams wrote that the category theorists are confused in that they 'express a doctrine which should surely be about sense in terms of reference'. But why can we not raise questions about the meaningfulness of ascribing certain predicates to certain entities? Williams said that what are categorially senseless, if anything is, are conjunctions of predicates; according to him what we should say is not that 'green' cannot be ascribed to a prime number but that 'green' and 'prime' cannot both be ascribed to the same thing. But this seems to beg the question. For *why* cannot 'green' and 'prime' together be sensibly (rather than falsely) ascribed to the same thing?

Here then are some important assumptions behind Strawson's claim that the concept of a person is primitive. In summary: (a) A concept's being primitive is compatible with its extension being a part of the extension of another concept. (b) Any ascription of a characterizing universal presupposes that the identification of the subject in terms of *a* sortal universal. (c) Concepts corresponding to sortal universals are intimately linked with the manner in which properties ascribed by characterizing predicates to objects belonging to the sortal are identified. (d) Every predicate presupposes a restricted domain in the sense that what it is that the predicate ascribes can only be understood with reference to a certain group of objects. And the category of persons is presupposed by the group of predicates which Strawson calls p-predicates.

3. For the rest of this essay I would like to develop one problem which relates to all of these four points and which I believe is important in clarifying the nature of the concept of person. One may call it the problem of the intension and extension of sortal concepts. The relationship between what Strawson calls characterizing universals and sortal universals seems to me to be much more complex than Strawson has indicated.

First as we have seen, an object falls under many sortal concepts and some sortal concepts obviously presuppose other sortal concepts. What I mean here by a sortal concept f presupposing a sortal concept g is that one cannot identify an object as falling under f without identifying it as a g. So it is not correct to say of *any* sortal universal that 'It presupposes no antecedent principle or method of individuating the particular it collects'. The sortal predicate 'philosopher' obviously presupposes the sortal predicate 'person', since one cannot individuate a philosopher without being aware that one individuates a person. This seems to be an epistemic feature of the use of the concept 'philosopher'.

Contrast this relations with that obtaining between the two sortals 'human being' and 'featherless biped'. Pascal, in his 'Esprit de Géometrie' (and Leibniz in the *New Essays*) criticized the definition of human being as a featherless biped popularly attributed to Plato. For, even if the two concepts were co-extensive—i.e. even if there were no person with amputated legs, and even if there never were or will be species other than man which are featherless and biped—the two concepts would be co-extensive only accidentally. We do not understand what a human being is by understanding what a featherless biped is. It is only because we assume we know what human beings are and that we discover the contingent fact that their class is co-extensive with that of featherless biped (if indeed it is).

How then do we understand what a human being is—and know when something is a human being?

In general we cannot have the concept corresponding to a sortal universal without knowing that the objects which fall under it necessarily instantiate certain kinds of characterizing universal, i.e. certain determinables. (To consider something as a material body in the sense of classical physics, for example, is to classify it as a kind of thing that has a certain mass, that has a spatial position at particular times, and that enters into various relations with other material bodies which can be subsumed under the laws of dynamics.) Thus falling under a sortal concept does not entail that the object falling under it instantiates any *specific* (determinate) characterizing universal, but it does entail that it instantiates a characterizing universal of some particular range. To identify something as a person is to judge that it has dispositions of certain kinds (beliefs, knowledge of various kinds) that it has abilities of a certain sort, that it enters into certain types of relationships with other persons. Yet when we understand what a person is, we do not have the complete set of characterizing universals (determinables) that distinguish persons from all other things.

In our acquisition of sortal concepts there is a subtle interplay between extension and intension, between our identifying objects that fall under the concept, and our then discovering that all these objects have a property which was not yet articulate in the concept. If we understand that the newly discovered properties follow necessarily (given the laws of nature we accept etc.) from the nature (of the objects) that are part of the concept, then we may enrich our conception and add the possession of these newly discovered properties to the concept. These are not arbitrary decisions how to redefine the sortal concept at each stage. Concepts of natural kinds may have a more or less fixed extension. As Professor Hilary Putnam has pointed out, what we do when we master the use of a natural kind term is to get the right extension. (Without getting into the debate whether a person is a natural kind or not, let us take this on trust about many sortal terms, including persons.) It is not up to us at a later stage to decide that certain properties which all the standard samples have are to count against their falling under the concept, and decide that we were not talking about the things we thought we were talking about. Part of how we identify concepts is by identifying what count as instances. We can take a hint here from Wittgenstein's claims that you must look for the use when you look for the meaning of the word. In understanding the concepts which correspond to the use of general terms, we are often guided by what objects they standardly designate.

For example, we have a working concept of an animal. Though I may not have a description of a set of features that would necessarily and sufficiently distinguish animals from other things, there are things I regard as standard examples. Of course there may be cases which do not fall clearly inside or outside the extension of the concept of animal that I think I share with others. I may have to consult authority or make decisions. On the other hand, I may find out that the description I gave of reproduction and which I thought was peculiar to animals, is satisfied by crystals. But crystals lack a whole cluster of properties which the things I consider as animals definitely have. I am not free to decide arbitrarily or piecemeal the status of the property of reproduction, as I had described it, within the concept *animal*, or simply make a decision that crystals are animals. The extension of the concept I had, which is given by the way I and others used the word 'animal', is my guide for the properties which I had not clearly articulated or described wrongly.

Just as in the case of individuals we can often agree about what or whom we are referring to without agreeing about all the descriptions the item satisfies, so also in the case of sortals it is enough for there to be sufficient agreement about the instances of the kind which we are talking about. It does not matter that we cannot spell out all of their distinguishing properties. In other words, even in the case of sortals, we do not always have to make decisions about the intension of a concept before we can get any agreement about the extension of the concept. And this point will support Strawson's contention that the concept of a person is primitive: we find ourselves using this sortal.

Professor Arthur Fine is right to have pointed out ('How to Compare Theories: Reference and Change', *Noûs*, 9, 1975) against Professor Kuhn, that if shift in theory and belief always shift the reference of general terms, then it rules out the possibility of people having mistaken beliefs or theories concerning the things they are talking about. Fine is quite right also to point out that fixing the reference is not a simple matter of ostension or some such unique introductory act. Let us agree that it is false that the extension of a general term is fixed once and for all by some act of introduction of the general term when one refers to an instantiation of it, and agree also that it is false that the intension of the general term must be determinate before we get to its extension. It does not follow, as Fine suggests, that we are therefore *free* at each stage *to decide* whether to keep the extension of the concept fixed and say we had false beliefs about the things in it, *or* keep the intension fixed and say we were wrong about the extension. In most cases we are simply not free to choose one way or another just as we please. In the case of the concept of person this is especially true. We agree about the entities which we think are indubitably persons, and this is not because we can articulate all the properties which all and only persons have. We want to treat those which are of the same nature (in a sense I hope to clarify later) as those we already recognize as persons, in certain agreed ways. It is because we *find* ourselves entering into certain kinds of relationships with them, that we understand something of what it is to be a person.

4. It will be helpful to recall here what Leibniz said about clear and confused ideas when he was arguing about a similar problem. According to Leibniz a complex idea may be both

clear and indistinct (confused) at the same time. Clarity does not always come together with distinctness. An idea is clear if we can clearly distinguish from others, things that fall under the idea. Yet the same idea may be indistinct if we do not understand the complex structure of the idea, i.e. if we do not know the properties that all and only these things which fall under the concept have. With ideas of abstract things like numbers it is hardly possible to have a clear idea without having a distinct idea. For example we cannot distinguish odd numbers from even numbers, without knowing what are the properties that are necessary and sufficient to make a number odd, but for most other kinds of things we have ideas that are not distinct. Thus Leibniz says 'we cannot give a definition of them. We make them known only by examples' (N. E. II, 29, 4). The position, is not simple as this remark of Leibniz might indicate, however. Even for material stuff concepts like 'gold' it is highly unlikely that we should have a clear idea unless we agreed on, or saw the prospect of agreeing on, a common distinct idea. This is because pointing to a sample does not by itself tell us how we decide that other objects are to count as being made of the same stuff as that sample. We might have been able so far to tell gold apart from other metals because every piece of gold we have encountered has been yellow and heavier than other metals. But if I encounter another alloy or another compound or even hitherto unknown metal which is of the same colour but heavier, how would I know whether it is to be considered the same metal or not? Without a knowledge of the relevant theory which would help me decide—i.e. without a distinct idea I would fail to distinguish gold from other metals. It is not enough to say that it is 'whatever bears a certain equivalence relation to the piece referred to as "this"'. We need to specify which equivalence relation it is or what it is to count as being of the same metal. Is an isotope of gold to count as the same kind of metal as this piece of gold? It is our theory about the sample in question which gives us the specific equivalence relation. So in many cases our clear ideas are also distinct ideas. cases our clear ideas are also distinct ideas.

When do we have clear but indistinct ideas? According to Leibniz, the best examples are ideas which correspond to Locke's secondary qualities. These ideas were simple ideas for

Locke, but for Leibniz these are complex ideas of complex properties. They are clear because we can distinguish things that fall under the idea *red* from other colours or hot things from cold things. They are nevertheless indistinct ideas because we do not understand the nature of the property of a thing's being red (e.g. that it reflects light waves of longest wave-length), or being hot (e.g. increased kinetic energy of the molecules). Those of us who have sight or sensation use our sight or touch to get things that are red or hot, rather than using a set of articulate criteria. Because our senses enable us to engage in discriminatory activities and a whole complex of activities dependent on these, we have a clear grasp of these properties which we cannot verbalize, having no grasp of the structure of things responsible for this property.

If we realize that there is a light wave with a wave length longer than that of light we hitherto called red light, we do not freely decide whether to think of this newly discovered light as red light. Red is the colour corresponding to certain perceptual experiences, and even if it was one of our beliefs that the colour was related to light of the longest wavelength, we *can* discover that our beliefs were wrong. Our senses, our perceptual experiences had more or less fixed the use of the term 'red', i.e. the extension of the concept.

5. I believe that it is similar in the case of the concept of a person. We do not recognize a person just by sight or by touch. But just as in the case of ideas of secondary qualities, we are hard put to define what a person is although we can more or less recognize one when we encounter one and see him act. By observing people we can discover various properties that all of them have. And even if on rare occasions we had to decide whether a being was a person on strength of its having or lacking certain property, there is normally no question of arbitrarily defining what goes into the concept of a person or what makes up its extension. We have some rough idea of what it is that we are committing ourselves to when we consider a being as a person. What matters to personhood of a being is the nature of the relations we find ourselves in, or decide to cultivate, or can even make ourselves see, however reluctantly, as being possible to establish with the being. We are obliged to consider it as a person whether we like it or not. Our ability to

communicate mutually and to understand or enter into various relations gives the extension of the concept of a person to which we believe we belong. And this does not have to wait for the moment when we have identified them as material bodies having a certain set of m-properties. (Our ascribing p-predicates to them presupposes rather than explains our regarding them as persons.)

Now obviously the fact that we treat certain objects in certain ways, and believe that we have entered into certain relation with them, does not by itself determine what kind of object they are. A fetichist's worship of an inanimate object, and his talking to it or engaging in various ritualized acts with it, does not turn an inanimate object into a person. Nor does the mere fact that certain people talk to and believe they communicate with dogs, goldfish, or even plants, establish that dogs, goldfish or plants are persons. Minimally personhood has to involve the possibility of entering into *mutual* relationship of the above kind. Nevertheless, it appears that the extension of the concept 'person' is determined not so much by our grasp of a clear set of characteristics which apply to a subset of animals as by our ability to enter into certain relationships or imagine ourselves doing so and realize in this way that they are of a kind with ourselves.

Strawson has written interestingly about this feature of human life (which he calls 'shared reactive attitudes') in his essays on *Freedom and Resentment* (British Academy Lecture 1962). It has been my purpose to connect it with the idea that the concept of a person is primitive relative to the concept of a material body. I have attempted to establish the link in three successive steps. (a) We get the concept person by some understanding of *ourselves* and of beings, typical beings, with whom we can identify ourselves as being of a kind. (b) This means that we can distinguish persons from other things without being able to articulate what kind of material objects they are by neutral physical features. (c) This in turn shows that it is indispensable that we have the sortal concept of a person. And, as I have said, I take the primitiveness of a concept to mean the indispensability of one sortal concept relative to another sortal concept. Of course (b) and (c) are compatible with the fact that there are some structural physical feature common to all those beings we consider as persons, as in the case of gold. But it does not entail this fact. What fall under the sortal *person* are not necessarily beings with the relevant genetic or physiological similarity to myself and standard persons—this may or may not turn out to be so—but beings who have the same range of dispositions, abilities, etc. Thus I would not like to commit myself to the view that a person is a natural kind. It may, for example, correspond to a disjunction of natural kinds, or one day include man-made beings which do not look like us. This will not affect the claim that the sortal concept is primitive.

People are sceptical about philosophical positions which start from *de facto* use of concepts. In the minds of many critics, the fact that people can obviously disagree about concepts or misuse them adds to the contingency of their uses. Yet, just as no theory of number would be worth defending if it did not minimally give an account of our entrenched practice of counting, no theory of persons would be worth defending if it did not capture our practice of regarding one another as persons. The necessary link between number theory and the practice of counting and doing sums is not destroyed by the fact that we occasionally miscount and miscalculate, nor by the fact that there are people who cannot learn to count. Similarly the necessary connection which must obtain between any philosophical concept of person and our practice of using the sortal concept is not weakened by the existence of disagreements and puzzles about personhood. Professor Strawson has reminded us of this truth.

Things Without the Mind—A Commentary upon Chapter Two of Strawson's *Individuals*

Gareth Evans

What is the connection between the idea of an objective world and the idea of a spatial world? If someone has a conception of a world, something whose existence and operations are independent of his experience of it, must he thereby conceive of a system of spatial relations in which both he and the phenomena he experiences have a place? This question can be put another way. We can imagine a series of judgements 'Warm now', 'Buzzing now', made by a subject in response to changes in his sensory state, which have no objective significance at all. But we can imagine a similar series of judgements, prompted by the same changes in the subject's sensory state, which do have such a significance: 'Now it's warm', 'Now there's a buzzing sound'—comments upon a changing world. What is involved in this change of significance? In particular, if 'Now it's warm' is interpreted as a report on the world prompted by experience, must it be tantamount to: 'Now it's warm *here*'?

The connection between space and objectivity lies so deep in our conceptual scheme that many philosophers pass from 'objective' to 'outer' without even noticing the question they beg. The subjective being regarded as what is 'in the mind', the objective becomes what is 'without the mind', and then it is easy to say with Hobbes that if we have a conception of a thing without the mind, we have a conception of space.[1]

In the second chapter of *Individuals*, Strawson probes this conceptual connection with great subtlety and imagination. He makes us aware of the potential gap between 'objective' and 'outer'—a gap which he then attempts to bridge with a fascinating argument. Strawson illustrates the argument by imagining the situation of a being whose experience is wholly auditory. He argues that the concepts of an objective world,

[1] Hobbes, *Elements of Philosophy*, II, 7, ii.

crucially the idea of existence unperceived, would not have any application in the experience of such a being unless that experience provides him with at least some analogue of space. Such an analogue can be provided in a purely auditory experience if each experience of a particular auditory phenomenon is accompanied by the experience of a master-sound—a constant sound whose variations in pitch enable the subject to give substance to the idea that he is moving. It is true that Strawson claims only that the master-sound provides an analogy of space. But it would be wrong to be misled by this, and by the fact that he labels the auditory universe a 'No-Space world', into thinking that Strawson is unsympathetic to the Kantian thesis that space is a necessary condition for objective experience. On the contrary, the chapter contains an argument for a slightly weakened version of that thesis.

Only part of the interest of the chapter lies here—in seeing how much is involved as an indispensable accompaniment to the idea of an objective world. The chapter is bold in another way. For if there is a frame of mind in which it is surprising how *much* is involved before the idea of objectivity can take root, there is an equally familiar frame of mind in which the surprise lies rather in how *little* a subject seems to need to think objectively. Certainly it is no part of Strawson's intention to derogate from the reality of things, but is our conception of our own world not just a little shaken by the thought that there could be a wholly auditory universe—by seeing how simply a tissue of reality can be woven out of regularities in experience?

I shall consider both these aspects of the chapter. I shall begin by considering whether Strawson successfully defends the Kantian thesis. After trying to show that the main line of argument is not successful, I go on to explore another line of argument also to be found in the chapter. In the final two sections, I elaborate two different reasons for doubting whether a subject whose experience was wholly auditory could be regarded as having a conception of an independent reality.

Before proceeding, there is one important preliminary. What sense does the phrase 'objective world' bear in the questions Strawson took to define his investigation, and which therefore define ours? Strawson is explicitly not concerned with an idea of objectivity which rests upon interpersonal agreement. For the purpose of focusing upon a manageable section of our over-all conceptual scheme rather than because it represents a genuine conceptual possibility, Strawson pretends that his subject makes no allowance for the existence of other observers. (Throughout, then, 'existence unperceived' is, effectively, 'existence unperceived by me'.) The idea which *does* concern Strawson is the idea of an experience's being *of* something distinct from it, and therefore the idea of something which is capable of existing independently of any experience of it.

Now Strawson dubs his investigation the elaboration of the conditions for a 'non-solipsistic consciousness'. But there is implicit in his notion of objectivity a restriction which precludes the application of the title 'theory of the objective world' to views which their proponents did not believe were solipsistic. The proponents of these views have a yet more general notion of objectivity in mind, according to which a theory has objective significance if it comprises propositions which, if true at a given time, are not true in virtue of the state of the subject at that time. This differs from Strawson's notion, for there may be no question of the subject's *experiencing* the reality which is constituted by the truths that do not belong in his biography.

For example, the subject's experience may be regular in a way which allows him to express various conditional or counterfactual propositions about what would be experienced were such and such else to be experienced. These propositions, if true at all, are not true in virtue of any actual occurrence in the subject's biography, and may be taken[2] as the basis of a claim that an objective reality is thereby allowed for. However this may be, it is not an objective reality in the sense which concerns Strawson:

> ... I shall mean by a non-solipsistic consciousness, the consciousness of a being who has a use for the distinction between himself and his states on the one hand, and something not himself, or a state of himself, *of which he has experience* on the other.[3]

---

[2] They have been so taken by phenomenalists. See, for example, C. I. Lewis, *An Analysis of Knowledge and Valuation* (Open Court, La Salle, Illinois, 1946), pp. 226–30, and *Mind and the World Order* (Dover, New York, 1956), pp. 135–9.

[3] *Individuals* (Methuen, London, 1959), pp. 69: my italics.

Things Without the Mind 79

For whatever it is that makes these purportedly 'objective' propositions true, it is not something of which the subject can be said to have experience.

PART ONE

Intertwined in the chapter are several ideas on which a defence of the Kantian thesis might rest, but the main line of argument is one in which the need for space arises from the requirement that the subject of experience (hereafter 'Hero') be able to reidentify the objects of his experience. As Strawson summarizes the results of this chapter in a later one:

> ... we had to introduce, in auditory terms, an analogue of space in order to make room for the idea of reidentifiable particulars ...[4]

A defence of the Kantian thesis on these lines must have two distinguishable stages; it has to be shown that the idea of reidentifiable objects is implicit in the idea of objectivity, and it has to be shown that criteria of reidentification, with the attendant distinction between qualitative and numerical identity, can only be framed in a spatial (or quasi-spatial)[5] world.

On the first stage of the argument, Strawson has this to say:

> ... to have a conceptual scheme in which a distinction is made between oneself or one's states and auditory items which are not states of oneself, is to have a conceptual scheme in which the existence of auditory items is logically independent of the existence of one's states or of oneself. Thus it is to have a conceptual scheme in which it is logically possible that such items should exist whether or not they were being observed, and hence should continue to exist through an interval during which they were not being observed. So it seems that it must be the case that there could be reidentifiable particulars in a purely auditory world if the conditions of a non-solipsistic consciousness could be fulfilled for such a world. Now it might further be said that it makes no sense to say that there logically could be reidentifiable particulars in a purely auditory world, unless criteria for reidentification can be framed or devised in purely auditory terms. And if this is correct, as it seems to be, we have the conclusion that the conditions of a non-solipsistic consciousness

---

[4] *Individuals*, p. 118.
[5] I shall drop this qualification in what follows; except where the context indicates otherwise, I shall use 'spatial' in the weak sense of 'spatial or quasi-spatial'.

can be satisfied in such a world only if we can describe in purely auditory terms criteria for reidentification of sound particulars.[6]

The second stage of the argument is not filled out in any great detail, but perhaps it is obvious how it would run. Hero has to be able to distinguish among later experiences of qualitatively indistinguishable phenomena those that are, and those that are not, later stages of the same phenomenon that he experienced earlier. This can only be done by taking into account the *relations* in which the phenomena stand; more specifically, relations which do not hold in virtue of the intrinsic non-relational character of the things related. And perhaps this may be seen as an abstract formal description of spatial relations.

Ingenious though this argument is, there is room for considerable doubt about its cogency, especially when it is interpreted in such a way that Strawson's auditory world provides an illustration of it. In that world, qualitatively identical sounds may be distinguished by their 'location at' (by being heard with) different pitch-levels of the master-sound. Given that this is the case, one may well feel that no genuine distinction between qualitative and numerical identity has been provided. Since different pitch-levels of the master-sound are qualitatively distinguishable, auditory presentations of numerically distinct sounds are never qualitatively indistinguishable, so long as a sufficiently inclusive view is taken of what to apply this concept to. But in the present context, a weaker point will suffice. If Strawson's Hero uses a genuine criterion of numerical identity, then space is not necessary for him to do so. Since his criterion does not make any real use of the dimensionality provided by the continuous variation in the pitch-levels of the master-sound we may suppose with equal legitimacy that criteria of reidentification can be framed in an auditory universe in which an *unordered* series of master-sounds plays the same distinguishing role as the ordered series of pitch-levels of Strawson's single master-sound.[7]

---

[6] *Individuals*, pp. 72–3.

[7] I assume here and throughout that the existence of an intrinsic ordering between 'places' is essential to a space or a quasi-space. This certainly seems to be the framework within which Strawson was working: 'We want the analogy of Space ... to provide for something like the idea of absence and presence—but not just of absence and presence in the most utterly general sense these words could bear, but absence or

The upshot of the weaker point is this: if the requirement deduced in the first stage of the argument can be satisfied in Strawson's auditory universe, the second stage of the argument cannot be completed. This difficulty stems from the quite unparalleled role played by the master-sound in generating the space of the auditory world. Since change of position is not logically tied to a change in the subject's relations to the occupants in the space, but rather is a change in one particular aspect of his experience, there is no reason why that feature of experience to which it is tied should mimic the dimensionality of space.

In addition to wrecking the argument, the master-sound is the source of extreme disanalogies with our own system of spatial relations. The space of Strawson's auditory universe is an absolute space, and not a framework constituted by the spatial relations of its occupants.[8] The fact that 'same place' in Strawson's auditory universe is not dependent upon 'same thing' is not merely a curiosity; it lays the whole scheme open to the most straightforward phenomenalistic reduction, since 'God save the Queen is now playing at position L' is apparently equivalent to 'If master-sound of pitch-level l were heard, God save the Queen would be heard'. But, as the Carnap of the *Aufbau* learned to his cost, in a universe where space is constituted by the spatial relations between things, there can be no phenomenal characterization of being at a particular position, since things can move and change.

Taking the master-sound illustration seriously, we are prevented from completing the intended defence of the Kantian thesis, or are committed to regarding as spatial a scheme of thought so radically unlike our own as seriously to undermine the interest of the conclusion, were we able satisfactorily to defend it. Moved by these connected considerations, we must surely suspect that it is the illustration that is at fault, and not the argument which it is intended to illustrate. And further

---

presence in a sense which would allow us to speak of something being to a greater or lesser degree removed from, or separated from, the point at which we are.'

[8] It is perhaps surprising that Strawson should invent such a space in Chapter Two, having emphasized in Chapter One the mutual identification–dependence, in our world, of things and places—a dependence which arises, on one side, from the fact that places are not intrinsically perceptible.

reflection appears to show the master-sound to be unnecessary even if an illustration of the argument is sought in a wholly auditory experience. For it may be held[9] that a one-dimensional space which is genuinely parallel to our own may be constructed out of an auditory experience (or, indeed, out of any experience) provided that experience exhibits such order and regularity that its course can be seen as simultaneously due to the way the world is laid out and to the subject's continuous motion through it. Provided the subject's experience is sufficiently regular to enable him to establish short-term generalizations of the form:

> An experience of kind k will intervene between any experience of kind k' and any experience of kind k''

it might appear that he can distil from its changing course a more or less detailed map of his world, with an object of kind κ between (in a 'travel-based' sense of this word) objects of kind κ' and κ''. Possessed of such a map, the subject can make empirical sense of the distinction between a change in his position and a change in the world, and being able effectively to apply this distinction, he can make revision of, and additions to, his map. That the resulting theory of the world has an interlocking, holistic character, as the subject simultaneously solves for the way the world is laid out and for the route he has taken through it, is no objection since it might reasonably be taken to mirror a feature of our own scheme. The holistic character of the resulting theory certainly renders it immune to any simple phenomenalistic reduction.[10]

More important for our immediate purpose, this way of introducing a spatial order into an auditory world seems to provide a much better illustration of the themes of Strawson's argument. Distinct but qualitatively indistinguishable sounds can now be distinguished by their positions in the 'travel-based' ordering, and, no matter how wide a segment of experience is taken, distinct sounds can present genuinely indistinguishable appearances. Furthermore, the second stage of the argument is not undercut since we run no risk of dimensionless parallels. To

---

[9] It has been held by Jonathan Bennett, in his *Kant's Analytic* (Cambridge University Press, Cambridge, 1966), p. 37.

[10] An illustration of this point will be developed later; see pp. 92–4.

construct a travel-based space is necessarily to construct an *ordering* of the objects or phenomena whose relations constitute the space.

In view of these considerations, let us suppose that Strawson would accept this as a better illustration of his argument. Eliminating the master-sound enables us to concentrate upon the nub of the argument—the connection between objectivity and reidentification. Here, too, I believe there is reason for scepticism.

My first objection, which does not run very deep, concerns the role which the concept of reidentification plays in the argument. The theories with which Strawson is concerned incorporate the idea that the subject has experience of phenomena which are independent of his experience of them. From this general acknowledgement of the independence of the world, Strawson is surely entitled to extract the corollary that the temporal dimensions of an experienced phenomenon may diverge from the temporal dimensions of any experience of it. Further it seems reasonable to suppose that Hero must be able to understand one particular application of this general idea, namely the possibility that the experienced phenomena should continue throughout a gap in his experience of them. Strawson expresses this idea in the language we use to talk about the persistence of material bodies, so that Hero is to think that he has experience of auditory *items* which continue to *exist* while unobserved and which may therefore be *reidentified*. But it is not clear that the concept of identity need be involved here at all, still less that it need be involved in just the way it is involved in our scheme of three-dimensional bodies.

In the first place, it seems that this particular application of the possibility of temporal divergence between phenomenon and experience can be captured with the concept of *continuity*, as it occurs in the thought that it may continue to rain after one falls asleep, or that it may rain continuously between the time one falls asleep and the time one awakes. It would appear that the idea of its raining continuously is prior to, and independent of, the idea of *a single rainstorm*, and that it is possible to enrich what Strawson calls a 'feature-placing' language with an operator having the force of 'continuously' without disturbing its ontological simplicity—without introducing quantification over, and reidentification of, particulars. If this is so, a theory of an objective world can be couched in a feature-placing language, and the concept of identity does not belong in Strawson's argument at all.[11]

Aside from this, there is a worry which arises even if we suppose that our Hero does express the idea of continuous sound by using the concept of identity. Let us suppose that Hero registers the independence of the world by allowing for the possibility of there being later, unheard parts of the same sound of which he has heard an earlier part, and therefore for the possibility of his hearing still later parts of the same sound of which, before an interruption, he has heard an earlier part. This is still not to think of an auditory *item* which *persists through time*, but rather of an auditory *process* which *is extended in time*. If the concept of reidentification is to be used in connection with processes, it must be understood that it is being used in a different sense from that which it has in connection with things. We reidentify a process when we hold that an occurrence encountered at one time is *part of* the same process as an occurrence encountered at another, but it is a distinctive (and some have thought incoherent) feature of our conceptual scheme of material bodies that we suppose an object to be both present *as a whole* on one occasion, and literally identical with an object present as a whole on another.

Now, a concept of reidentification can be used in connection with processes, and Strawson's detailed discussion of the auditory universe makes it clear that this is the concept which he intends.[12] Nevertheless, in the absence of any explanation or qualification, the use of the concept of reidentification which was originally introduced in the description of our conceptual

[11] In view of Strawson's defence of the coherence of a feature-placing scheme of thought later on in the book (pp. 202–13), it is perhaps surprising that he gives the impression in this chapter that he has demonstrated that any coherent scheme of thought about the objective world must involve the idea of reidentifiable particulars. Strawson does occasionally appear to restrict his question to schemes of thought involving particulars (as in: 'What are the most general statable conditions of knowledge of objective particulars?'—p. 62) but to defend the formulation of the argument by taking this restriction seriously is to do so at the cost of significantly reducing its interest.

[12] '... identified as *part of* the same particular M as that of which the previously heard instance of A was a *part* ...' (p. 70); 'There is a clear criterion for distinguishing the case of hearing a *later part* of a particular unitary sound-sequence of which the *earlier part* has been heard previously ...' (p. 77) etc. etc. (My italics.)

scheme of material bodies carried with it the suggestion of a greater parallel between that scheme and the scheme of the auditory universe than is strictly warranted—a parallel which can only be purchased at the cost of ignoring the considerable difference between things and processes.

Identity is, indeed, a double irrelevance, since it appears not only that continuity can be registered without it, but also that identity can be recognized in the absence of continuity—at least where processes are concerned. We can quite intelligibly hold that later occurrences are parts of the same extended game as earlier occurrences to which they are not linked by any continuous series of game stages. This point has been raised in objection to Strawson's argument, for it seems to open the possibility of thinking reidentifyingly without thinking objectively.[13] The obvious reply is that the criteria of reidentification mentioned in the argument must be restricted to those which require continuity; but if this reply is made the concept of identity once again drops out of the argument, in favour of that of continuity.

The reason why I said that this objection was not very deep was that it seems simply to invite a restatement of the argument in terms of the concept of continuity. Hero must be able to make sense of the idea that, after his perception has ceased, there should be ϕ-ing stages continuous with the ϕ-ing stages which he perceived, and therefore that some such stage may be encountered later. But not just any later ϕ-ing stage is continuous with a given earlier one. So, Hero must have a way of drawing a distinction between those later ϕ-ing stages that are, and those that are not, continuous with a given earlier stage. Is this distinction not exactly parallel with our distinction between qualitative and numerical identity, and will it not similarly presuppose space?

I do not believe that this argument is successful, for it seems to beg the question against a No-Space world in a subtle but decisive way.

In a spatial world there is no absolute notion of (temporal) continuity; we can only speak of spatio-temporal continuity. Now, in order to affirm upon the basis of a later perception of

---

[13] See Don Locke, 'Strawson's Auditory Universe', *Philosophical Review lxx* (1961), pp. 518–32.

φ-ing that the φ-ing one experienced at t did continue (did have later stages) one has to be sure, not merely that the later φ-ing is continuous with *some* φ-ing in existence at time t, but also that it is continuous with the particular φ-ing experienced. For, in a spatial world, and possibly only in a spatial world, there can be distinct but simultaneous instances of the same universal. Thus, to be sure that the toy I saw at time t survived until time t', it is not enough to be sure (i) that the indistinguishable toy I see at t' was in existence at time t, one must in addition be sure (ii) that the route by which it arrived at its position at t' was one which started from its occupation at t of the position in which I saw a toy.

Compare this with a very much simpler way of thinking—one which does not admit of the possibility of distinct but simultaneous instances of the same universal. The objectivity of φ-ing is recognized in this scheme (that is to say, it is intelligible that it be φ-ing when no φ-ing is perceived) but if, at any time, φ-ing *is* perceived, then that is all the φ-ing that the universe affords. Justice is done to this conception of reality by utterances of the unrestricted form 'It's now φ-ing'. Now, if Hero thinks in these terms, he will certainly make sense of the idea that the φ-ing that he is perceiving might continue, but by this he means no more than that it may φ for all times between the time at which his experience of φ-ing ceases, and some later time. And while in the spatial scheme he would have two questions to ask upon encountering φ-ing after a gap, now he has just one: 'Was this φ-ing going on continuously between the time I ceased, and the time I began, to experience φ-ing?', for by this he means: 'Was it φ-ing for all times between the time I ceased, and the time I began, to experience φ-ing?'. In this crude way of thinking there is no parallel to the second question of the spatial scheme, no analogue to the distinction between qualitative and numerical identity, and therefore no need for a criterion employing quasi-spatial considerations to assist Hero in drawing it.

If this is correct, then the space Strawson extracted out of the concept of objectivity is the space he smuggled into it, by limiting his attention to those theories of the objective that allow for distinct but simultaneous instances of the same universal. It is not surprising if such theories can be shown to be implicitly spatial; it is precisely for this reason that we were prepared to allow that the second stage of the argument might be completed. Perhaps there is some hidden incoherence in the crude and limited way of thinking, but that has to be shown, and if it can be shown the Kantian thesis can be established directly and Strawson's argument becomes an unnecessary circuit.

It is true that there is a distinction which someone thinking in these very crude terms must understand: namely, between the case where it is, and the case where it is not uninterruptedly ϕ-ing during a gap in his ϕ-experience. For in this sense, it remains true that 'not just any later ϕ-ing stage is continuous with a given earlier one'. But space does not appear to be involved in this distinction in any obvious way, and if it is involved in some unobvious way, this also has to be shown. It certainly cannot be shown by gesturing towards a distinction in which space is involved—the distinction between qualitative and numerical identity—but to which the required distinction is not remotely analogous.

To defend the Kantian thesis, the idea of space must be shown to be implicitly involved in the very idea of existence unperceived, even as it is embedded in such a purported scheme as this. It is possible to find in Strawson's chapter materials for another line of defence of the Kantian thesis—a line of defence which would have just this effect.

PART TWO

Strawson suggests that thinking of an auditory experience as experience of an objective world confronts our Hero with the problem of 'making sense of' the idea of sounds existing unperceived. He maintains that 'the most familiar and easily understood sense in which there exist sounds which I do not now hear is this: that there are places at which those sounds are audible but at which I am not now stationed.'[14] Space is clearly one way in which this difficulty can be resolved. Various other ways in which *we* 'make sense of' the idea of unheard sounds are mentioned, namely those which bring into play the idea of one sound *drowning* another, and the idea of deafness, but Strawson maintains that Hero cannot make use of them.

[14] *Individuals*, p. 74.

This is obviously a sketch of a line of argument rather than the argument itself, and in the text it is woven together with the argument we have just considered in a way which makes it difficult to disentangle, but I think that it is interesting and distinct, and I shall try to elaborate it. What, then, is the problem, and why should space be thought indispensable to its solution?

Hero must be able to understand the hypothesis, even if, in fact, he never believes it to be the case, that the phenomena of which he has experience should occur unperceived. Now, the idea of unperceived existence, or rather, the idea of existence now perceived, now unperceived, is not an idea that can stand on its own, stand without any surrounding theory. How is it possible that phenomena *of the very same kind as* those of which he has experience should occur in the absence of any experience? Such phenomena are evidently *perceptible*; why should they not be perceived? To answer this question, some rudimentary theory, or form of a theory, of perception is required. This is the indispensable surrounding for the idea of existence unperceived, and so, of existence perceived. (It is not to be thought that the idea of existence unperceived is an additional hurdle to be surmounted after the idea of existence perceived has been understood; the two ideas are sides of a single idea: the idea of an objective world.)

The same point can be put in other words. We might pretend for a moment that we are tracing the development, in a child's thought, of an utterance 'It's ϕ-ing', originally tied to a recurring pattern of his experience—a cry with which experiences of a certain kind are greeted.[15] For an utterance like 'It's ϕ-ing', originating in this way, to become an assertion about an objective world, it must loosen its tie with experience, so that it makes sense to suppose that it is true even when no experience occurs. But, although it must loosen its tie with experience, the tie must not be severed; that which is potentially true in the absence of any experience must be the very same statement as may, on occasion, be affirmed upon the basis of experience. There must be no question of allowing for 'It's ϕ-ing' to be true in the absence of experience by introducing a new sufficient

[15] I do not mean to suggest that this is the way all concepts of the objective world originate; far from it. See Part Three below.

condition for its truth, unconnected with its existing basis. This would merely produce ambiguity, so that what is required would not yet have been accomplished—sense has not been made of the idea of the very same state of affairs that is on occasion experienced obtaining in the absence of experience. Now, we can detach 'It's ϕ-ing' from experience, without pulling the concept apart, only if that in virtue of which 'It's ϕ-ing' is true is connected with experience by some condition which is sometimes, but not always, satisfied. The proposition 'It's ϕ-ing' will then be understood to entail that, if that condition is satisfied, it may be perceived to be true. In the formulation of the condition there lies a theory, or the form of a theory, of perception.

Provided that he is capable of telling whether or not this condition is satisfied, such a connection with experience allows Hero to give empirical content to the supposition that it is now ϕ-ing, irrespective of whether he currently perceives that it is ϕ-ing. If it is true that it is now ϕ-ing, then it must be the case that if the condition is satisfied, he will perceive it to be ϕ.[16]

This, then, is what it is to 'make sense of' the idea of existence unperceived. And the requirement that Hero have a conception of the world of sufficient complexity to enable him to understand why what is perceivable should sometimes be, and sometimes not be, perceived will surely rule out some purported theories of the world of excessive simplicity. But have we any reason for thinking that it will rule out all but the spatial theories; that 'the most familiar and easily understood sense' in which there exist unperceived phenomena is the only sense?

There are two kinds of explanation of why a perceptible phenomenon may not be perceived, if we exclude those that obviously rely upon spatial notions, such as the observer's being in the wrong position, or having the wrong orientation, or

---

[16] Do not say: empirical sense has not been given to the supposition that *it is ϕ-ing unperceived*—i.e. that it is ϕ-ing and the opportunity to establish whether or not it is ϕ-ing is not taken up. All that can be required is that empirical content be given to the hypothesis that *it is ϕ-ing*, and in such a way that it may be the case that it is ϕ-ing unperceived. The supposition that *it is ϕ-ing unperceived* is one whose intelligibility is consequential upon such a way of giving sense to the simple supposition that it is ϕ-ing, but it is obviously not in its turn a supposition that needs to be given empirical content in the sense of conditions under which one can conclusively establish that it obtains.

there being something in the way. There are those that cite deficiencies in the perceiver, such as that he is inattentive, unreceptive in the proper modality, unconscious, or asleep. And there are those which cite the absence of factors in the world which are causally necessary for perception, as the absence of light is cited to explain why we cannot see a table. For reasons which I try to explain in the next section, explanations of this second kind do not represent a very promising avenue for exploration, if we are trying to find a non-spatial way of making sense of existence unperceived. Very briefly: we can make sense of the idea of a *material* object or substance existing in the absence of conditions causally necessary for its perception, but we cannot do the same for sensory objects; a rainbow cannot exist in the darkness, even if, were there to be light, a rainbow would be visible. And it appears that, if our Hero is to think of his experience as of a world, and this world is not to be a spatial world, it will be a world composed of phenomena analogous to our sounds, smells, and rainbows, rather than to our material substances.

But there does not appear to be any parallel reason why Hero should not make sense of the idea of unperceived sounds (or, more generally, phenomena) by thinking in terms of some block of unreceptivity in himself. 'Perhaps', he thinks, 'there are sounds which I do not now hear, because I am unreceptive; if I was to become receptive, I would be able to hear them.'

Let us suppose that this abstract form of a theory is filled out in the following way. Let us suppose that Hero's prior experience had been of the unceasing auditory sequence 'tick tock tick tock...', but that upon one occasion the sequence in experience had been 'tick tock   tock tick...'. Why should Hero not use ordinary canons of scientific inference (let us not inquire too closely into what they are) to hypothesize that there was a tick which he did not hear, and understand this hypothesis in turn by supposing that he must have been unreceptive?

The objection Strawson would make to the coherence of this scheme of thought must be gathered from the following extract drawn from the passage in which he discusses various ways in which *we* make sense of the idea of unperceived sounds:

Alternatively, they turn upon such an idea as that of failing sensory powers. But why do we think of our powers failing rather than the world fading? This choice cannot be used to explain a conception it presupposes.[17]

I am not at all sure what objection Strawson has in mind here, but perhaps it is this. 'If one asks oneself why, in any particular case, one supposes that one's sensory apparatus is defective, it is clear that such a judgement cannot rest only upon internal features of one's experience (e.g. hearing nothing, or hearing things fainter and fainter), since it cannot be logically ruled out that there should be nothing to hear, or that what there is to hear is getting fainter and fainter. A judgement that one's sensory apparatus is defective must *rest upon* a view that this or that thing is there to be heard. Since the view that one's apparatus is defective ('this choice') must rest upon ('presuppose') a view as to what objectively exists, it cannot be used to give the indispensable surrounding ('explain a conception') which the idea of what objectively exists was discovered to require.'

If this *is* the objection, then it appears wrong in principle. It is right to insist that all of the elements of the theory of an objective world should be present, but wrong to insist that they be independently intelligible. It is true that the idea of a perceptual breakdown presupposes the idea of an objective reality, and that, upon the envisaged scheme at least, the idea of an objective reality presupposes the idea of a perceptual breakdown (or lack of receptivity). The ideas form a circle, and any theory constructed with their aid will have a holistic character as a result. Propositions about how the world is will be derivable from propositions about the course of Hero's experience only when they are taken together with propositions about when he was, and when he was not, receptive, while propositions of this latter kind will in their turn depend both upon propositions about what Hero is (or is not) experiencing, and also upon propositions about what there is to be experienced. Hero must see the course of his experience as simultaneously determined by the way the world is and his changing receptivity to it; each is connected to experience, but only as modified by the other. All this is correct. What is not correct is that there is anything objectionable in principle in such an arrangement.

[17] *Individuals*, p. 74.

The best possible reason against objecting to such a structure in Hero's theory is that it can also be discerned in a spatial theory. In the modified version of a spatial scheme in the auditory universe, Hero can tell that he has changed position by the changing course of his experience, but only when this is taken together with a map of a fairly stable world. But that map, in its turn, can only have been established, and must constantly be revised, by Hero's adopting views as to where and when he is moving. (In the somewhat Cartesian setting of the auditory universe, in the absence of other subjects to whom Hero and his movements can be objects of perception, all it can mean for him to be at a position is for him to perceive what is audible at that position.) The parallel between these two kinds of theories is not complete, since, in the place of an absolute notion of receptivity – present or absent at a time –, the spatial theory effectively employs a relativized notion: receptive to (= located at) this or that position. But this greater complexity does not prevent its central concepts from having that interlocking character which would appear to expose it to Strawson's criticism, if that criticism was well founded.

In fact, a stronger point might be suggested, namely that it is not merely permissible, but positively necessary, for that condition which is to account for the presence or absence of perception to be connected *a priori* with, and therefore, known to be satisfied only upon the basis of, propositions about the way the world is. For it was precisely this feature of the revised spatial theory of the auditory world which secured for it an immunity to that simple phenomenalistic reduction which threatened the master-sound theory. (In the master-sound theory, the subject's changing position is definitionally tried to a change in one phenomenally identifiable aspect of his experience.)[18]

Although each person in a large circle of people can be sitting upon the knees of the person behind him, this is not a feat which only two or three people can manage. Perhaps the objection is not that there is a circle in a theory relying upon deafness or unreceptivity to give sense to the idea of existence unperceived, but that the circle is too small. For, while it is true in the spatial theory that deciding whether or not one has moved (and there-

[18] I shall discuss the significance of this irreducibility below; see pp. 114–15.

fore deciding whether a change in one's experience signals objective change at some given place) requires taking as given certain propositions about the way the world is, these are not the very propositions about the world whose truth one is required to establish, but rather propositions about how it is with adjacent places. (This reveals another part of the structure of the theory: the subject can only move continuously through space). Of course doubt might be raised about the condition of these adjacent places, which could be resolved in the same way provided weight is shifted on to knowledge of still other places; an indefinite series of such challenges could bring us back to the place from which we started. However, the theory, though interlocking, has enough structure to get off the ground; one who holds it can meet a challenge parallel to the challenge in Strawson's rhetorical question:

But why do we think our position changing rather than the world changing?

Compare this with the scheme using receptivity. Hero is supposed to be able to make sense of the idea of its now ϕ-being unperceived by relying upon the concept of receptivity, and in particular, by supposing that, if he were now to become receptive, he would perceive ϕ-ing. However, this only gives content to the idea that a sound now exists unperceived if there is some criterion of Hero's now becoming receptive, other than his perceiving ϕ-ing. But what could it be?

Equally, Hero was supposed to be able to understand the hypothesis that there was an unperceived tick by using the supposition that he was unreceptive. But the past regularity in his experience cannot be regarded by Hero as conclusively establishing the hypothesis that there was an unperceived tick. If it does, this would not be because Hero had made the uniformity of nature a logical truth – no one could do that. It would simply be that he had established a new, and independent, sufficient condition for the statement that there is a tick, and therefore failed to give sense to one and the same state of affairs existing both perceived and unperceived. But, if the inductive considerations fail conclusively to establish the hypothesis of an unperceived tick, then Hero must be able to distinguish, at least in thought, between the case in which the regularity was perpetuated, and the case in which it was not. Here we should like Hero to be able to appeal to the counterfactual conditional 'If I had been receptive, I would have/would-not have heard a tick'. But such a conditional is quite vacuous if the only possible conception that he can have of his being receptive at that time is simply that of being able to hear what is there to be heard.

Here, surely, are the materials for a possible line of defence of the Kantian thesis – a line of defence which rests upon the idea that only a spatial theory can satisfy the demand that the factor accounting for the presence or absence of perception of perceptible phenomena should be at once *a priori* connected with the propositions about the world, and yet subject to significant empirical control. I shall not now pursue this line any further; to do so would involve the consideration of a variety of alternative schemes[19] in a detail which is not perhaps commensurate with their interest. The principle of the argument should be clear, and if it is clear, we have perhaps derived such illumination of the role of space in *our* thinking as it is in the power of this, or any, defence of the Kantian thesis to afford. After all, as Strawson himself emphasizes, this is the object of the exercise.

Instead, in the remaining two sections, I want to turn to what must be a brief, and I fear rather dogmatic, consideration of the question of whether a coherent theory of an objective world can be constructed upon the basis of an experience that is wholly auditory, even when that experience exhibits whatever degree of order and connectedness is necessary for the subject to apply 'travel-based' spatial notions to it. There does not appear to be any concept parallel to that of matter or material substance which can be framed in the auditory universe. The first question I want to ask is: Can there be a world without substance?

PART THREE

It seems possible to draw a distinction between two kinds of properties which objects may have, though a complete elabora-

---

[19] A spatial scheme is not the only scheme to employ a relativized receptivity condition, with the possibilities of additional empirical control which that provides; we can make sense, perhaps, of the idea of being ϕ-*receptive*, where receptivity is relativized to a universal. And there are other possibilities.

tion and defence of the distinction would be a very difficult task. Into the first kind fall those properties which are dispositions to affect sensitive beings with certain experiences – these we might call *sensory properties*, or, in deference to a long-standing tradition in philosophy, *secondary properties*. For an object to have such a property is for it to be such that, if certain sensitive beings were suitably situated, they would be affected with certain experiences, though this property may, in its turn, be identified with what we should normally regard as the ground of the disposition. However, in the first instance, a sensory property is a dispositional property.

It is not necessary for our immediate purpose to have any other characterization of primary properties than as non-sensory properties of objects. So defined, the class is extremely heterogeneous. What *is* important, though, is that the properties constitutive of the idea of material substance as *space-occupying stuff* should be acknowledged to be primary. These include properties of bodies immediately consequential upon the idea of space-occupation – position, shape, size, motion; properties applicable to a body in virtue of the primary properties of its spatial parts; and properties definable when these properties are combined with the idea of force (e.g. mass, weight, hardness). The way these properties relate to experience is quite different from the way sensory properties relate to it. To grasp these primary properties, one must master a set of interconnected principles which make up an elementary theory – of primitive mechanics – into which these properties fit, and which alone gives them sense. One must grasp the idea of a unitary spatial framework in which both oneself and the bodies of which one has experience have a place, and through which they move continuously. One must learn of the conservation of matter in different shapes, of the identity of matter perceived from different points of view and through different modalities, and of the persistence of matter through gaps in observation. One must learn how bodies compete for the occupancy of positions in space, and of the resistance one body may afford to the motion of another. And so on.

To say that these primary properties of matter are theoretical is not to explain or to mystify, but to highlight an analogy between the way our grasp of them rests upon implicit knowledge of a set of interconnected principles in which they are employed, and the way our understanding of such a property as electric charge rests upon explicit knowledge of a set of propositions more familiarly regarded as a theory. Certainly, to deny that these primary properties are *sensory* is not at all to deny that they are *sensible* or *observable*, for we are obviously able, after the appropriate training to perceive the shape, motion, and hardness of things. The point is rather that it is not possible to distil the concept of hardness solely out of the experiences produced by deformation of the skin which is brought into contact with a hard object, for it is not possible to distil out of such an experience the theory into which the concept fits. It is no more possible to have a purely sensory concept of hardness than it is to have a purely kinaesthetic conception of what it is for one's legs to be crossed, or to have a purely muscular conception of the motion of one's body, or to master the concept of electricity solely by learning to recognize electric shocks. And, though this is less obvious, it does not appear to be possible to regard the conception of the shape of a material thing – with all the propositions about its characteristic behaviour and interaction with other bodies which that implies – as the same as whatever shape concepts might be grounded in the colour mosaic thought to be given in immediate visual experience. This would certainly seem to be suggested if we can demonstrate, as I believe we can, that the blind are capable of a perfectly adequate mastery of shape concepts, and of spatial concepts generally, for no single *sensory* property can be defined in relation to different senses.[20] Berkeley[21] and Mill[22] both saw this point but, constrained by a theory of concept formation that would not allow for the formation of ideas of any other than sensory properties, they concluded that these spatial concepts were sensory concepts, but related to the sense of touch as heat is. This is possible only by supposing that the concept of solidity is a sensory concept, as we have seen that it is not, and further, by supposing that the concept of the motion of the subject, and of the parts of his body,

---

[20] The issue of the spatial concepts of the blind surfaces again in Part IV below.
[21] Berkeley, *An Essay Towards a New Theory of Vision*.
[22] J. S. Mill, *An Examination of Sir William Hamilton's Philosophy* (Longmans, London, 1872), pp. 270–313.

are concepts of kinaesthetic experience, which they are not.[23] I wish to stress my divergence from Berkeley and Mill on this point in order to guard against a serious misunderstanding. The distinction we shall presently find between Hero's conception of his world and our conception of the material world, does not at all reside in whatever difference is to be found between auditory, and tactuo-kinaesthetic experience. On the contrary, it resides in the difference between a conception of the world which is directly and exclusively, and a conception of the world which is neither directly nor exclusively, woven out of materials given in experience.

I do not take myself to be saying anything new in drawing the primary/secondary quality distinction in this way, since it is almost exactly the way Thomas Reid explains the distinction in his *An Inquiry into the Human Mind*.[24] Consider, for example, the following remarks on hardness:

> When the parts of the body adhere so firmly that it cannot easily be made to change its figure, we call it hard; when its parts are easily displaced we call it soft. This is the notion which all mankind have of hardness and softness; they are neither sensations nor like any sensations ...
>
> Hardness is a quality of which we have as clear and distinct a conception as of anything whatever. The cohesion of the parts of a body with more or less force is perfectly understood though its cause is not: we know what it is as well as how it affects the touch. It is therefore a quality of a quite different order from those secondary qualities, whereof we know no more naturally, than that they are adapted to raise certain sensations in us.[25]

In the words of a recent commentator:

> Reid tries to show that our concepts of certain primary qualities are bound up in an elementary theory of bodies, a natively given primitive mechanics. Since the primitive mechanics gives us various ways of telling when and where the primary qualities are present, then we can

---

[23] Further, any attempt to explain spatial concepts in this way runs into the objection that it only provides 'serial' and not 'simultaneous' spatial concepts. For this distinction, and the significance of the objection, see Part IV below. For Mill's wrestling with the issue of simultaneity, and his conclusion ('The idea of Space is at bottom one of time') see ibid., pp. 278–83.

[24] *An Inquiry into the Human Mind* (ed. Duggan) (University of Chicago Press, Chicago, 1970), pp. 61 and 69.

[25] Op. cit.

develop and apply these concepts independently of our having all the corresponding sensations.[26]

With such an excellent and detailed discussion to appeal to, I feel easier in giving nothing but a very brief sketch of the distinction.[27]

All it can amount to for something to be red is that it be such that, if looked at in the normal conditions, it will appear red. This formulation embodies what we might call the dispositional route from subjective experience to objective property, a route with which we are already familiar.[28] Philosophers have tried to provide a different account of what it is for a colour ascription to be true which does not so much involve a different route, as an attempt to make the most direct possible leap from subjective experience to objective property. They have tried to make sense of the idea of a property of redness which is both an abiding property of the object, both perceived and unperceived, and yet 'exactly as we experience redness to be'. By concentrating upon one's experience of colour, one is supposed thereby to know what it is for an object to have this property: 'This', one is to say, referring neither to the experience nor to any primary property of the thing, 'this, just as it is, can exist in the absence of any observer'.[29]

But the leap gets us nowhere, for it inevitably involves an attempt to make sense of an exemplification of a property of *experience* in the absence of any experience. Wittgenstein once imagined a world in which there were places which affected everyone painfully, so that pains were located at places in the

[26] Norman Daniels, *Thomas Reid's Enquiry* (Burt Franklin, New York, 1974), xiv; see also Ch. IV.

[27] This way of drawing the distinction also echoes recent work; on the interconnection between the primary properties and the idea of space see A. M. Quinton 'Matter and Space', *Mind*, lxxiii (1964); on the idea of secondary qualities as dispositions to affect us with experiences see J. Bennett, *Locke, Berkeley, Hume* (Clarendon Press, Oxford, 1971), Ch. IV. I differ from Bennett in not making the dispositional character of the secondary qualities a matter of the meaning of sentences ascribing secondary qualities, but relying instead upon the obscurer notion of that in which their truth consists. It seems decisive against any dispositional account of the meaning of such a term as 'red' that the only way to characterize the experiences red objects produce in us is as such.

[28] See pp. 88–9 above.

[29] See, for example, J. L. Mackie, *Problems from Locke* (Clarendon Press, Oxford, 1976), Ch. 1. Mackie regards such a concept as intelligible, and used by the common man, though in fact Mackie himself does not believe there is any scientific use for it. In these views, he follows Locke.

way we locate smells. Suppose this fantasy came true. Would it then make sense to give a non-dispositional account of what it is for there to be a pain at such and such a spot; to suppose a 'pain as we feel it' existing in the absence of any observer? What can the latter form of words mean save that something awful is going on there, and how can that be, when there is no one who is hurt? To modify a dictum of Wittgenstein, conceiving of a pain which no one feels upon the model of a pain which one does feel is none too easy a thing to do.

We may ask a philosopher who claims to find intelligible the idea of an objective property extracted from our experiences of colour in this direct way, whether or not such a colour property can characterize an object in the dark. He can hardly say 'Yes', since it would be quite obscure how a 'colour-as-we-see-it' can exist when we cannot see it, and how our experiences of colour would enable us to form a conception of such a state of affairs. Further, it would have to be explained in what the difference between such an objective colour property, and the dispositional property, consists. Observing the results of switching on the light merely tests for the dispositional property; what could show whether or not objects did in fact retain these other colour properties in the dark? To maintain, on the other hand, that such colour properties cannot be true of objects in an unlit cellar seems to undermine the status of the property to being an objective property of a body, since it seems to depend for its existence upon the conditions necessary for the human perception of it. Further, the concept is *said* to be different from a dispositional property but it is difficult to see in what a grasp of the supposed residue would consist. Presumably, it is conceivable that objects which are not really 'red-as-we-see-them' should appear red to us; indeed, this appears to be the situation Locke supposed actually to obtain. But what one conceives, when one conceives that objects which appear red to us are, in addition, really red, or are, in addition, not really red, and how one might manifest, either verbally or behaviourally, these supposed conceptions, is quite opaque.[30]

---

[30] These remarks are equally directed against those 'hard nosed' philosophers who wish to maintain that "science has shown that objects are not really red". Such a position would equally require the *intelligibility* of a non-dispositional concept directly fashioned from experience, which I am trying to deny.

The idea that objects lose their colour properties in the dark suggests a diagnosis of the position – it suggests that it arises because philosophers are being led astray by their imaginations. We must suspect that the philosophers who claim to find intelligible an objective but non-dispositional colour property try to conceive of an object's possessing such a property in the absence of any observer by imagining a red object which no one sees – a feat of the imagination which is impeded if part of the imagined story is that the object exists in a pitch-black cellar. Now, if the conceivability of an object's having such properties in the absence of any observer comes to this, then Berkeley's arguments against taking those imaginings as at their face value is decisive. What, after all, is being imagined but experiencing a red object unseen by anyone *else*?[31]

In our world, auditory properties are sensory properties, and auditory phenomena are sensory phenomena, and since they are imagined to rest upon the same basis in experience, they cannot be different for Hero, who inhabits a purely auditory universe. For both Hero and ourselves, the truth of a proposition to the effect that there is a sound at such and such a position must consist in this: if someone was to go to that position, he would have certain auditory experiences, or rather, to bring out the force of the conditional, if someone was to go to that position, he would thereby be caused to have certain

---

[31] This argument is found both in Berkeley's *Principles of Human Knowledge* Section 23, and in the first of the *Three Dialogues Between Hylas and Philonus*. In general I take Berkeley to have been quite correct to argue against Locke's contention that we can form an idea of a world existing independently of observers out of the ideas of primary properties which Locke provided, since they remained sensory concepts. Cf. M. R. Ayers, 'Introduction' to *Berkeley's Philosophical Works* (Dent, London, 1975) '... the only case of conceiving a thing's intrinsic properties that Locke can suggest ... is conceiving of its 'primary properties', the ideas of which, as he himself holds, are acquired through sense. Thus the real issue between them [Locke and Berkeley] is whether we get, or could possibly get a *sensory* concept through which we could conceive of reality in a *sense-independent* way' (p. xiii). Reid saw that Berkeley was right about this, but thought that, rather than reject the material world, we should reject the poverty of the mechanisms of concept formation which the empiricists recognized: 'The very existence of our conceptions of extension, figure, and motion, since they are neither ideas of sensations nor reflection overturns the whole ideal system by which the material world hath been tried and condemned ...' (op. cit. p. 79). Actually, Berkeley's idealism doesn't follow immediately, even within the empiricist framework, since there is the 'dispositional route' from experience to objective property which the phenomenalists later explored.

auditory experiences.[32] But there is a difference, for we have, and Hero does not have, the resources to make sense of the idea of the persisting categorical basis or ground of that disposition, in the object, or at the place, to which it is ascribed. Unlike Hero, we have the concept of substance, of space-occupying matter, for we have the concepts of the primary properties of matter.

In order to make this difference clear, we must make another difference clear. Michael Dummett has drawn attention to the fact that, for every proposition which is true, we like to think that there is something that makes it true, and further, that we do not like to think that conditional propositions can be *barely true*, that is to say, we do not regard that in virtue of which a conditional proposition is true as specifiable only by a repetition of that proposition. Now, there are two different kinds of non-conditional statements in whose truth the truth of a conditional may be taken to consist, and therefore two different kinds of ground for a disposition. The first kind of ground is simply the generalization whose truth we normally regard as evidence for the conditional. Hero's propositions about the world, true in the first instance in virtue of the truth of a conditional, need not be regarded as barely true, for they can be regarded as having a ground of this kind; the truth of the proposition 'There is now a ϕ-sound at p' can be regarded as true in virtue of the truth of the generalization 'Whenever in the recent past I have gone to p, I have had ϕ-experiences', or perhaps more complicated generalizations from which the conditional may be derived.

There is another kind of ground for a disposition, namely a relatively abiding property of the object to which the disposition is ascribed, capable of being characterized independently of the disposition, and therefore capable of providing, when taken together with the antecedent of the conditional (and perhaps certain other conditions understood as normal) a causal explanation of the occurrence which the consequent of the conditional reports. It is a ground of this kind which we

---

[32] Since going to the position must produce the experiences if the place is to have the dispositional property, it is possible for Hero to make some sort of distinction between veridical and hallucinatory perception, the latter consisting of experiences which are not causally dependent upon his position.

suppose a disposition like fragility has in the arrangement and binding of molecules; more relevantly, we suppose that any disposition of a place to affect us with certain experiences has a ground of this kind in the occupation of that place by a matter of a certain sort. Now, Hero can have no idea of such a ground for the dispositions which places have to affect him in a certain way. He has no resources, or at any rate has not obviously been provided with resources, for forming the idea of any property of the world that is not a disposition of the world to affect him in a certain way.

It is important to appreciate the difference between these two kinds of ground for a conditional if we are to gain a proper understanding of phenomenalism. Sir Isaiah Berlin has objected to phenomenalism that it reduces categorical existence to the truth of subjunctive conditionals which are not, in their turn, grounded in anything else.[33] Dummett has replied, on behalf of the phenomenalist, that, provided he gives up bivalence for statements concerning material objects in remote parts of the world, there is no reason why he should suppose that any subjunctive conditionals are barely true, since he can maintain that propositions about the explored material world are true in virtue of observed regularities in our experience. But it is clear that Dummett is not offering what Berlin was missing, namely a ground of the second kind for these subjunctive conditionals—a relatively abiding property of an object or place which, together with a subject's presence, could be used to explain his experiences. Whether or not it is something that would or should worry the phenomenalist, Berlin certainly put his finger upon a deep conceptual prejudice of ours that is offended by dispositional properties without categorical grounds of the second kind. The sense of disquiet which we feel at the idea of two glasses which are exactly alike in all that is abiding, yet different in that if one is struck it will emit middle C, and if the other is struck it will not, is not at all diminished by citing the generalization upon which the proposition may be asserted, namely, that whenever in the past one has been struck, it has emitted middle C, and whenever in the past the other has been struck, it has not. And this prejudice is equally offended by the idea of two places alike in what

[33] I. Berlin, 'Empirical Propositions and Entailment Statements', *Mind*, lix (1950).

occupies them between visits, yet of which one is such that if one goes to it, one will have certain experiences, and the other is not.

This is just the situation that Hero must accept in his world; places have powers that cannot be identified with anything continuously occupying them, so that going to a place is just a basic, causally relevant factor in the explanation of the course of his experience. However, I do not want at this point to examine whether there is more to our resistance to such an idea than mere prejudice, but rather turn to this question: if this is the situation, can we continue to suppose that Hero has a coherent theory which incorporates the idea that he has experience of an objective world?

The notion of objectivity arises as a result of conceiving a situation in which a subject has experience as involving a duality: on the one hand, there is *that of which there is an experience* (part of the world) and, on the other, there is *the experience of it* (an event in the subject's biography). We have been exploring the consequences of this duality, especially the consequence that, though the temporal dimensions of these two elements overlap, they need not coincide. And, if the situation does comprise these two elements, they are not unconnected—they are not two distinct states of affairs existing simultaneously by accident or as the result of pre-established harmony. Thus unconnected, the one could not be regarded as an experience *of* the other, as a way of gaining knowledge of it, and thereby, of the world of which it is a part.

Now, can these features be recapitulated in Hero's scheme—in a scheme where that in virtue of which the 'objective proposition is true can only be generalizations about the past course of Hero's experiences? The answer is surely 'No'. We do not have two states of affairs existing simultaneously, and related causally. All that exists at the position is Hero and his experiences. The only cause of Hero's having those experiences on going to that position *is* his going to that position. That which makes the 'objective proposition' true cannot be cited as a cause. If it is regarded as a barely true dispositional property of a position, then it is ineliminably characterized in terms which logically connect it to the event that is to be explained. It is no improvement to consider the 'objective proposition' not as barely true, but as true in virtue of the past regularity in Hero's experience, for the regularity can hardly be regarded as something which causes those events which perpetuate it, nor can it sensibly be regarded as something Hero *experiences*.

In fact, without ideas corresponding to our ideas of the primary properties of matter, Hero cannot make sense of the same thing existing both experienced and unexperienced, for he cannot recognize any unexperienced *existence* at all. It may hold good of a place when no one occupies it that *if* one was to go there, one would be affected with such and such experiences, but *that* patently does not report any contemporaneous existence, nor, when we inquire into its ground, do we discover any contemporaneous existence there either; all we have are generalizations. Hero is forced to think as the phenomenalist would have us always think, and the remark Berlin made about the phenomenalist's scheme applies equally well to Hero's:

> ... what troubles the plain man is the thought that if the hypotheticals are unfulfilled, if no observers were in fact observing, then, if the phenomenalist analysis is in fact correct, there was ... nothing at all.[34]

We can think of sounds as perceptible phenomena, phenomena that are independent of us, and that can exist unperceived, because we have the resources for thinking of the abiding stuff in whose changes the truth of the proposition that there is a sound can be regarded as consisting. A fly is moving its wings; this is an event which we perceive, partly in an auditory way, and which is naïvely regarded as the ground of the proposition that, if one goes into a certain room one will hear a buzzing. (More knowledgeable thinkers would locate the ground in the movement of the air molecules which these events produce.) And the event of a fly's moving its wings is not even in the first instance a sensory phenomenon; it is an event consisting in space-occupying objects, possessed of qualities characterized independently of observers, moving in relation to one another. The sensory phenomena we typically recognize are, in fact, properties of things or stuffs—persisting space-occupying

---

[34] Op. cit., This passage makes it clear that Berlin was lamenting the absence of a contemporaneously existing categorical ground for the hypothetical propositions.

substances—in whose primary qualities, or primary quality changes, the dispositions to produce experiences may be regarded as grounded. It is these substances which we perceive as coloured, or as making a sound.

There is a passage in the chapter in which Strawson seems to be expressing similar thoughts:

It helps us to think of one particular M being drowned or submerged by the stridencies which intervene . . . ; and thus to think that there were there to be heard, would have been heard but for these stridencies. But now we have only to think of the reasons, the evidence, we have for thinking something like this in real life—the visible but inaudible scrapings of the street violinist as the street band marches by, and then we lose interest in the suggested criterion for the case of the purely auditory world.[35]

We find here the idea that what enables us to think of sounds as being drowned out, and in this way, existing though unperceived, is the knowledge that their categorical basis—the scrapings—continues; this is, on the whole, the point I have been making. I would want to guard against the misunderstanding that might be involved in thinking of the scrapings as particularly *visible*, as though the difficulty could be surmounted by providing Hero with a richer network of correlations between his experiences. But the main idea is surely there, together with the critical equation upon which it rests: 'was there to be heard / would have been heard'. I disagree with Strawson only in that I go further, and see the difficulty he points to as arising for Hero in *any* attempt he makes at the idea of an unheard sound. Exactly the same background is necessary for making sense of the idea of a sound's existing unheard at a place; the place must be occupied by an object characterized in other than sensory terms, and in whose states and doings (scrapings) the existence of an unheard sound may be taken to consist.[36]

---

[35] *Individuals*, p. 71.

[36] It might be worth pointing out that considerations similar to those of the present section bear upon the question of how Hero conceives of himself. Presumably Hero must be able to make sense of his *existing unperceiving*—located in space although asleep. In the first instance, Hero can understand such location in terms of dispositions: 'If I had been awake, I would have had experiences as of position p'. But if Hero's being at a position is to be cited in the explanation of Hero's experiences, when he does perceive the world, this disposition must have a ground which can be independently characterized, and this can presumably be found only in the occupation of that position by

This is the first respect in which I believe that Strawson does not provide the subject of auditory experience with a coherent conception of external reality—the conception is one constructed exclusively out of sensory concepts. However, even if it is now clear that such a conception of an independent reality is not possible, it may be less clear why the conception by a subject of auditory experience of his world must take this form. After all, I have stressed that our ideas of matter are independent of any particular kind of experience, for example, tactual experience. So why can there be no analogue to the idea of matter in an auditory universe?

The issues raised by this question are enormous, and I should not be able to deal with them in this paper, even if I knew how. If the hypothetical theory is to follow ours at all closely, sounds would have to *occupy* space, and not merely be located in it, so that the notions of force and impenetrability would somehow have to have a place, and we may well wonder whether we can make sense of this without providing Hero with an impenetrable body and allowing him to be an agent in, and manipulator of, his world. But perhaps this is the wrong line to pursue. Perhaps we should explore the possibility of a theory more closely analogous to the field theory of some physicists, or even a physical theory working on principles quite different from any we have knowledge of. Unsurprisingly, I cannot myself conceive of such a theory nor do I know how one might set about demonstrating its possibility, nor whether a search for such a demonstration is even coherent. What I hope to have pointed out is the need for some physical theory over and above the ideas which Strawson attributed to his subject; not that such a supplementation cannot be provided. Though my conclusion is limited, I believe that it is worth drawing. For it is extremely tempting, upon first reading Wittgenstein's fantasy about locatable pains, to think: "How simple! This is all that separates the inner from the outer—this is all that is required to make an object, and hence a world, out of experience." Liberat-

---

something which is identical with Hero, and, since it exists unperceived, something which is characterized by primary properties.

Strawson made a half-hearted attempt to provide Hero with an audible body (pp. 84–5) but, since it does not have primary properties, it does not meet the need here indicated.

ing and appealing though this thought may be, it does not appear to be correct.

PART FOUR

I shall raise the second doubt I have about Strawson's auditory 'universe' rather obliquely, taking as my starting point a debate about the spatial concepts of the blind. For some centuries now, philosophers and psychologists have disagreed over whether and to what extent the spatial concepts of the blind are similar to those of the sighted. There have been those who have maintained that the blind do not, strictly speaking, have genuine spatial concepts at all; as Lotze puts it:

... the space of a blind man may not be so much what we mean by space, as an artificial system of conceptions of movement time and effort ...[37]

This position is also taken by Platner:

In reality, it is time that serves, for the man born blind, as space. Remoteness and proximity only mean to him the time, more or less long, and the number, more or less, of intermediaries which he needs in passing from one tactual impression to another.[38]

Occupying a middle position are those who agree that the distance concept of the blind is essentially a concept of the time and bodily movement necessary to traverse the distance, but who deny that in this fact there is any ground of difference from the sighted, since their spatial concepts have exactly the same feature. This is Mill's position.[39] And although I do not know of any text in which Poincaré specifically addressed himself to the question of the blind, he is committed by his general views on the concepts of space to occupying this position:

To localize an object simply means to represent oneself the movements that would be necessary to reach it. It is not a question of representing the movements themselves in space, but solely of representing to oneself the muscular sensations which accompany

[37] H. Lotze, *Metaphysic*, Vol. II (Clarendon Press, Oxford, 1887), pp. 272–3.

[38] E. Platner, *Philosophische Aphorismen* (1793), Vol. i, Sect. 765, p. 439. Quoted in J. S. Mill, op. cit., pp. 283–4. The most extreme and dogmatic version of this position is found in von Senden's book *Space and Sight* (Methuen, London, 1960).

[39] Op. cit., pp. 274–86.

these movements and which do not presuppose the existence of space.⁴⁰

The other group opposed to the idea that the spatial concepts of the blind are *toto caelo* different from those of the sighted accept that the only genuine spatial concepts are those that are instanced in an array of simultaneously existing objects, and thus that are paradigmatically applicable to a simultaneously presented array, but deny that such concepts are inaccessible to the blind. According to this last group, while it is true that the blind must receive information about the spatial arrangement of the world successively, it is possible for them to organize the information they receive into a form in which genuine spatial concepts are used, or to which they may be applied. This point has been made with particular reference to the haptic perception of an object like a chair, too large to be encompassed by the hand, but presumably the point would also apply to the blind man's conception of the room or city in which he lives. Revesz puts the point about haptic perception like this:

... But even when the details have been touched, the total form is not yet given. The parts which are touched must be finally unified in a total form, in a complete impression. This synthesis presupposes a specific constructive process which we see in the visual sphere only occasionally... Thinking and fantasy exert their effects together with intuition. The parts of a figure grasped haptically become fixated abstractly.⁴¹

It is difficult not to think of this synthesis in terms of the formation of an image, and this is the way in which Pierre Villey, a Montesquieu scholar who was himself blind, put the point:

The image which a blind man receives by touch rids itself very easily of the characteristics which constitute the modalities peculiar to tactual sensation... The residue which it keeps, if it does not contain colouring which is absolutely foreign to tactile nerves, and if it be less rich than the contents of the visual image, may frequently not include any element which is not in the visual image, and may coincide very nearly with that.

⁴⁰ *The Value of Science* (Dover, New York, 1958), p. 47.
⁴¹ Revesz, *The Human Hand* (Routledge and Kegan Paul, London, 1958), p. 26.

He acknowledges that his tactual perception of the chair is successive while visual perception is simultaneous, but goes on:

> But if, an hour after feeling it, I search in my consciousness for the memory of the vanished chair ... I do not reconstruct it by means of fragmentary and successive images. It appears immediately and as a whole in its essential parts ... There is no procession, even rapid, of representations ... I couldn't tell in what order the parts were perceived by me ... What is the residue of this work? The limit towards which they tend, and which they appear to reach, is simply form.[42]

I do not mean to engage in this fascinating dispute now, but to get a little closer to my objective by extracting from it the distinction between two different kinds of spatial concepts which it highlights. On the one hand, we have what I shall call *serial* spatial concepts—concepts explained in terms of the succession or sequence of the subject's perceptions, and any muscular or kinaesthetic sensations accompanying these changes, whether they arise from the movement of the whole, or merely part, of the subject's body. I shall call these concepts 'spatial', but in view of the scepticism that is to follow, neither this term, nor the corresponding term 'travel-based' ought to be taken too seriously. For, as Poincaré said, the 'movements' can be characterized in terms which do not presuppose the existence of space.

Distinguished from these are what I shall call *simultaneous* spatial concepts, a notion which is much more difficult to make precise. Perhaps we may characterize them as relational concepts the situation for whose most direct application is one in which the elements related by them are simultaneously presented or perceived.[43] Relative to this characterization, the dispute about blind men is a dispute about whether someone who has no capacity to make the most direct application of a concept *to the world* might nevertheless possess it, and how this possession might be manifested.

However exactly the distinction between these two kinds of spatial concepts is to be drawn, that there is such a distinction

[42] Pierre Villey, *The World of the Blind* (Simpkin, Marshall, Hamilton, Kent; London, 1922), p. 183.
[43] In view of the discussion of the concepts of primary properties at the beginning of the preceding part, this characterization must in no way be taken to suggest that such concepts can be *extracted from* just an experience in which distinct elements are simultaneously presented.

seems fairly clear. It seems fairly clear, that is to say, that there are two quite different ways in which, for example, the fact that three objects a, b, and c lie, in that order, upon a straight line might be established. Someone might be able to tell that the line connecting the objects was straight by means of the kind of bodily movement necessary to pass from one to another, and that b lay between a and c by means of the temporal relation between the experience of a, b, and c. On the other hand, someone who was able to see, might be able simply to *see* that such an arrangement existed. Equally, it seems fairly clear that we can identify, in these different ways of detecting spatial facts, the application of different kinds of spatial concepts, which have different presuppositions and which sustain different kinds of reasoning. Someone who had information given in, or stored with the use of, concepts of one kind, or in a form to which concepts of one kind would be directly applicable, would find certain problems easier, and certain problems harder, to solve than one who relied on concepts of the other kind.[44]

Armed with this distinction, let us return to the auditory universe, and ask what kind of spatial concepts its inhabitant has been provided with. So far, in fact, Hero has a theory of perhaps excessive simplicity, since it concerns a space of just one dimension, in which distance is only measurable upon an ordinal scale. It uses just one primitive spatial concept—'x is between y and z'—and as it was introduced, the concept is serial or travel-based. What it *means* to say that x is between y and z is simply that an experience of x will intervene between any experience of y which is followed by an experience of z and conversely.

If we were to provide Hero with analogues to our more complicated spatial concepts, such as 'arranged in a square', 'forming a circle' etc.—something that would be necessary if we were able to contemplate a generalization to a two-dimensional auditory universe—then we should have to pro-

[44] In fact, the distinction between serial and simultaneous spatial concepts is implicit in much of the psychological literature upon spatial perception and behaviour, especially since Tolman argued for the use of the notion of a *cognitive map* in psychological explanation. For an explicit use of the distinction see F. N. Shemyakin, 'Orientation in Space' in B. G. Ananyev *et al.* (eds.), *Psychological Science in the U.S.S.R.*, Vol. I (Office of Technical Services, Washington, 1962), pp. 186–225.

vide Hero with some way of estimating the passage of time, so that a notion of distance permitting measurement upon a ratio scale could be understood in terms of the time of normal travel. (The presence of the word 'normal' is to signal that the estimate of distance, like the estimate of position, would be subject to revision in the light of considerations from elsewhere in the theory, which would therefore retain its holistic character.) The notion of a straight line could then be defined in terms of the shortest distance between two points, but the scheme would presumably be practically unworkable unless Hero could make provisional judgements of the straightness of the path he was following upon the basis of 'bodily sensations'. (In a parallel way, our holistic scheme of re-identifiable bodies and places would be practically unworkable unless we had the ability to make provisional judgements of the identity of bodies by recognizing them.) We have not been supposing that Hero has these conceptual riches, but for present purposes it would not matter if we had, since his concepts of space would remain serial.

Now, whether or not a subject in an auditory universe could have a use for simultaneous spatial concepts is a difficult question, partly overlapping with the question about the spatial concepts of the blind which I mentioned earlier. But Strawson did not suppose that the subject in the auditory universe could, and it is this that gives me the ground of my disagreement. Strawson was quite well aware of the distinction between the different kinds of spatial concepts, and he in fact elaborates an objection to his discussion which is based upon the premiss that the subject in his auditory world would not have simultaneous spatial concepts. However exactly it is that Strawson does deal with this objection he raises to himself, it is not by denying the premiss.

The objector Strawson imagines begins by pointing out that, in visual perception, we are simultaneously presented with objects in a seen spatial array:

... these simultaneously presented elements ... are simultaneously presented as being related in another respect: viz. in a respect which leads us to characterize one as being *above* or *below* or to the *left* or to the *right* of another ...[45]

[45] *Individuals*, p. 79.

112 *Gareth Evans*

He then goes on to object:

> But relations between elements in respect of the auditory analogue of the spatial dimension cannot be presented simultaneously, all at once. They turn essentially upon change.[46]

When Jonathan Bennett discusses this objection, he says that Strawson treats it much too tolerantly. This is wrong; there is a deep objection to the serial nature of the spatial concepts of the auditory universe, and Strawson does not treat it at all. The objection which Strawson does answer, or rather, shows that he does not need to answer, is one to the effect that serial spatial concepts are not *sufficiently analogous* to our simultaneous concepts. But, *even as Strawson presents it*, the objection has a much deeper thrust, for it calls into question the claim that a theory couched in serial spatial terms can genuinely embody the idea of an independently existing objective world:

> But surely the idea of the simultaneous existence of the perceived and the unperceived is linked with this idea of the simultaneous presentation of elements, each of a definite character, but simultaneously exhibiting a system of relations over and above those which arise from the definite character of each. Surely the former idea is necessarily an extension of the latter, is just the idea of such a system of relations extending beyond the limits of observation.[47]

And to this objection, which expresses the doubt I have been approaching by such a circuitous route, Strawson offers no answer.[48]

Certainly, any theory using simultaneous spatial concepts does genuinely embody the idea of an independently existing reality, the idea of the perceived and the unperceived existing simultaneously, and in exactly the same sense. If a, b, and c are envisaged to lie upon a straight line, when what is envisaged is an instance of the simultaneous concept—a concept whose most direct application lies in a presentation of the three elements a, b, and c together—then a, b, and c must thereby be conceived to exist in exactly the same way. If a, b, and c are believed to exist in such an arrangement when b is perceived

---

[46] *Individuals*, pp. 79–80.
[47] *Individuals*, p. 80.
[48] More accurately: he offers no answer which he does not answer himself.

and a and c are not, then a and c are conceived to exist, though not perceived, in exactly the sense in which b, now perceived, exists.[49]

It is just this idea of the simultaneous existence of the perceived and the unperceived that we illegitimately import into the auditory universe by misinterpreting Hero's serial propositions as simultaneous, for example, by crediting him with something like a *map* of the world in which the information about succession and sequence is synthesized into a unitary framework. Tempting though this further step of interpretation may be, there is no warrant for it. The serial spatial propositions are once again conditional in form: if such and such an experience is had, followed by such and such another, then an experience of still a third kind will intervene between them. If this is the stuff of which the theory is made, how can it register the existence of anything going on unperceived? Unlike simultaneous spatial propositions, serial spatial propositions are not at a level different from, and therefore potentially explanatory of, propositions about order in experience. Strawson's Hero does not have the resources to rise above the level of the explicandum.

This sceptical point must be put with some delicacy. It will not do to say: 'the fact that I will have an experience *of b* between any times I have an experience *of a* and *of c* (and vice versa) does not guarantee that a and c exist now, when, for example, I am perceiving b.' By speaking in tems of the experience *of b*, etc. the trick has already been given away, and the scepticism can only be expressed in the unwanted, and possibly incoherent form: 'Why may it not be that a springs into existence when I come to have experience of it?' Nor will it do to say that, while simultaneous spatial concepts could relate things existing simultaneously, serial spatial concepts could relate things existing at different times. Once again this turns the objection into a worry about objects 'springing into existence'. The objection is rather this: because serial spatial concepts do not provide us with a way or thinking about simultaneously

---

[49] Someone who thinks of time *spatially* pictures the time series as a totality any member of which could be observed from a position outside the series. Precisely for this reason to think of time in this way is to think of the past and future events existing in the same way as do present events.

existing objects, they are not obviously concepts of relations between (independently existing) objects at all.[50]

Against the background of this scepticism, the immunity of the 'travel-based' theory to a simple phenomenalist reduction takes on a new complexion. Any proposition 'spatially' relating specified, preceivable 'objects' is reducible in a straightforward way to a proposition about the sequence of experiences; such irreducibility as there is comes only when Hero introduces expressions referring to 'places' whose identity conditions are tied to the whole network of propositions previously mentioned, but to no one taken individually. But it is hard to believe that an ontology appropriate to a theory of an objective world is introduced by Hero's supposed version of 'It's ϕ-ing at position p', if it is not already involved in the propositions of the form 'It's ϕ-ing between where it is ψ-ing and where it is χ-ing.'

The situation is really no different from this. There is a group of currencies each actively traded against the others in a situation of floating exchange rates. The basic propositions for describing this system will be of the form '£1 = $1.75 at the end of ... day's trading'. But we can imagine the description enriched by the introduction of the idea of *the value of the £*, something which is reckoned to be increasing, decreasing or constant by means of some averaging of its relation to all other currencies. Just as in the 'spatial' case, there is sufficient *de facto* stability in the relations between most currencies from day to day to provide the background against which it makes sense to discriminate those changes in the £–$ exchange rate which are due to the pound's falling, and those that are due to the dollar's rising. Now, a proposition to the effect that the value of the pound has declined is not reducible to any one proposition of the form 'At the end of day d, £1 = n units of X currency, and at the end of day $d+1$, £1 = $n-k$ units of X currency.' Such a proposition is not necessary, since X may be a currency moving down with the £, and it is not sufficient, since X may be moving up rather than the £ moving down.

If this does provide a parallel for the relation between the

---

[50] If the line of reasoning expressed in these paragraphs is correct, those who deny simultaneous spatial concepts to the blind are committed to denying that they have a conception of an independently existing reality at all, which is surely very difficult to accept.

basic propositions of Hero's travel-based theory, and those which mention or quantify over 'positions', it is hard to take the theory's immunity to a simple phenomenalistic reduction seriously. While a genuine theory of an independent reality will be thus irreducible, not every theory thus irreducible is a genuine theory of an independent reality.

It is a little surprising that Strawson does not treat the objection to his auditory universe which we have been considering with more understanding, for the point upon which it rests is one which Strawson himself emphasized in defence of the Kantian thesis:

'... we must have a dimension other than the temporal in which to house the at present unheard sensory particulars if we are to give a satisfactory sense to their existing now unperceived ...'[51]

... we want an analogy of distance—of nearer to and farther away from—for only, at least, under this condition would we have anything like the idea of a dimension other than the temporal in which unperceived particulars could be thought of as simultaneously existing in some kind of systematic relation to each other and to perceived particulars.[52]

The objector is simply taking this point, and insisting that, if space is to provide this system of relations, it must be a space constituted by simultaneous spatial relations; that if Hero is to think of unperceived particulars existing simultaneously with, and in relation to, perceived particulars, he must have simultaneous spatial concepts, and not those that 'turn essentially upon change'.

I may have given the impression that I disagree with all the most important points which Strawson makes in his second chapter. But this does not seem to me to be so. As important as any point I have so far discussed is something implicit in the entire procedure of discussion, something implicit in what, if he would not shrink from such a word, might be called Strawson's methodology. This is the idea that the connections between the fundamental concepts of our conceptual scheme are central objects of philosophical investigation, and that exploratory pressure may have to be put upon these connections by

[51] *Individuals*, p. 74.   [52] *Individuals*, p. 75.

imagining situations radically unlike our own. (Hero must not take on a life of his own, so that speculations about him are misinterpreted as speculations 'about what would really happen in certain remote contingencies'; Hero and his 'world' are devices for 'testing and strengthening our own reflective understanding of our own conceptual structure'.) As a model of how to pursue this essentially imaginative exploration, Strawson's chapter is unsurpassed.[53]

[53] I am grateful to Crispin Wright, David Pears, and John McDowell for reading an earlier draft of this paper and offering helpful comments.

Meaning, Communication, and Knowledge[1]
John McDowell

1. According to theorists of communication-intention, we should explain what meaning is in terms of the audience-directed intentions of speakers. According to theorists of formal semantics, the functioning of language can be illuminated by considering a certain sort of formal theory of a particular language: namely, a theory competent to specify truth-conditions for all of the language's indicative sentences. It seems likely that there is something to be gained from both these ways of thinking, but it is rare for much attention to be devoted to the question how they are related. However, a welcome exception is P. F. Strawson's provocative inaugural lecture,[2] from which the above characterizations are drawn.

Strawson's major thesis is this. The notion of truth-conditions is the fundamental notion of formal semantics, and the idea that meanings can be specified in terms of truth-conditions is all very well as far as it goes. But it does not go far enough. Further explanation of the notion of truth-conditions is called for; and this turns out to require an appeal to the characteristic conceptions of the communication-intention theorist. So while neither tradition is incorrect, the theorist of communication-intention can claim to be closer to the philosophical foundations.

In more detail, Strawson's central argument is as follows. The theorist of communication-intention can concede that 'in almost all the things we should count as sentences there is a substantial central core of meaning which is explicable either in terms of truth-conditions or in terms of some related notion

[1] I should like to express my thanks for help with this paper to Brian Loar, Stephen Schiffer, and especially Gareth Evans.
[2] *Meaning and Truth* (OUP, Oxford, 1970); reprinted in *Logico-Linguistic Papers* (Methuen, London, 1971), p. 170. Page references are to *Logico-Linguistic Papers*.

quite simply derivable from that of a truth-condition' (p. 178); and hence that theories of meaning for particular languages can hinge on the notion of truth. With its generality over languages, this concession constitutes, we might suppose, a potentially illuminating thesis about meaning in general; and it is one in which the explanatory weight rests on the notion of truth. But 'we still cannot be satisfied that we have an adequate general account of the notion of meaning unless we are satisfied that we have an adequate general understanding of the notion of truth' (p. 180). Now when we look for accounts of truth in general—as opposed to the sort of account of truth in this or that particular language which semantic theories themselves provide—the best we can come up with seems to be such platitudes as this: 'one who makes a statement or assertion makes a true statement or assertion if and only if things are as, in making that statement, he states them to be' (p. 180). If we combine this platitude with the concession that meanings can be specified in terms of truth-conditions, we arrive at the following conclusion: to specify the meaning of an indicative sentence is to specify how things are stated to be by someone who makes a statement by uttering it. (Presumably other sorts of sentence can have their meanings explained in some derivative way.) So we have arrived at the notion of the content of such centrally important speech acts as statement-making. Strawson goes on:

> And here the theorist of communication-intention sees his chance. There is no hope, he says, of elucidating the notion of the content of such speech acts without paying some attention to the notions of those speech acts themselves ... And we cannot, the theorist maintains, elucidate the notion of stating or asserting except in terms of audience-directed intention. For the fundamental case of stating or asserting, in terms of which all variants must be understood, is that of uttering a sentence with a certain intention ... which can be incompletely described as that of letting an audience know, or getting it to think, that the speaker has a certain belief... (p. 181).[3]

To determine the meaning of an indicative sentence is to

[3] This incompletely described intention is (at least in the version formulated in terms of getting the audience to think ...) a component of H. P. Grice's analysis of utterer's meaning: see 'Meaning', *Philosophical Review*, lxvii (1957), 377, and the modifications proposed in 'Utterer's Meaning and Intentions', *Philosophical Review*, lxxviii (1969), 147.

determine what statement can be made by uttering it; and that is just to determine what belief the sentence can be used to get audiences to think the speaker has. Strawson concludes that the concession, 'so far from being an alternative to a communication theory of meaning, leads us straight in to such a theory of meaning' (p. 182).

According to this argument, then, theories of meaning for particular languages might be essentially as theorists of formal semantics propose. But the work of explaining the concept of meaning is done, not by the central notion of such theories, the notion of truth, but by the conceptual apparatus required for the further elucidation of the notion of truth; and that is the favoured conceptual apparatus of the communication-intention theorist.

2. In Strawson's debate, the theorist of formal semantics is depicted as resisting pressure to appeal to the communicative nature of linguistic behaviour in order to underpin his interest in truth. But this misrepresents at least some of those who think about language within the tradition Strawson is considering. There is an attractive way to defend the philosophical interest of formal semantics, as applied to natural languages, which involves no such resistance.

Someone who understands a language can hear utterances in it, not just as productions of sound, but as significant speech acts. What he has is an information-processing capacity. His senses furnish him with information to the effect that people are uttering such-and-such sounds—information which is available equally to someone who does not understand the language. What is special about someone who does understand the language is that his sensory intake yields him, in addition, knowledge as to what speech acts, with what content, are being performed. The property which distinguishes him, then, would be captured by a theory with the following powers: given a suitable non-interpreting description of any possible utterance in the language—a formulation of information available equally, on hearing the utterance, to someone who understands the language and to someone who does not—the theory would enable anyone who knew it to derive that interpreting description under which someone who understands the language would be capable of recognizing the action performed.[4] Such a theory would compendiously describe the extra contribution, over and above the sharable sensory intake, which his competence with the language makes to his cognitive position on any of the relevant occasions. For any possible utterance in the language, it would yield a route from a non-interpreting description of it to an interpreting description. Thus it would reveal the relations between sound and—to speak intuitively—significance which, in a sense, constitute the language. It is hard to see what could have a better claim to count as a theory of meaning for a language.

If, for the moment, we ignore moods other than the indicative, we can restrict the scope of a theory of the envisaged sort to sayings. The theory would need, then, to make someone who knew it capable of specifying, for any indicative sentence in the language it dealt with, the content of the saying which an utterance of the sentence would be taken to be by someone who understood the language. This content-specification might be made possible by a theory which met the following description: for each object-language sentence, it entails a theorem whose form we can represent schematically as 's...p', where 's' is replaced by a suitable designation of the object-language sentence and 'p' by a sentence, in the language in which the theory is stated, suitable for expressing what can be said by uttering 's'. (We shall consider what goes in place of the dots shortly.)

We want to be able to see the content expressible by uttering a sentence as the upshot of contributions from repeatable parts or aspects of it. It seems inconceivable that a theory could yield specifications of content for all possible indicative sentences in a language whose complexity approached that of a natural language, unless the theory were organized in such a way as to meet something like that desideratum: the theorems would need to be deducible on the basis of the structure of the object-language sentences, in such a way that the premiss which

[4] There is no implication that the theory is known by a possessor of the capacity it describes. Nor need the language in which the interpreting descriptions are given be understood by him: a monoglot Frenchman can be taken by us to recognize another Frenchman as, for instance, saying that it is likely to snow. For the conception of a theory of a language expressed here, cf., e.g., Donald Davidson, 'Radical Interpretation', *Dialectica*, xxvii (1973), 313; and my 'On the Sense and Reference of a Proper Name', *Mind*, lxxxvi (1977), 159.

registers the contribution of, say, a word to a given sentence figures also in derivations which reveal its contribution to other sentences in which it occurs.

Now suppose a theory for a given language can meet these requirements by taking this shape: what the replacements for 'p' do, in the theorems, is to state necessary and sufficient conditions for the application of some predicate to the object-language sentences. One of the requirements is that replacements for 'p' are to express what can be said by uttering the relevant object-language sentences. By way of something like Strawson's platitude (§1), this guarantees the weaker claim that the extension of the envisaged predicate is that of a truth-predicate. The envisaged theory would not be false if the predicate were written 'true'.[5]

Reintroduction of non-indicative moods need not radically alter the picture. The task of generating sentences suitable for content-specifying can still be assigned to a component of the total theory which deals only with indicative sentences. If the object language has more than one mood, a theory competent to impose interpreting descriptions on all possible utterances in it will need to be able to classify utterances as performances of speech acts of this or that kind (assertion, question, command, or whatever). We can require the principles which effect this classification to be written in such a way that, in the case of a non-assertoric utterance, besides enabling us to identify the kind of speech act performed, they also equip us with an indicative sentence, related to the sentence uttered in such a way that the right-hand side of its theorem in the simple theory considered above—a sentence apt for expressing the content of sayings effected by uttering the indicative sentence—will equally serve (perhaps with minor syntactic modification) to express the content of the non-assertoric speech act performed by uttering a non-indicative counterpart. The relevant relations between sentences are quite systematic, and there is no reason to suppose they could not be codified in a theory.

The argument I have outlined does not purport to show that it is compulsory to formulate the central component of a theory

[5] Cf. Davidson, 'Truth and Meaning', *Synthese*, xvii (1967), 304, especially at pp. 310–11. Indexicality introduces a complication; but one which is surmountable, as Strawson notes (pp. 179–80).

of a language—that component which yields sentences suitable to specify the contents of utterances—as a characterization of a predicate. Nor does it guarantee that it is possible to do so; we know it is possible for languages with certain syntactic structures, but it is an open question whether we can wrench all of a natural language into syntactic forms which are amenable. But the policy of trying to do it this way, if possible, offers advantages. For it suggests a model of the kind of thing to aim at, in the truth characterizations which Tarski showed how to construct for certain sorts of formalized language.[6] And Tarskian truth characterizations have special attractions for those concerned with how languages relate to reality: they allow us to lay bare, in derivations of truth-conditions from semantic properties of sentence-constituents, how a sentence's bearing on the world is dependent on specific word-world relations involving its parts, and thus to meet a version of the desideratum mentioned three paragraphs back.

3. The appearance of the debate should now be somewhat altered. A theorist of formal semantics who defends his approach on the lines I have just sketched differs from his counterpart, in the dispute which Strawson stages, in this crucial respect: he evinces no reluctance to appeal to the notion of a communicative performance in what he offers in the way of general remarks about meaning—namely, a description of the shape which a theory of meaning for any particular language might take. On the contrary, the notion of the content of a saying is centrally important in his position. If one counts as a communication-intention theorist by virtue of thinking it unavoidable, in any adequate general account of meaning, to mention kinds of action which are standardly intentional and directed towards audiences, then Strawson's battle seems after all not to be joined. But this is not to say that the theorist of formal semantics I envisage concedes, in advance, the specific outcome of Strawson's debate.

Strawson's predominant picture involves the progressive extension of an analysis. At the first stage, the theorist of formal semantics offers an analysis of the notion of sentence-meaning

[6] Alfred Tarski, 'The Concept of Truth in Formalized Languages', in *Logic, Semantics, Metamathematics* (Clarendon Press, Oxford, 1956), p. 152.

in terms of the notion of truth-conditions. On behalf of the theorist of communication-intention, Strawson insists that the analysans stands in need of further analysis, and that the further analysis takes us to a second stage, at which the notion of sentence-meaning is analysed in terms of the notion of the content of an assertion. Given the aim of analysis, it looks suspect to stop at this point, with an analysis in terms of an overtly linguistic notion; an analysis should decompose a notion into conceptually prior components, and the notion of assertion seems to be on a level with the notion of sentence-meaning—too much so for analytic progress to have been achieved. As Strawson sets things out, such considerations may seem to render obligatory a third stage, in which the notion of assertion is itself analysed in non-linguistic terms—as in the account of assertoric communication, in terms of intention and belief, which Strawson recommends.[7]

Strawson's theorist of formal semantics sticks at the first stage of this progression. Anyone who had arrived at the second stage would be ill-placed to baulk at the third; and my theorist, as noted above, does not hesitate to appeal to the notion of the content of a saying. But it would be a mistake to suppose that this places him at the second stage of Strawson's debate. For he is not, like Strawson's disputant, driven to the notion of saying in order to underpin employment of the concept of truth in a first-stage analysis of the concept of sentence-meaning. Indeed, any such suggestion reverses the order of his reflections, in which the notion of truth enters only at the end. The predicate characterized, in its application to sentences of a given language, by a theory of the sort which he envisages would be a truth-predicate; but this thesis appears, not as a purported analysis—even an interim analysis—of the notion of sentence-meaning, but as a subsequently-noticed consequence of what gives such theories their claim to count as components of theories of meaning.

It might be thought that my theorist is still not entitled to

[7] The full analysis would include more than the partial specification of intention quoted above. Not only would more need to be said about the intention (so far only 'incompletely described'); the idea is that a fuller account would also introduce the notion of a conventional way of executing the intentions in question (see pp. 173–5). I am sceptical about the idea that linguistic behaviour is conventional, but in this paper I shall not consider that element in Strawson's recommended analysis.

appeal to an unanalysed notion of saying, even if his doing so does not correspond to the second stage of Strawson's debate. But what seemed, in that context, to make it compulsory to attempt a reductive analysis of assertion—one which makes no use of notions essentially connected with language—was a thought about conceptual levels which is not so much as relevant if analysis is not the aim. Strawson himself remarks (though he relegates the remark to a footnote) that when one sets out to give a philosophical account of something, conceptual analysis is not the only option (p. 172). Now nothing in the position sketched in §2 commits my theorist to analytic aspirations. And we lack an argument that meaning constitutes the sort of philosophical problem which requires analysis for its solution. The ability to understand a language is an ability to know what people are doing, in the way of performing significant speech acts, when they speak in it; if there is a problem about this, it is not unfamiliarity, or resistance to comprehension, on the part of the concepts employed in saying, occasion by occasion, what someone who understands a speech act knows, but rather an initial unclarity about how the general ability can be specifically described with a degree of systematic articulation sufficient to match the systematic way in which it evidently functions. What we need, on this view, is not conceptual analysis, but a perspicuous mapping of interrelations between concepts which, so far as this exercise goes, can be taken to be already perfectly well understood.

It is a striking fact that in the mapping offered by my theorist, the concept of meaning as such does not even appear. So far from analysing the notion of meaning, he suggests the radical thought that in describing the understanding of a language we can get along without it.

4. There is, however, a different line of argument available to Strawson: one which does not depend on the idea that what we need is analysis of the concept of meaning. It seems fair to claim that a satisfying general account of how language functions should make clear the peculiar importance which language has in human lives; and it seems obvious that one could not achieve that goal without making it clear that language is essentially communicative—that speaking and

understanding are primarily the issuing and the reception of communication. Now the position outlined in §2 does not involve denying the essentially communicative nature of language; it is not liable to the devastating objections which Strawson deploys against any such denial. But there would be justice in the complaint that more needs saying about what exactly communication is. (We might hope that this would have some bearing on the question when the application of an interpreting description to a speech act is acceptable—a question to which the position of §2 requires us to have some answer.) Strawson equates assertoric communication with the fulfilment of an intention of the kind which figures in his favoured account of saying or asserting: that is, an intention which can be partly specified as that of getting an audience to believe that the communicator has a certain belief.[8] Here, then, we have a starting-point for an argument, quite distinct from one which appeals to the conditions for a satisfactory analysis, for accepting not just the innocuous concession to communication-intention theories implicit in §2 and remarked on in the first paragraph of §3, but something more like the specific communication-intention theory which Strawson recommends.

But the proposed account of assertoric communication, from which this line of argument starts, is questionable.

5. According to the proposal, a partial account of what it is for a communicator (C) to communicate to an audience (A) that p by ϕ-ing is as follows: C fulfils an intention that A, through awareness of C's ϕ-ing, should come to believe that C believes that p.[9]

The form 'communicate that p' is perhaps mildly barbarous. It may help to have in mind some plausible substitute for 'communicate'; perhaps 'get it across' will do. But if it will, the suggestion is in doubt, for this reason: it seems that one cannot get it across that p if it is not the case that p. Thus the analysan-

[8] Strawson's formulation (p. 181) actually says 'letting an audience know, or getting it to think, that the speaker has a certain belief'. The former phrase introduces a quite different notion. See §5, and n. 12, below.

[9] Only a partial account. The main omission here, in comparison with the account which Strawson outlines, is a requirement of overtness in the intention. On this, see §6 below.

dum requires the truth of what replaces 'p', whereas the partial analysans obviously does not; and it does not seem that a more precise formulation of the analysans could repair the deficiency, so long as the operative notion remains the notion of inducing beliefs. (Simply adding 'p' as a conjunct seems too *ad hoc* to be satisfactory.)

In the mildly barbarous idiom I am considering, then, 'communicate' belongs to a class of verbs V whose defining property is that a sentence of the form 'S V's that p' entails the truth of its embedded sentence. (Compare 'disclose', 'reveal', 'convey'.) Now Peter Unger has put forward the following attractive hypothesis: what makes a verb belong to this class is that it 'yields us a decision as to the presence or absence of knowledge'.[10] (Unger in fact restricts his hypothesis to lexically unstructured verbs, in order to avoid obvious counter-examples like 'guess correctly'; but it seems reasonable to suppose that the structure of 'get it across' is not of a disqualifying sort.) In the case of 'communicate', understood as tantamount to 'get it across', it is presumably the presence rather than the absence of knowledge which is determined by the true applicability of the verb. This suggests the suspicion: perhaps we should think of communication as the instilling not of beliefs but of knowledge.[11]

The suspicion is one which we might have wanted to entertain in any case, even without the detour through the dubious idiom. We can find it plausible, with Strawson, that the primary intention of a statement-maker, in 'the fundamental case of stating or asserting' (p. 181), is to communicate something, to get something across. But we surely ought not to find it plausible that his primary intention is to induce someone else to form a belief about his belief. Consider what seems to be the corresponding thesis about questions: namely, that the intention of an inquirer, in the most fundamental case of inquiring, is to induce an audience to induce in the inquirer a belief about

[10] 'Propositional Verbs and Knowledge', *Journal of Philosophy*, lxix (1972), 301; the quotation is from p. 307.

[11] 'Suggests' only: Unger's hypothesis would require no more than that a communicator should have knowledge (on the assumption that it is the presence rather than the absence of knowledge which is at issue). But given that the concept of communication requires that a communicator should have knowledge, it seems irresistible to suppose that what he is doing when he communicates is sharing the knowledge.

the audience's belief. Surely any such claim would be absurd. The primary point of asking questions is not to acquire beliefs about one's interlocutor's beliefs, but to find out how things are. Correspondingly, the primary point of making assertions is not to instil into others beliefs about one's own beliefs, but to inform others—to let them know—about the subject matter of one's assertions (which need not be, though of course it may be, the asserter's beliefs).[12]

Strawson's proposal represents a communicator as engaged in the manipulation of his audience's beliefs.[13] Whether the manipulation is in the audience's interest is simply left open. Of course a belief about another person's belief is sometimes a good thing to have; it might afford—if true—insight into the other person, and—if his belief is true as well—an argument to a truth about the world. But this view of communication yields no general presumption that communication, as such, is beneficial to its recipient. That depends on the goodwill, reliability, and so forth of the communicator. If communication is conceived, by contrast, as the sharing of knowledge, it will not seem an accidental fact about communication that is potentially helpful to its recipient; communication, of its very nature, confers potential benefits, whose usefulness is grounded in that interest in how things are which no agent can lack.

6. Of course an assertoric linguistic repertoire can be exploited manipulatively—to mislead rather than to inform. Moreover, a statement-maker can be honestly mistaken even if his intention is informative. This, together with the existence of speech acts which are not assertoric at all, forces us to complicate the picture somewhat, if we are to combine the thesis that communication is the sharing of knowledge with the thesis that linguistic behaviour is essentially communicative in character.

A version of the latter thesis can still be defended on the

[12] On the importance of the notion of letting someone know something, in an account of communication, see Strawson's article 'Intention and Convention in Speech Acts', *Philosophical Review*, lxxiii (1964), 439, reprinted in *Logico-Linguistic Papers*, p. 149, at p. 156 of the reprinted version. But here, as in 'Meaning and Truth' (see n. 8 above), Strawson slides (p. 157) into a formulation in terms of getting something to think something. (Even if we ignore 'or getting it to think', the account in 'Meaning and Truth' is still unsatisfactory from the present standpoint, in that it restricts the content of the knowledge instilled to the communicator's beliefs.)

[13] I owe this thought to Thomas Ricketts.

following lines. We can say that a perceptual capacity is essentially a capacity to acquire knowledge, without committing ourselves to the false claim that knowledge is acquired in every exercise of a perceptual capacity; the concept of misperception is, precisely, the concept of a defective exercise of a capacity whose non-defective exercises issue in knowledge. In a similar way, we can say that the essential character of the assertoric use of language lies in its availability for communicating, in the sense of transmitting knowledge about the subject matter of assertions, without denying the possibility of using assertions to deceive. Communication, in the sense of the transmission of knowledge about the topic of discourse, need not actually take place in every exercise of the repertoire; nevertheless it can be essential to the repertoire that it is apt for communicating in that sense. (Indeed, we might say, it is precisely by purporting to communicate in that sense that a deceiver deceives.)

If we left it at that, however, we would be simply denying—highly implausibly—that communication takes place in deceptive or misguided uses of assertoric language. So far, moreover, we have no inkling how the concept of knowledge-sharing might be extended to non-assertoric uses of language. But the implication of our minimal concession to communication-intention theories (§§2, 3) was that, simply by virtue of being intentional and directed towards audiences, speech acts were quite generally communicative. So faithfulness to the concession requires us to find a further application for the concept of communication, one in which it is not restricted to actually informative assertions but true of speech acts in general. We shall see that we can preserve the idea that communication is the instilling of knowledge.

I shall approach the topic by way of the special overtness which is characteristic of linguistic communication.

A concept at least closely akin to the concept of knowledge-transmission applies to modes of behaviour which we can ascribe to creatures to which we would not think of ascribing intentional action. Absence of intentional action is no bar to possession of sensory capacities; that is, capacities for the acquisition of states of informedness about the environment, in the intuitively satisfactory sense of states, resulting from a systematic sensitivity to features of the environment, which enable behaviour to be suited, in the light of needs or goals, to the way the environment actually is. Such capacities obviously have survival value. Similar survival value would attach also to any behavioural disposition whose effect was to spread, among several individuals, the beneficial results of one individual's exercises of its perceptual capacities. A bird, say, might instinctively emit a characteristic sort of squawk on seeing a predator; other birds might acquire, on hearing such a squawk, a propensity towards behaviour appropriate to the proximity of a predator (flight, increased caution in feeding, or whatever). This propensity might match a propensity they would have acquired if they had seen the predator themselves. In such a case it would be natural to regard the squawk as a further mode of sensitivity to the presence of predators, over and above more direct kinds of perception. The upshot of this further mode of sensitivity is no less appropriately thought of as possession of information (or misinformation if things have gone wrong) than is the state which standardly results from perceiving a predator. We might jib at the word 'knowledge', but there is no risk of overpsychologizing our account of the birds—crediting them with an inner life—if we regard such behaviour as effecting the transmission of information, and hence as constituting a kind of communication.

Now a conspicuous difference between linguistic behaviour and this kind of information-transmission lies in the intentions which are overt in speech. In successful linguistic exchange speaker and hearer are mutually aware of the speaker's intentions, in a way which could have no counterpart in merely instinctive responses to stimuli.

Strawson indeed employs the notion of overtness, when he formulates a component of his favoured account of communicative intentions which I have so far passed over. In Strawson's sketch, the communicator's intention that the audience should form a certain belief about the communicator's belief is 'wholly overt', in this sense: the communicator intends this very intention to be recognized by the audience (pp. 172–3).

It is open to question, however, whether this formulation successfully captures the special transparency of intention which is characteristic of linguistic communication. Such mutual awareness of intention as is involved in the overtness which Strawson describes could be fully achieved even though the intention which is alleged to be the communicative intention is not fulfilled: the audience might recognize the communicator's intention that he, the audience, should adopt a certain belief about the communicator's belief, but fail, or refuse, to oblige. Thus making the communicative intention overt—securing mutual awareness of it between speaker and hearer—is represented as independent of communicative success. What seems plausible, however, is this: the appropriate mutual awareness is actually what is aimed at by the speaker's primary communicative intention, so that securing the mutual awareness is not, as in Strawson's picture, a fallible means to communicative success, but rather constitutes it. This suggests the following position. The primary communicative intention is the intention, for instance, to say such-and-such to the audience. The appropriate mutual awareness is awareness that the speaker has indeed said such-and-such to the audience. Speech acts are publications of intentions: the primary aim of a speech act is to produce an object—the speech act itself—which is perceptible publicly, and in particular to the audience, embodying an intention whose content is precisely a recognizable performance of that very speech act. Recognition by an audience that such an intention has been made public in this way leaves nothing further needing to happen for the intention to be fulfilled.[14]

The notion of an intentional performance is more fundamental in this context than the notion of the intention to perform it. One can sometimes divine an intention to say such-and-such behind a bungled performance, but correctly executed speech acts carry their intentions on their surface; normal understanding of correct speech is not a matter of divination. And an account of the understanding of language must start with the understanding of correct speech.

Now intentions of this sort—intentions whose content is the publication of themselves—are communicative in a sense which involves no departure from the idea that communication is the instilling of knowledge. The intention to make such an

[14] For the idea of speech acts as intentional acts such that the recognition of the intention is its fulfilment, see John R. Searle, *Speech Acts* (CUP, 1969), p. 47.

intention public is the intention to let an audience know what speech act is being performed. Here, then, we have our required further application for the concept of communication. The concept applies, we can now say, at two levels. At the first level, communication takes place, as before, only when information is actually transmitted about the topic of discourse. But at the second level, the information whose sharing is relevant to the question whether communication is taking place concerns, not the topic of discourse, but the nature of the speaker's intentions; and when a properly executed speech act is understood, such information is always transmitted—not only in informative assertions but also in assertions by which information is not transmitted and in speech acts which are not assertoric at all.

If we take it that the content of the intention made public in a speech act—an intention which is communicative at the second level if not at the first—essentially involves the concept of the kind of speech act in question (it is the intention, for instance, to say such-and-such), then we cannot hope for a reductive account of kinds of speech act in terms of the intentions of their performers. But once we have turned our backs on analysis of the concept of meaning (§3), we have no obvious reason to regret this renunciation.

7. Strawson's debate has the centrality of assertoric speech acts as an undisputed background; the idea is that, if we can acceptably explain the notion of the content of these central speech acts, there should be no special difficulty about the content of other sorts of speech act. Now at the beginning of §6 I considered the thesis that availability for first-level communication—transmission of information about the topic of discourse—is of the essence of an assertoric repertoire. I suggested that this thesis cannot be quickly ruled out on the score that assertions need not transmit information; but we lack, as yet, a positive reason for accepting the thesis. Perhaps finding one would be finding a way of domesticating, within a position in which reductive ambitions are renounced, Strawson's thought that 'there is no hope ... of elucidating the notion of the content of such speech acts without paying some attention to the notions of those speech acts themselves' (p. 181).

To specify the meaning of an indicative sentence, according

to Strawson's concession to theorists of formal semantics (§1), is to specify conditions under which it could be used to assert the truth. Now Michael Dummett has argued that to connect meaning with truth-conditions in this way is merely superficial as long as the notion of truth is simply taken for granted. More specifically, such a connection is unilluminating if it is allowed to seem that truth and falsehood are simply a pair of co-ordinate properties, one or the other of which an indicative sentence will happen to have.[15] The implication is that such a connection might be illuminating if reinforced by an account of the special interest which attaches to the question whether a sentence is true or false: an account which makes clear a relation between the point of the classification of sentences into true and false, on the one hand, and the possession of content by sentences, on the other. In the pre-*Tractatus Notebooks*, Wittgenstein associates the fact that sentences represent states of affairs with their possession of a true–false polarity;[16] another way of putting what appears to be Dummett's suggestion is that if any such association is to be illuminating about how indicative sentences represent states of affairs, it must be reinforced by an explanation of the fact that the true–false polarity is not a matter of indifference.

Such considerations seem obviously akin to those which Strawson brings to bear against the theorist of formal semantics who figures in his debate—one who proposes an analysis of the concept of meaning in terms of the concept of truth-conditions. Their relevance to the different position outlined in §2, which claims no particular conceptual illumination from the notion of truth as such, is less obvious. However, that position seems vulnerable to an analogous accusation of superficiality. The Tractarian association has its attraction in the context of questions like this: 'How can a sentence, which is after all a mere complex of lifeless sounds or marks, represent reality as constituted a certain way?' What Dummett stigmatizes as superficial is a purported answer to this question which appeals to the notion of truth-conditions but takes the notion of truth for granted. In the position of §2, what we find instead is an appeal

---

[15] See 'Truth', *Proceedings of the Aristotelian Society*, lix (1958–9), 141.
[16] *Notebooks, 1914–1916* (Blackwell, Oxford, 1961), p. 94 (cf. *Tractatus Logico-Philosophicus* (Routledge and Kegan Paul, London, 1961), e.g. 4.022–4.024).

to the notion of the content of an assertion or a saying, again—so far—without further explanation. But if the question puzzles us, the modification can hardly be an improvement. As long as we take the notion of content for granted, we are open to the accusation of simply refusing to feel the perplexity which the question aims to express: a perplexity about how mere objects can have content at all.

(If the point is generalized like this, it becomes, after all, doubtful whether it is congenial to the position which Strawson recommends. If we are not to take the notion of the content of an assertion for granted, because our perplexity is about the notion of content in general, then how do we make progress by moving to a position in which we take for granted, as Strawson seems to, the notion of the content of a belief? Here we may need to work at resisting an insidious temptation: the temptation to think of the representing of states of affairs as a quasi-magical feat, most easily comprehended, or at least accepted, as effected by mental states, conceived as configurations in an ethereal medium whose properties can be as mysterious as we like. But Strawson is surely not subject to this temptation.)

What Dummett suggests, as a way of beginning to cure the superficiality, is this: the point of the classification of sentences into true and false lies in the fact that we aim at making true statements. But it is not obvious that this suggestion is correct. Truth is not always our aim in statement-making. Nevertheless, the statements we make with deceptive intent still put themselves forward, so to speak, as representing things the way they are; content and truth-conditions seem no differently connected in their case. A modified version of the thesis about aims might at any rate be true: perhaps truth is the normal, or the proper, aim of a statement-maker. But the connection between content and truth-conditions seems to be exceptionless. It is natural to suspect that facts about the normal or proper aims of statement-makers are not themselves what we are looking for. (Perhaps they are consequences of it.)

A different possibility is suggested by the idea that communication is the instilling of information. Consider, first, instinctive communicative behaviour like that of the birds described in §6. The function of such behaviour is to furnish information about the environment to birds which witness it; here 'function' occurs in something like the sense in which it is the function of the heart, say, to circulate the blood. When what gets transmitted is misinformation, there has been a malfunction of a natural process. A malfunction is as such a defect (even if, on occasion, misinformation is better for its recipient than information would have been). In this case, then, the non-indifference of the distinction between truth and falsehood is simply the non-indifference of the distinction between proper functioning and malfunction. Aims pursued in communicating do not enter the story. There are no such aims, since the behaviour is instinctive. But in an account of the (no doubt rudimentary) notion of content which seems undeniably applicable in this case, the natural function of the behavioural repertoire can serve, as it were, instead; it can occupy a position analogous to the position which was supposed to be occupied, in an account of the notion of the content of an assertion, by the alleged fact that in making assertions we aim at truth.

When the communicative process functions properly, sensory confrontation with a piece of communicative behaviour has the same impact on the cognitive state of a perceiver as sensory confrontation with the state of affairs which the behaviour, as we may say, represents; elements of the communicative repertoire serve as epistemic surrogates for represented states of affairs. It is hard to see what perplexity there could be, about the application of the notion of content to pieces of behaviour of this kind, which would persist entirely unalleviated by this thought: elements of such a repertoire represent states of affairs by virtue of standing in for them in a creature's cognitive dealings with the world.

It is plausible that the assertoric core of linguistic behaviour is a descendant, now under intentional control, of the sort of instinctive communicative repertoire we have been considering. This would account for the plausibility of the suggestion that availability for transmission of knowledge is an essential characteristic of the assertoric component of a language (§6). Of course assertions can serve purposes other than the purpose of supplying information; once the behavioural repertoire is responsive to a variety of non-informative intentions, it no longer seems appropriate to think of the transmission of information as the natural function of its exercises. However, it remains a striking fact about assertions that knowledge can be acquired at second hand. If someone knows that p and says that p, then typically someone who hears and understands him is in a position to know that p. It seems unpromising to suppose that knowledge by hearsay owes its status as knowledge, quite generally, to the knower's possessing a cogent argument to the truth of what he knows from the supposed reliability of the speaker. A more attractive line of thought is that the linguistic repertoire retains, through the alteration of nature involved in the onset of self-consciousness, a form of the characteristic which was essential to its pre-linguistic ancestor: in suitable circumstances (to be spelled out in any fuller elaboration of this idea) its exercises are cognitive stand-ins for the states of affairs which they represent. An assertion will actually have that epistemological role only if the circumstances are right. But all standard assertions—excluding, that is, special cases like irony —purport to have it. Thus their possession of content— their capacity for representing states of affairs—is intelligible in terms of a suitable modification of the simple idea which seemed appropriate in the case of instinctive communication.

8. I have been ignoring the belief-expressing aspect of assertion on which Strawson concentrates. I have no wish to deny the central importance, in any account of what gives language its special place in our lives, of the way it enables us to reveal our states of mind to one another. Indeed, the belief-expressing aspect of assertion would be crucial in empirically assessing a theory of a language of the sort envisaged in §2. A theory of that sort is acceptable if the interpreting descriptions of linguistic behaviour which it yields make the behaviour intelligible; the test of intelligibility is the question whether we can make sense of the behaviour, as described, in terms of propositional attitudes which the speakers' behaviour and circumstances permit us to attribute to them, and we typically make sense of assertions as expressive of beliefs. But to concede all this is not necessarily to conclude, with Strawson, that we must understand the possession of significance by indicative sentences in terms of their admitted availability for the expression of beliefs. In fact §7 suggests the possibility of a position in which things are the other way round.

The acquisition of linguistic competence by a contemporary human being may be expected to recapitulate, in some salient respects, the evolution of language from instinctive communicative behaviour found plausible in §7, with the learning of new dispositions taking the place of the evolution of increasingly complex instincts.[17] According to such a view, when an individual language-learner has become fully *au fait* with the practice of making assertions, that component in his competence which consists in his ability to treat assertions as representing states of affairs is a continuation of something which was already present in his behavioural dispositions at an earlier stage, before his operations with his repertoire were self-conscious. (This mirrors the evolutionary suggestion made at the end of §7.) What accounts for the possession of content—the capacity to represent states of affairs—on the part of pieces of behaviour of the kind which, in the fully-fledged competence, he recognizes as assertions is the part played by some such pieces of behaviour—for instance, utterances by his parents—in his acquisition of knowledge; a part which such pieces of behaviour were already playing before the competence was fully-fledged. Then this possession of content, on the part of pieces of behaviour of the relevant kind, can in turn account for the fact that they become capable of being taken as expressive of belief when the individual's dealings with the repertoire become self-conscious.

Exercises of instinctive communicative repertoires do not give expression to states of mind; there are no states of mind, in the relevant sense, to be expressed. Something similar is true if the repertoire is not instinctive but, as in the early stages of language-learning, a matter of something like conditioned reflex. A piece of communicative behaviour of a non-intentional kind simply represents reality, or misrepresents it if something goes wrong. But once communicative behaviour is under the

---

[17] Here, as in the speculation about evolution in §7, I ignore that use of what, in due course, becomes a linguistic repertoire in which its effect is to get others to do things. No doubt this would be important in any account of these issues which was less sketchy and impressionistic than the present one. But in concentrating on the assertoric, I am at any rate no worse off than Strawson. (And it might plausibly be argued that in the absence of anything assertoric, there would be no reason to regard the sort of behaviour I am ignoring as communicative, in any interesting sense, rather than simply a particular way of making the environment more congenial.)

intentional control of the communicator, so that deliberate misrepresentation of reality is possible, the communicating self joins external circumstances as a possible object of representation, or (now) purported representation. To go through the motions of supplying an audience with knowledge of some circumstance which one takes to be otherwise is potentially to mislead, not only about the circumstances, but also about the cast of one's thought—one's belief, in a sense which seems to apply only when questions arise in this way about the sincerity or insincerity of its expressions.[18] (I say 'potentially' not just because an audience may see through one's deception, but also because an audience whose operations with the repertoire—responses as well as exercises—are still no more than conditioned reflex will not be capable of being misled about the second topic.) Now the suggestion is that it is because indicative sentences have the capacity of representing reality as constituted in certain ways—this being independently accounted for in terms of the pre-linguistic role of some of them in knowledge-acquisition—that they are available for representing their utterers as believing that reality is constituted in those ways, once dealings with the repertoire become self-conscious. It is not that their capacity for use as expressive of belief breathes into them the life which enables them to represent reality, but rather that their antecedent capacity to represent reality is what makes them capable of expressing beliefs.

Children start acquiring knowledge by being told things, long before they are capable of so much as raising questions about the sincerity and reliability of their informants.[19] Thus the utterances which they hear on the relevant occasions impinge on them with content, so to speak, in advance of being taken as expressive of belief, in the sense of 'belief' mentioned in the last paragraph. There is a complication: if sentences contain terms which have their life in the context of some body of theory (a description which perhaps fits all sentences), then comprehension of their content is initially incomplete, and the knowledge is commensurately imperfect. What the child really has is a sentence which is confidently accepted though not

---

[18] See Bernard Williams, 'Deciding to Believe', in *Problems of the Self* (CUP, 1973), p. 136.
[19] See Wittgenstein, *On Certainty* (Blackwell, Oxford, 1969), §§143, 160.

properly understood. But what is needed for full exposure to the significance of the sentence is not thoughts about the mental state of the original informant, but acceptance of the further sentences which form the required theoretical context, and a capacity to employ them appropriately in connected conversation.[20] Once the child has worked his way into a fair competence with an appreciable amount of a language, he will surely be engaged in, and sensitive to, assertion as expressive of belief. But it is not because belief-expression is by then in his picture of his dealings with language that content, gradually more fully understood, has for some time been an appropriate constituent of our picture of his dealings with language. Content is in our picture, rather, because the child's operations with sentences have fitted into his life in such a way as to permit us to suppose that the sentences have been serving as vehicles for the transmission of knowledge.

(Anyone who is inclined to suppose that this cannot be right, and that possession of content must be grounded in availability for belief-expression, needs to resist the temptation to rely on the dubious thought mentioned in §7: the thought that the possession of content is too mysterious to be understood except in terms of the peculiar properties of an ethereal medium, conceived as the stuff of which mental states are composed.)

9. The objects to which a formal semantic theory assigns semantic properties tend naturally to be rather formal objects: objects arrived at, then, by abstracting ruthlessly from the concrete detail of actual behaviour. In an access of mathematical enthusiasm about these formal objects and their formally assigned properties, it is possible to forget, or even deny, the anchoring of the discipline in the realities of speech or sufficiently speech-like behaviour. But semantics, formal or otherwise, is secondary to the theory of communication in at least this sense: if there were no subject matter for the theory of communication, there would be nothing for semantic theories to be about. Strawson goes further than this. He endorses a specific proposal about the nature of communication which I have found questionable. And in keeping with this view of communication, he takes the dependence of semantics on the

[20] 'Light dawns gradually over the whole': Wittgenstein, op. cit., §141.

theory of communication to involve a possibility of analysing, in purely psychological terms, the properties which fit words and sentences to be objects of semantic theories; whereas I have suggested that such reductive analysis is not compulsory, and that it misleads about what must be understood in terms of what. Strawson's main aim, however, in the lecture I have discussed, is to recall formal semantics from platonistic excess, and remind it that a semantic theory is nothing if not a component in an account of actual or possible communicative behaviour. That he is correct in this is the unquestioned foundation of the suggestions, divergent in detail from the position he recommends, which I have made in this paper.

The Individuation of Proper Names

L. Jonathan Cohen

Some of Sir Peter Strawson's most interesting work has been in connection with the ways in which certain features of natural language differ from the representations of them that are prevalent among formal logicians. The following is a latter-day effort that tends in a similar direction.

I

There are two different conceptions of a proper name. According to one, which I shall call the 'linguistic' conception, proper names are, and ought to be, individuated by their phonological form. Thus *Aristotle* is a different name from *Plato*, but the given name of the philosopher who tutored Alexander the Great is quite properly, and without any taint of equivocation, the same as that of the shipowner who married President Kennedy's widow. According to the other conception, which I shall call the 'idiosyncratic' one, proper names are, or would ideally be, individuated by their form-and-bearer. On this view it is either said that the philosopher's given name is different from that of the shipowner or, alternatively, that the form *Aristotle* is unfortunately at least two ways homonymous. The present paper is concerned to strengthen[1] the case for adopting the linguistic rather than the idiosyncratic conception, and to articulate some of the implications of so doing.

The idiosyncratic conception has been adopted by many modern logicians. Frege, like Russell, thought not only that in a logically perfect language every proper name would designate just one object, but also, presumably, that where a natural-

[1] Some arguments in its favour were sketched in L. Jonathan Cohen, 'Searle's Theory of Speech Acts', *Philosophical Review*, lxxix, 1970, pp. 547–50. A further development of it was given by Tyler Burge, 'Reference and Proper Names', *Journal of Philosophy*, lxx, 1973, pp. 425–39 and by J. J. Katz, 'A Proper Theory of Names', *Philosophical Studies*, xxxi, 1977, pp. 1–80; but both Burge's and Katz's proposals are unsatisfactory in certain respects, which are discussed below.

language proper name designated now one, now another, object this was an imperfection and a kind of homonymy.[2] Quine wanted to replace *Socrates* by 'a general term that is true of just one object'.[3] Though Dummett admits that the doctrine 'requires qualification in many respects before it becomes a realistic picture of our actual employment of names', he thinks that in principle 'a proper name possesses a unique and specific sense, common to all users of the name, which determines its reference'.[4] According to Kripke the main problem about proper names is whether such a name determines its characteristically unique reference by virtue of its sense, as Frege thought, or in some other way.[5] According to David Lewis 'we would distinguish the name of London (England) from the homonymous name of London (Ontario)'.[6] And within the framework of the idiosyncratic concept an immense amount of controversy has been generated by the question whether a natural-language proper name has a sense as well as a designation. On the one hand the assignment of a sense, or even of a disjunction of senses, seems to restrict the range of possibilities that can be considered. If *Aristotle* means the philosopher who tutored Alexander the Great, we cannot self-consistently consider what might have happened if Aristotle had not performed that task. On the other hand, if a proper name has no sense, it seems to have nothing with which to pick out a unique designation, in the way that the meaning of a common name like *cat* picks out the manifold extension of that name. So causal theories are constructed which tend, as soon as their details are made sufficiently determinate, to be too easily confounded by counter-examples.

The linguistic conception side-steps this tiresome controversy altogether, and guides us towards a less problematic semantical characterization. At least three considerations

---

[2] Cf. 'On Sense and Reference', *passim*, in *Translations from the Writings of Gottlob Frege*, ed. P. Geach and M. Black, esp. p. 70.

[3] W. V. O. Quine, *Word and Object*, 1960, p. 179.

[4] M. Dummett, *Frege: Philosophy of Language*, 1973, p. 142. Cf. also 'What is a Theory of Meaning?' in *Mind and Language*, ed. S. Guttenplan, 1975, p. 132, where Dummett's argument against Davidson presupposes the validity of the idiosyncratic conception of proper names.

[5] S. A. Kripke, 'Naming and Necessity', in *Semantics of Natural Language*, ed. D. Davidson and G. Harman, 1972, pp. 252 ff.

[6] David Lewis, 'Truth in Fiction', *Amer. Philos. Quart.* V, 1978, p. 39.

stand in its favour. The first two are easily stated: the third requires greater elaboration.

II

First, it is of fundamental importance to grasp that the properness of proper names is a feature—in Saussurean terms—of 'parole', not of 'langue'. In a particular utterance or sequence of utterances the name *Smith*, when functioning as a singular term, is typically peculiar to the person it names: it designates just one person. If more people of that name are at issue and the name is used without a distinguishing verbal or non-verbal context, then the use is ambiguous and deviant. But within any given natural language each proper name is normally available, on appropriately different occasions, for naming any number of entities of the appropriate category. During the course of one day a single speaker of English could unambiguously designate six different people by the name *Smith* if he managed to have six conversations that differed appropriately in their circumstances.

Perhaps someone will object that we should think of each such conversation as taking place in an appropriate sub-language of English, so that *Smith* can be conceived to have a unique designation in each sub-language. But this objection cannot be sustained. No doubt it seems flattering: it makes brilliant linguists of us all. But the flattery is empty, because for many other theoretical purposes, whether synchronic or diachronic, we shall want a less extravagant method of individuating languages. A theory of language in such a Pickwickian sense of *language* would have rather poor explanatory value. It is methodologically unrewarding to have to sacrifice the unity of the larger entity (a language) in order to preserve that of the smaller one (a proper name's designation). Moreover, if you speak one language when you refer to your neighbour by *Smith* and a second when you refer to your colleague by that name, then what language are you speaking when they both come to your party and you proudly announce

> There are two Smiths here this evening,

or when, as does happen sometimes, you find occasion to refer separately to both of them in the same conversation? Someone may perhaps speculate that in the small groups in which he supposes language to have originated the philological ancestors of modern proper names had unique designations. But our task is to describe language as we know it is now, not as we speculate it to have been in the remote and unknowable past.

Convenience, not logical principle, is the main factor determining how many objects bear the same name. For example, the larger and better known the object, the more important that its name should not be widely shared. Only a few towns in the world are called London, but many English villages are called Coombe, and even more Englishmen are called John. Occasionally special scruples prevent reuse of a name, as in the case of Japanese emperors' names, but such scruples are religious or ethical rather than linguistic. It is misleading to describe this versatility of proper names as a form of homonymy, since all proper names are intrinsically versatile whereas homonymy, as in *bank* or *bat*, is an inconvenience from which almost all words of a particular grammatical category—almost all common-noun-forms, almost all verb-forms, almost all adjective-forms, etc.—are normally free. Admittedly languages sometimes extend the meanings of common nouns, verbs or adjectives, so that *blue* comes to signify a certain state of mind or a certain type of film, for example, as well as a certain colour. But this is an event in the history of the 'langue'—not an event in the history of 'parole', like giving an old name to a new baby or a new ship: it is characteristically recorded by dictionaries, not by newspapers. The idiosyncratic conception of a proper name therefore carries with it the suggestion, as in Frege's writings, that natural-language proper names have drifted away from univocation, and deviated into homonymy, by some series of philological accidents or through the ignorance, laziness, carelessness, or improvidence of those who baptize children, name towns, etc. Yet in fact it is an immense convenience to have a reusable reservoir of phonologically acceptable speech-forms, divided perhaps into several categories, which parents of children, founders of cities or discoverers of mountains can draw on when they need.

Of course, we must distinguish between simple proper names and compound ones. The simple proper names of a language—sometimes called its proper nouns—are listed in dictionaries of male given names, female given names, surnames, field-names, place-names, etc. for that language. They are a species of word, co-ordinate with common nouns, verbs and the other traditional parts of speech, in any language in which these distinctions are syntactically important. On the other hand, the compound proper names of a language, which should perhaps be called its proper noun-phrases, are constructed out of its proper nouns or other words according to a variety of patterns. Thus we can have in English such compounds as *The Open University*, *Mount Everest*, *The New York Guaranty Trust Company* and *Charles Algernon Montgomery Smith*. But even compound proper names are reusable. Though it may be illegal for you to name your little school *The Open University*, you have not committed any linguistic solecism. Similarly, if Smith's parents failed to give him a sufficient number of personal names to distinguish him from all past, present, and future bearers of the same surname, they may have been deficient in parental care, but scarcely in linguistic propriety. And, after all, Smith's date and place of birth can always eke out identification when this does need to be unique, as on a passport.

Thus it is far from being the case, as the idiosyncratic conception implies, that a natural-language proper name normally has a unique designation, or that in an ideal natural language it would have one. Just the opposite. It would be a real *im*perfection in a natural language to prohibit the reuse of any proper name. Such a prohibition might be workable in a small, static community over a short period. But the phonological inventiveness it would require within any other kind of speech-community would be quite beyond normal human powers. Just as language economizes a speaker's effort in saying different things by allowing an infinite variety of sentences to be composed out of a finite number of words, so too it economizes his effort in naming different objects by allowing an infinite number of objects to be designatable (though not all at once) with a finite set of proper names. The idiosyncratic conception of proper names obstructs awareness of this immensely convenient feature of human language. If a logician's linguistic intuition generates that conception, rather than the linguistic one, he would do well to disregard his intuition.

III

The second consideration that stands in favour of the linguistic conception of proper names is the nature of human knowledge about them. That the philosopher who tutored Alexander was called Aristotle is normally accepted as being a matter of historical fact, not of language. People who do not know that philosopher's name, when asked, are taken to show historical ignorance, not linguistic imperfection, and the same is true if they do not know the name of a living person who is pointed out to them. Learning the given names of our new neighbours, or even their full names, does not necessarily add anything to our knowledge of English: we might well have known already that the names *John* and *Mary*—which our new neighbours happen to have—are English names. But when we learn our new neighbours' names we have at least then learned a fact that we need to know in order to avoid excessive formality in addressing them.

It is therefore important not to be misled by the partial parallelism between the function of a proper name in natural language and that of an individual constant in an interpreted formal system. If you don't know what the individual constant designates, you haven't got a complete knowledge of this artificial language. But you can have a complete knowledge of English, including even its whole present-day vocabulary of proper names, and still not know what given name or what surname—let alone what full name—any particular person has. Certainly there is a sense in which a particular individual constant in an interpreted formal system could have had a different designation. But to have given it that other designation would have constituted an alteration in the artificial language-system; so, relative to the original system, the constant could not have had a different designation from the one it in fact had. On the other hand our new neighbour's parents could perfectly well have decided not to call their son John, or could have changed the family surname, without changing any feature whatever of their natural language.[7] The name that he has is as much a contingent fact about him (changeable by deed

---

[7] This is implicitly denied by S. Kripke, 'Identity and Necessity', in M. K. Munitz, *Identity and Individuation*, p. 155, where he assumes that a renaming of planets entails a change of language.

poll) as the colour of his car (changeable by respray). Our language would be volatile indeed if every time anyone got married and changed his or her name they thereby changed the language! Versatility, not volatility, is the hallmark of natural language.

It follows that where a mountain, a person or any other object has been given two different names, or where a person or corporation has adopted an alias, a statement asserting the identity of what the one name designates with what the other does is typically a contingent truth, not a necessary one. To describe it as a necessary, though a posteriori truth, would be to treat proper names in a natural language as if they were individual constants in an unalterable artificial language-system. When we learn the two names we learn two facts about an object which need not stand in any form of necessary connection with one another. Of course, some cultures might have elaborate rules for naming children that generated a form of necessary truth for the utterance of an appropriate identity-sentence in an appropriate context. Maybe in some remote Pacific island, peopled by English castaways, social conventions require that a man's name is John if and only if he is also called George. Once we know the rule we know, in a particular case, that John <u>must</u> be George. But the conceivability of such a bizarre culture serves merely to highlight the contingency of ordinary name-name identifications in natural language. If the ordinary ones were not contingent there would be no point in saying, on the Pacific island, that John <u>must</u> be George. More familiarly, perhaps, in the ancient Roman Republic anyone who bore the 'cognomen' *Cicero* was necessarily also named *Tullius*, since the Cicero family was part of the Tullian gens. But by these standards it is quite contingent for someone named *Nixon* to be also called *Richard*.

Philosophers who deny the contingency of any name-name identifications have tended to concentrate their attention on notoriously true identifications. Their thesis is intuitively less plausible when applied to false ones, like

(1)   Bacon is identical with Shakespeare.

It scarcely seems impossible to imagine a course of events by which Nicholas Bacon's youngest son was born at Stratford and wrote the plays under a pseudonym as well as the *Novum Organum* under his own name. But these events never actually occurred, so (1) is contingently false. We therefore cannot say that if (1) were true it would be necessarily true: if (1) were true it would be contingently true. Equally, denials of true identity statements often seem eminently plausible candidates for contingent falsehood. If I say

(2) Hesperus is not identical with Phosphorus,

I may well be imagining a possible system of planetary revolutions that allows for this non-identity. Perhaps you wrote off your natural inclination to take

(3) Hesperus is identical with Phosphorus

as a contingent truth, on the ground that the apparent contingency of (3) is due to its announcement of an empirical discovery. But (2) announces no such discovery. Its assertion could well be a piece of unempirical dogmatism. So the natural inclination to take (2) as a contingent falsehood cannot so easily be written off; and if (2) is contingent so is (3).

It follows that there is bound to be a fallacy somewhere in any argument designed to show that all true name-name identifications are necessarily true. One such argument, for example,[8] proceeds from the premiss that everything has the property of being necessarily identical with itself. Hence George has the property of being necessarily identical with George. And if John is identical with George, John must have every property that George has. Therefore, it is claimed, John has the property of being necessarily identical with George. But the argument is essentially question-begging in that it assumes the sharing of properties, which goes along with identity, to include properties involving modalities. Or, alternatively, when the argument is set out formally, we can say that the fallacy consists in allowing modal operators to appear within substituends for predicate variables. Not that this procedure ought always to be formally impermissible. But it should

[8] Cf. S. Kripke, op. cit., pp. 135 ff.

not occur in a formal system that is designed to represent the logical structure of natural language.⁹ Each syntactically differentiated kind of symbol-occurrence in such a formal system should be reserved, in the intended interpretation, for the performance of just one linguistic function, and just one kind of symbol-occurrence for each function: predicates for predicates, operators for operators, and so on. Go against this principle in your formalizations, if you please; but you are not then entitled to use your consequentially distorted representation of natural language as a basis for drawing related conclusions about what natural language is really like, as if you had not introduced any relevant distortions by your very system for representing its structure. After all, you would not judge your own appearance from its image in a distorting mirror.

Perhaps it will be objected that *necessarily* can occur within substituends for natural-language predicate variables if it occurs as a predicate modifier to express modality de re, and not as a sentential operator to express modality de dicto, and that its availability for use as such a predicate modifier is supported by the semantics for that use which has now been constructed.¹⁰ But, in order to show that *necessarily* actually functions as a predicate modifier in relevant contexts in natural language, we need rather better reasons than the existence of this semantics. We need to be shown not merely what the semantics of such a modal predicate-modifier would be if the modifier were part of natural language. We need to be shown also that it is a relevant part of natural language. We need to be told of a statement like

Hesperus is necessarily identical with Phosphorus

that would have to be recognized both as true, and as having a thus modified predicate, even by those who adopt a semantics for proper names like the one detailed here: otherwise the objection would be question-begging. And the anti-essentialist has in effect always denied that any such statements exist.

---

⁹ The fallacy here is discussed at greater length, and in relation to other examples, in L. Jonathan Cohen, *The Implications of Induction*, 1970, pp. 211 ff.

¹⁰ D. Wiggins, 'The *De Re* "Must": a Note on the Logical Form of Essentialist Claims' in *Truth and Meaning*, ed. G. Evans and J. McDowell, 1976, pp. 285 ff., and C. Peacocke, 'An Appendix to David Wiggins' "Note"', ibid., pp. 313 ff.

IV

The third consideration in favour of the linguistic, rather than the idiosyncratic, concept of proper names is their actual mode of linguistic operation. In order to understand how proper names normally function in a natural language one has to grasp that this is a form of indexical, or token-reflexive usage. Logicians are ready enough to grant that demonstrative pronouns (like *he, outside, to-day, hereafter*), temporally tensed verbs (like *jumps* and *jumped*), or temporally oriented adjectives (like *present* and *future*) can have their designations determined, in actual speech, by their context of utterance. But they have generally been reluctant to recognize that this is how proper names normally function also.

Admittedly Tyler Burge[11] has recently argued that proper names function both as demonstratives (in *Alfred studies in Princeton*) and as predicates or general terms (in *There are relatively few Alfreds in Princeton*). But even this does not get it quite right. The concept of a demonstrative is a fairly clear-cut one, which loses a lot of its value if we blur it in order to include proper names within its extension. Demonstratives have their designations determined by their context of utterance without the benefit of any previous baptismal ceremonies, official registrations, etc. They are extremely adaptable tools of reference which a speaker can use without having any previous knowledge whatever about the entity designated (except perhaps knowledge of some highly general feature such as its sex). For example, the demonstrative *I* can be used in this way, without any impropriety or risk of misunderstanding, by a known amnesiac. But demonstratives pay the price for their extreme adaptability by being rather more difficult to use when the speaker is at a distance—in time, space, or subject-matter—from what he wishes to designate. Demonstratives are typically helped to achieve their designation by their relative proximity, along one dimension or another, to what they designate: the easiest things to direct attention to, for purposes of

---

[11] Op. cit. Burge's theory is endorsed by J. Hornsby, 'Singular Terms in Contexts of Propositional Attitude', *Mind*, lxxxvi, 1977, p. 42, and criticized (from another point of view than mine) by S. E. Boër, 'Proper Names as Predicates', *Philosophical Studies*, 27, 1975, pp. 389–400.

mutual understanding, are what you and your addressee can both see or have just been discussing.[12] The use of a proper name, on the other hand, does not depend in any way on proximity to what it designates. No doubt proper names are substantially less flexible than demonstratives, and their optimally effective use requires both the speaker and his addressee to have stored in their memory certain appropriate items of non-linguistic knowledge. But proper names have the countervailing advantage that they can be used to designate entities which are far beyond the speaker's current range of pointing out. No useful purpose, therefore, can be served by confounding together two such valuably different categories of words. Even if we were to classify proper names as a species of 'demonstrative', in some extended sense of that word, we should still need another term to cover those 'demonstratives' that are not proper names.

Nor is it particularly significant, as Burge seems to imply, that proper names sometimes function as predicates or general terms, in sentences like

There are relatively few Alfreds in Princeton.

Burge objects to treating such uses as special ones, and wishes to regard modified and unmodified occurrences of proper-names as co-ordinate types of usage. But Burge offers no evidence that the modified use of proper names occurs in most natural languages: all his examples are from English. And the fact is that all forms of indexical expression tend to lend themselves, at least in some languages, to de-indexicalization. This certainly happens with ordinary English demonstratives, though Burge seems unaware of it.[13] Compare, for example,

(4) That cat is a *he*[14]

or

(5) The *outside* world is unknown to us

or

[12] In its original, now obsolete sense, the English verb *to demonstrate* meant to point out or indicate.

[13] His treatment of ordinary demonstratives makes no mention of it: cf. T. Burge, 'Demonstrative Construction, Reference and Truth', *Journal of Philosophy*, lxxi, 1974, pp. 205 ff.

[14] This usage has a paragraph to itself in the *Oxford English Dictionary* (Compact edition, 1971, vol. i, p. 1269).

(6) *To-day*'s problem is always more exciting than *yesterday*'s

or

(7) Some people fear the *hereafter*.

And it also happens with temporally tensed verbs, as in

(8) Kittens *jump* when startled,

or with temporally oriented adjectives, as in

(9) *Present* love has *present* laughter.

In sum, ability to function as a descriptive term has not been established as a feature of proper names that distinguishes them from other indexically usable expressions;[15] and a technique for formalizing sentences that include proper names is obliged to represent a connection between their indexical and descriptive uses only so far as it also needs to represent a connection between sentences like

> That cat is a he

and

> He is purring.

Indeed, so far as it is the task of logical formalizations to represent such connections, one might think it more important to connect the designatory potential of proper names with their vocative use. Proper names are very commonly used to request or arouse the attention of the persons to whom they can, in those contexts, also be used to refer. Burge does not mention this use, though it is much more closely confined to proper names, among indexically usable expressions, than is de-indexicalization: perhaps the second person pronoun is the only demonstrative that regularly functions thus. Yet any formalization of imperative sentences like

> John, come here!

must be capable of representing vocatives.

[15] Not that there are not other kinds of English word of which it seems more appropriate to say, as Burge says of proper names, that usage A is just an indexicalization of usage B, rather than that usage B is just a deindexicalization of usage A. The names for days of the week are a typical example, as in (usage A) *He will arrive on Sunday*, as distinct from (usage B) *Sundays are sacred*.

V

How then does the context of a proper name's utterance determine its designation? We need to distinguish at the outset here between the object that a speaker intends to designate by his utterance of a proper name, the object that is actually designated, and the object that the addressee takes to be designated.

By a slip of the tongue, or as a result of originally mishearing, or later misremembering, the Peripatetic philosopher's name you might utter the sentence

(10)   Aristophanes tutored a great conqueror.

You have it clearly in mind that Alexander was tutored by a philosopher, about whom you know a number of facts such as that he was born at Stagirus in 384 BC and walked about while lecturing; and you certainly do not think that Alexander was tutored by a very aged comic playwright. Whom does the name *Aristophanes* in your utterance designate? According to many logicians[16] it designates the person you had in mind or meant, viz. Aristotle. But 'designates' here is in any case a technical term and we have to adopt those criteria for its predication that are appropriate to the theoretical function of statements about designations. And these statements must at least give the facts that are needed for truth-assessments, if statements about truth-conditions form at least a part of any adequate semantics for a natural-language. Hence 'designates' must be so defined that what *Aristophanes* designates in your utterance of (10) must, if and only if your utterance is true, be an entity satisfying the predicate *tutored a great conqueror*. So we need to decide whether to call your utterance of (10) true, or false. Well, what did you say? You said that Aristophanes tutored a great conqueror. You may have intended to say that Aristotle did this, but what you actually said was that Aristophanes did it. No court of law, no jury of your colleagues, no verdict of public opinion, would describe what you said otherwise. Reformulation of your utterance in indirect speech supplies a decisive basis for truth-assessment. After all this is the basis on which the biconditionals of truth-conditional semantics are constructed. The sentence 'Snow is white' is held to be true, for any speaker at any

[16] e.g. M. Devitt, 'Singular Terms', *Journal of philosophy*, lxxi, 1974, p. 188.

time, if and only if snow is white, just because, whatever such a speaker intends to say, what he actually says is that snow is white. It follows that, irrespective of your intentions or of your beliefs or of what you had in mind or of the causal origins of your mistake, your utterance of (10) was false. The name *Aristophanes* in your utterance did not designate the man whom you had in mind or meant. It is just the same with demonstrative pronouns. Suppose you say

(11) He is coming with me,

having John in mind and pointing over your shoulder, since you think that John is behind you; and suppose that Jim, not John, is the man behind you. Despite what you intended, what you have actually said is that Jim is coming with you and the demonstrative pronoun *he* in your utterance of (11) designated Jim, not John.[17] The objective designation of your pronoun depends not on what you yourself happened to believe, but on what an observer of your gesture might reasonably presume that you knew.

No doubt there is a sense in which you were referring to Aristotle, when you unfortunately used the wrong name for him, and to John, when you pointed in the wrong direction. But, even though it would be quite true, in one ordinary, everyday sense of *refer* to say this, that sense of *refer* is not the one needed to do the technical job for which I have been using the word *designate*. In the pragmatic, or speech-act, sense of *refer*, people and their utterances refer, and frequently what they refer to doesn't even exist, though they may think it does, like the book which Professor X referred to in his lectures and which turns out never to have been written. In the usual semantic, or logical, sense of *refer*, however—i.e. in the sense expressed by *designate* in the present paper—it is only words, phrases, individual constants, class-abstracts, etc. that refer, and existence is arguably a necessary condition for being referred to.[18] Again, in the everyday, pragmatic sense of *refer* you have not referred to John, but addressed him, when you say

[17] J. J. Katz, 'A Proper Theory of Names', *Philosophical Studies*, xxxi, 1977, pp. 1–80, has a linguistic token-reflexive theory of proper names, but spoils it by identifying the actual reference of a proper name's utterance with its intended reference.

[18] On the difference between these two senses of *refer*, see further L. Jonathan Cohen, 'What is the ability to refer to things, as a constituent of a language-speaker's competence?', in R. Jakobson *et al.*, *Linguaggi nella Società e nella Tecnica*, 1970, pp. 259 ff.

John, come here!

Yet this need not prevent our saying that the first word of your utterance designates the subject of its imperative verb-form.

Very similar considerations refute other psychologizing accounts. For example, even though the person with whom you are talking is familiar with your tendency to say 'Aristophanes' when you mean 'Aristotle', it does not follow from that fact that the proper-name token in your utterance of (1) actually designates Aristotle. We have to distinguish here between the linguistic meaning of your utterance and the message that it successfully communicated.

How then is it determined what such or such an occurrence of a particular proper name actually designates? Four factors seem capable of playing a critical part, though they are not equally important in every utterance: the topic under discussion, the speaker's knowledge about what entities within that topic have the name in question, his addressee's knowledge about what entities within the topic have the name in question, and any relevant events, circumstances, etc. that are present at the time and place of the utterance and may be reasonably presumed to be known to the speaker and his addressee. In a book, for example, where the author of the text is rather remote from his readers and the readers may be rather heterogeneous in their education, the designation of a proper name will be primarily determined by the book's topic. In a history of logic *Aristotle* denotes the Stagirite: in memoirs of the twentieth century jet set it denotes the shipowner. In the course of a brief conversation, however, the topic of a remark may be insufficiently clear to fix the designation of a particular proper name, and the determining consideration may be the fact that only one person of that name is known to both the speaker and his addressee. Nor need they both have precisely the same knowledge. Maybe the speaker knows only that the founder of the Peripatetic school of philosophy had the name *Aristotle*, while his addressee knows only that the most famous person to be born in Stagirus had that name. But in virtue of knowing these two things they both know enough to establish the name's designation. Or perhaps the speaker and his addressee share knowledge of several people with the name in question, and the presumably observed arrival of one such person is the critical consideration. Of course, two or more of these factors may sometimes conflict with one another. But on those occasions the proper name's designation is ambiguous. And, if none of the four factors is appropriately operative, the designation is empty and the utterance correspondingly defective.

Note that it is the addressee who counts here, not the hearer. The background knowledge of casual eavesdroppers is irrelevant. But we can think of a normal bystander as adopting a neutral and independent position between the speaker and the addressee. He arbitrates on the actual, objective designation as distinct from the one subjective designation that is intended by the speaker or the other subjective designation that is imputed by the addressee. So any causal chains that have to connect the speaker's state of mind with the name's original assignment to its bearer must be matched by causal chains connecting the addressee's state of mind with this. Nor are these causal chains something special to proper-name designation. They are relevant here just because, first, all knowledge of fact entails some causal connection between the facts that are known and the belief implicit in the knowledge,[19] while, secondly, speaker's and addressee's knowledge about a name are two of the four factors that determine its designation.

Again, the uniquely identifying descriptions that some logicians have wished to associate with proper names do not belong to these names as such, any more than similar descriptions belong to demonstratives. But when we talk of the speaker's or hearer's knowledge that goes to determine a proper name's designation we must think of this as containing relevant descriptive items, such as that Aristotle was the founder of the Peripatetic school of philosophy or the most famous person born in Stagirus.

Thus it is excessively restrictive to suppose, as some logicians have done,[20] that a proper name achieves its designation of a

---

[19] This is obviously too big a claim to be defended here. But so far as perceptual knowledge is concerned cf. L. Jonathan Cohen, 'The Causal Theory of Perception', *Proceedings of the Aristotelian Society*, Supp. Vol. li, 1977 pp. 127 ff. ; and so far as non-perceptual knowledge is concerned this seems the only way to account for the knowledge of the examinee who mistakenly thinks that he is only guessing.

[20] e.g. G. Evans, 'The Causal Theory of Names', *Proc. Arist. Soc.*, Supp. Vol. xlvii, 1973, p. 202.

particular object via the existence of a community in which it is common knowledge that members of the community have in their repertoire the procedure of using the name to refer to the object. There is no reason at all why the use of a particular name to designate a particular object should not be private to a single speaker. For example, suppose a hermit calls his cat *Aristotle*. Then *Aristotle* is certainly the name of that cat, even if no one else ever knows this. The hermit has certainly succeeded in using a proper name to designate the cat without the existence of any community of the above-mentioned kind. To require the existence of such a community is to assimilate naming far too closely to meaning. It is the opposite error to that of those (perhaps legendary) philosophers who are supposed to have conceived all meaning on the model of naming—the notorious 'Fido'-Fido fallacy. Proper names are no more parasitic on the existence of such a community than are demonstratives. Some assignments of proper names are socially sanctioned and widely known, others are private to a few people, and yet others are quite individual and personal, like some love-names, nicknames, or pets' names. Similarly some occurrences of demonstratives achieve their designations via the use of gestures that enjoy a conventional significance within this or that sub-culture of a speech-community, while other occurrences of demonstratives, like most occurrences of the first person singular pronoun, need no such sub-cultural props. Certainly neither proper names nor demonstratives nor any other linguistic form could have designatory potential unless a community existed in which it was common knowledge that members of the community include the referential use of such sound-patterns within their communicational repertoire. But it is this general ability to use proper names referentially that needs to be included in a community's self-conscious repertoire, for just the same reasons as the other components of semantic competence need to be. Without such tacit conventions it is impossible to achieve communication by any system of meaningful signals, let alone by language.[21]

Perhaps it will be objected that the hermit's name for his cat is not a real counter-example. 'His usage is parasitic', we may

[21] Cf. L. Jonathan Cohen, *The Diversity of Meaning*, 1962, pp. 38 ff. The issue is investigated in detail in D. K. Lewis, *Convention: A Philosophical Study*, 1969.

be told, 'upon acceptance of a standard procedure for naming in the community at large. The hermit just constitutes a one-membered sub-community in which it is common knowledge that all members of the sub-community have in their repertoire the procedure of using the name to refer to the object.' Well, such an objection runs the risk of trivializing the thesis that it sets out to defend. We can agree that the hermit's usage is parasitic upon acceptance of a standard procedure for naming in the community at large. But it is not obviously parasitic upon acceptance that a particular name is not normally used in a sub-community unless it is common knowledge that all members of the sub-community have in their repertoire the procedure of using the name to refer to its bearer. And in any case consider a situation where more than one person is involved and the speaker does not know what the addressee knows about the name in question. Suppose the topic of a guide's lecture is clearly ancient Greek culture, and the guide asserts (in any language) to his audience of exotic tourists

(12)   Aristotle is a philosopher.

Such a speaker may well be the first person to inform that particular audience about the existence of a famous ancient Greek called *Aristotle*. But the name's designation in his remark remains unaffected thereby. Despite the historical ignorance of his audience, the guide must still be construed to have asserted that Aristotle (the ancient Greek) was a philosopher.

'That is beside the point', the objector may now claim. 'Nothing gets a name in the first place except by the existence of a community in which it is common knowledge that members of the community have in their repertoire the procedure of using the name to refer to its bearer.' But this is to look at the issue through the wrong end of the long telescope of time. What is at stake is not how an entity acquires its proper name, but how a particular occurrence of the name, perhaps centuries later, or continents away, obtains its designation. Some of the factors determining this designation do indeed relate to knowledge that a certain entity once acquired a certain name. But we must not confound the knowledge-conditions appropriate to name-acquisition with the knowledge conditions appropriate to name-use. Ideally both speaker and addressee should know about the fact of name-acquisition, but neither need know that the other knows. A bystander could always determine the designation by looking only at the four factors already listed.

Finally we shall perhaps be told that, if the speaker wishes to use a proper name in a successful linguistic communication, he must know that the addressee knows the name's bearer, and that, if the addressee is to interpret the speaker's utterance correctly, he must know that the speaker knows the name's bearer: so in general there must be common knowledge that members of the community have in their repertoire the procedure of using the name to refer to the object. But one needs to distinguish here between the conditions requisite for a successful act of communication in which a proper name is employed, and the conditions determining what the proper name actually designates. It is just because the latter may include the first-order knowledge-states of speaker and addressee that the former may have to include knowledge about these knowledge-states. To know what the name's occurrence designates, one must know what relevant conditions are present.

VI

The idiosyncratic conception of proper names, therefore, with its projected individuation of them by form-and-bearer, gains no support from considerations about the way in which natural language actually functions. Nevertheless the requirements of theoretical systematization often force us to oversimplify. Ideal gases, lines that have length without breadth, and perhaps also truth-functional connectives, are familiar examples of such well-motivated regimentation. They constitute misrepresentations only so far as we have some good reason to conceive our theories as descriptions, rather than idealizations, of their several domains. So logicians might be tempted to defend an idiosyncratic conception of proper names on the ground that it allows a very simple and straightforward procedure for the formalization of sentences containing proper names. Each proper name, when individuated by form-and-bearer, is assumed to correlate with a distinct individual constant in the formalism.

Now there is certainly no logical harm in this mode of formalization. It will not lead us from true premisses to false conclusions; and, given a sufficiently inexhaustible supply of individual constants, our formal language can represent thus (other things being equal) any argument that is constructable in natural language with the help of proper names or demonstratives. Indeed this mode of formalization is ideal for logical exercises and for the analysis of particular pieces of actual reasoning. But it will not serve as a satisfactory representation of how proper names function in natural language because, when operating as such a representation, it individuates proper names quite incorrectly and does not reveal the essentially indexical, or token-reflexive way in which their designations are determined. Nor, correspondingly, should this mode of formalization be used in the construction of a truth-conditional semantics for a natural language, if the theorems of that semantics are to state truth-conditions for sentences of the language that are identified and individuated by their appropriate structural description.

One method of dealing with proper names in a truth-conditional semantics, on a non-idiosyncratic basis, has been proposed by Burge.[22] It exploits the point that all English proper names have a descriptive or predicative use. His analysans for a sentence like (12) is a formal paraphrase of the sentence

> For all x and y, if x is an act of reference by a speaker s at time t to y with the first occurrence of *Aristotle* in *Aristotle is a philosopher*, then *Aristotle is a philosopher* is true with respect to s at t just in case the object which is y and is an Aristotle is a philosopher.

However, not only are Burge's proposals of dubious value for languages other than English. They also depend essentially on the mistaken assumption that what is relevant to the truth of an utterance is the speaker's subjective act of referring rather than the objective designation that a normal bystander would attribute to the utterance. Only on the former assumption would it be reasonable to restrict the relativization of a proper name's

---

[22] 'Reference and Proper Names', *Journal of Philosophy*, lxx, 1973, p. 433. I am accepting for present purposes the general framework of truth-conditional semantics, as a way of talking about meanings in natural language, though in a more extended discussion this acceptance would have to be subject to some important qualifications.

reference to relativization for a speaker-at-a-time. Nor, in any case, is there much illumination to be gained from an analysans which assumes that we already (prior to evaluating the analysis) know the conditions under which the utterance of a certain proper name by a speaker s at time t is an act of reference to a certain entity.[23]

If instead we are right to suppose, for reasons already given, that we must represent the objective designation, we shall have to construct an analysans that increases the degree of relativization by acknowledging the four determining factors listed above. What a proper name designates in any given utterance will normally be relative to the subject-matter of the utterance, to the speaker's and addressee's knowledge, and to relevant features of the non-linguistic context. Thus the truth-conditions for a sentence like (12) will be given by a formal paraphrase of

(13) For all e, u, d, s, a and x, if e is the English sentence *Aristotle is a philosopher*, u is an utterance of e as an English sentence by speaker s to addressee a about domain of discourse d, and there is just one entity y such that y is identical with x and satisfies one or more of the following four conditions

(i) y has the name *Aristotle* and falls within d,
(ii) s knows y to have the name *Aristotle* and to fall within d,
(iii) a knows y to have the name *Aristotle* and to fall within d, or
(iv) circumstances of u that are presumably known to s and a make it appropriate for u to include a mention of y,

then u is an utterance of a true saying if and only if x is a philosopher.

But the descriptive or predicative use of a proper name can be represented much more simply. For example, the truth-condition for a sentence like

---

[23] A similar criticism may be made of the analysis of demonstratives suggested by D. Davidson, 'Truth and Meaning', *Synthese*, 17, 1967, pp. 310–20, where Davidson claims that *That book was stolen* is true as (potentially) spoken by p at t if and only if the book demonstrated by p at t is stolen prior to t. A minor fault in Davidson's analysis is that according to it someone can know the semantics of English, in terms of the appropriate T-sentences, without knowing any relevant difference between *this* and *that*.

At least two Aristotles are philosophers

will be given by a formal paraphrase of

> For all x and y, if x and y both have the name *Aristotle*, then an utterance of the English sentence *At least two Aristotles are philosophers* is an utterance of a true saying if and only if x is not identical with y and both x and y are philosophers.

(I am assuming that *two Aristotles* here is synonymous with *two people who each have the name 'Aristotle'* and not with *two members of the Aristotle family* or with *two people who resemble Aristotle*.)

It is possible that I have underestimated the number and variety of factors that go to determine the objective designations of proper names. Perhaps the details of (13) need to be even more complicated. But the guiding principle on which (13) is constructed will still be unaffected. Proper names will just be even more token-reflexive than I have allowed for, and the idiosyncratic conception of them will be even more inappropriate than I have claimed in a semantics for natural language.

Perhaps it is also worth remarking that demonstratives and demonstrative phrases are not the only other types of expression for which, *mutatis mutandis*, an analysis like (13) is applicable. Titles (of books, plays, poems, stories, musical compositions, or works of visual art) may also be treated in this way. Titles may include proper names, as with *The Perils of Pauline*, but they need not, as with *Persuasion* and *Principia Mathematica*. They certainly differ from proper names in being substantially less adaptable than proper names as instruments of reference, just as proper names are themselves less adaptable than demonstratives. This is because titles, unlike proper names, create the presumption that they carry some information about what they entitle: *Hamlet*'s leading character is presumably a man of that name. But there is nothing in language to stop people from using the same title to designate different books, plays, paintings, etc. Title plagiarism may be a literary sin, just as company-name copying may be a legal wrong, but neither is a linguistic solecism. So a truth-conditional semantics for natural language has to relativize the designations of titles in much the same way as it relativizes those of proper names.

What should we say about Pegasus, Pickwick, 'et hoc genus omne'? Proper names may be given not only to actual persons, animals, places and events, but also to deities, angels and devils, to mythological heroes, to the persons and places of creative fiction, to military operations that may well be cancelled before they take place, or even to numbers that may one day be proved not to exist (like the lowest even number that is not the sum of two primes, which we might name *Eldorado*).

It is sometimes suggested that the problem of fictional reference may be solved by assuming that all references in works of fiction are pretended ones. What we should have to consider, on this view, are not some special, fictional truth conditions for the sentence *Spenlow came out of the house* that might be used to make the fictional reference to a Mr Spenlow, but just ordinary truth-conditions for a sentence asserting Charles Dicken's pretence that Spenlow came out of the house. But this suggestion will hardly work. Very few of the problematic references are pretended ones. Even in novels the author very rarely pretends to be referring to real people. To make such a pretence seriously, he needs to cite alleged sources or print photographs of mimeographed police dossiers, and so on. Most modern novels instead print an explicit disclaimer of any intention to refer to a real person, living or dead, so as to avoid the consequences of possible libel actions. One does not want to lose the distinction between fiction which pretends to be history and fiction which does not (or even denies that it is). In any case the generals who name an operation that they later have to cancel are not necessarily pretending anything when they refer to the operation by name in discussing its strategy and logistics: planning does not necessarily entail make-believe.

Indeed, one really should not be concerned, in an analysis of natural language, with the different domains of discourse to which speakers of the language devote their attention on different occasions. It is no business of linguistics to give some kind of priority to the physical over the spiritual, the historical over the fictitious, the achieved over the merely intended, or the confirmed over the merely hypothesized. Metaphysics should not be allowed to intrude into the semantics of natural language. Language is an all-purpose instrument and allows references to be made, in appropriate contexts, to the elements of any conceivable domain. So all that needs to be said about (13) in this connection is that the term 'entity' in it should be taken to permit a corresponding latitude. Since one of the four determining factors for a proper name's designation is the subject-matter of the utterance in which it occurs, we are entitled to suppose that the entity designated merely has to fall within the utterance's domain of discourse. Of course, occasions occur when even this requirement is not satisfied. Genuine mistakes are sometimes made as to whether a particular domain of discourse contains an entity bearing such-or-such a proper name. But it is of no relevance to the present enquiry whether one should adopt a Russellian or a quasi-Strawsonian method of dealing with those eventualities. In (13) truth-conditions are given only for cases where the existential condition is satisfied; and acceptance of (13) leaves it an open question whether utterance of (12) should be regarded as an assertion of a false saying in the other cases, where the existential condition is not satisfied, or as an assertion of a saying with a neutral truth-value.

One final qualification needs to be added, however. Some languages divide their proper names into morphologically distinct categories, whereby people and places, for example, or men and women, can never bear the same names. Where this happens, the proper names have a good claim to be attributed corresponding meanings.[24] Thus in Latin the names *Julia* and *Julius* might be said to differ in meaning because their bearers must always differ in sex. But the point is easily represented within an analysans like (13). If English is such a language and *Aristotle* a male person's name within it, all that needs to be done to (13) is to replace 'entity' by 'male person'.

---

[24] Exact translation of a proper name, from one language to another, may thus be rendered rather difficult. But in any case it is only by a rather crude convention that we assume the Stagirite to have been given the name *Aristotle* rather than its Greek original, which was a different speech-form and therefore a different name. The crudity of this convention generates serious problems for the analysis of indirect discourse, which are interestingly discussed in Saul Kripke, 'A Puzzle about Belief', in *Meaning and Use*, ed. A. Margalit (1979), pp. 239–83.

The Variable and Its Place in Reference

W. V. Quine

... The idea is that (A) ['Socrates performs swimming'] or (B) ['Socrates possesses bravery'] *commit* us, as regards swimming and bravery, in a way in which we are not at all committed by (a) 'Socrates swims' or by (b) 'Socrates is brave'.

But this is absurd. The theory of 'commitment' by noun, but not by adjective or verb, is as absolutely implausible as any philosophical view could be.

Strawson, Subject and Predicate, p. 33.

He was right about the implausibility and absurdity of the idea, but wrong in supposing, if he did, that the idea was mine. The difference between (A) and (a) or between (B) and (b) is, as he rightly suggests, 'simply a matter of stylistic variation'. Clearly it is too frail a reed to bear the weight of an ontology. Occurrence of a word in a meaningful sentence gives no presumption that the word designates anything, and the circumstance that the word is a singular term is still too casual a circumstance to make the difference.

But we do like to think of sentences as telling about things. How then are we to distinguish between the words that adduce the things and the words that tell about them? Such is the business of Strawson's notion of 'identificatory force'—which, however, issues finally not in a distinction but in a matter of degree,[1] And we easily see that it might. Since we say something about a subject matter already in specifying it, what significant separation can we expect between that information and what comes after? There are differences in phrasing, granted—but so there were between (A) and (a), or (B) and (b). Thus one may say that one's pompous husband is an ass, or that one's hus-

---

[1] Op. cit., pp. 106 ff. Also he seems to recognize (p. 109) that identificatory force can be carried by predicates.

band is a pompous ass. In French it is usual even to specify the protagonist in a prefatory phrase before the grammatical subject is broached: *Ma pauvre tante, elle ne sort jamais*. Japanese has a particle *wa* to mark such a phrase. In respect of cognitive content, however, the distinction between the identificatory information and the ampliative information remains as empty as that between (A) and (a), or (B) and (b). It is a rhetorical difference, a difference in *force*, as Strawson well describes it.

The quest for points of objective reference in sentences is beset, we see, with *ignes fatui*. But the French construction deserves a closer look. The French speaker is at pains to strip away all the information, identificatory and ampliative alike, and designate his protagonist by a purely referential, utterly uninformative *elle*. The pronoun connotes only the sex, and scarcely that; witness *la peau, la forêt*. The French speaker certainly does separate the identificatory characterization (*ma pauvre tante*) from the ampliative characterization (*ne sort jamais*), dimly rhetorical though the distinction be; but he sees both characterizations, rightly I think, as equally peripheral to the referential function, which he reserves to *elle*. The distinction between the identificatory and the ampliative is one thing, however dim, and the distinction between reference and characterization is another. The identificatory information and the ampliative together make up the characterization, while the pronoun stands by for pure and simple reference. The pronoun is the tenable linguistic counterpart of the untenable old metaphysical notion of a bare particular.

Were it not for pronouns, or other devices to similar effect, I could make no sense of objective reference. Were it not for an indirect effect traceable to pronouns, I would see no relevant distinction between designative terms and any other meaningful constituents of sentences. I would see no ontologically relevant distinction between a so-called name and an adverb or preposition. Let me trace, then, that indirect effect of pronouns.

The use of pronouns that is basic to our present concerns is their use in abstracting relative clauses. The power and flexibility of our language is due overwhelmingly to the relative clause, taken in the restrictive sense. Thus consider any sentence, however complex, containing a name of anything. It may be built up of many clauses, some of them attaching one or another predicate to the name in question, others of them treating of quite other matters. Now this whole conglomerate sentence can be transformed into a single predication, having the name in question as its subject and a relative clause as predicate—a conglomerate relative clause, embodying the full complexity of the original sentence. The clause is formed from the original or *source* sentence by supplanting the name in question by a relative pronoun and its recurrences by an ordinary pronoun and adjusting the word order. Everything that any sentence says about something can be packaged thus in a single complex predicate; such is the relative clause.

Grammatically it may be viewed as an adjective phrase.[2] Strictly speaking it is used only attributively, rather than predicatively, and is preceded by the substantive that it governs. But we can form a substantive from it by prefixing a dummy substantive ('thing', 'person') and then we can predicate the whole with help of 'is a'. Not that we want to; the predication would simply be equivalent to a source sentence of the relative clause, thus getting us nowhere. The reason to contemplate predicating relative clauses is just in order to explain the relative clause, as I did, by saying that the predication is equivalent to the corresponding source sentence. The relative clause has its utility rather in attributive uses that do not resolve out thus through predication.

I said that the use of pronouns basic to our inquiry into reference, or ontology, is the use in relative clauses. Here the pronoun is the relative pronoun 'that' or 'which' (or 'who' or 'whom'), together with its recurrences in the guise 'it' (or 'he' or 'she' or 'him' or 'her'). A variant of the relative clause, favoured by mathematicians for the simplicity of its syntax, is the 'such that' construction; the form 'which ... it ...' gives way to 'such that ... it ... it ...'. This form spares us the contortions of word order that are called for in manœuvring the relative pronoun into an early position. Also it facilitates the introduction of variables in lieu of pronouns so as to keep cross-references

[2] In 'Quine's syntactical insights' (D. Davidson and J. Hintikka, eds., *Words and Objections*, Reidel, 1969, pp. 146–57). Peter Geach has ably argued that the relative clause in English is not adjectival, nor even a grammatically coherent whole. The anomalies he adduces may afford clues to the genesis of the construction. The utility of relative clauses is best understood, even so, by thinking of them as complex general terms, adjectival in form, derived from sentences.

under control in the complex cases so typical of mathematics. This use of variables, in lieu of the relative pronoun and its recurrences, is the basic use of bound variables.

If pronouns were used only in the fashion of what Geach distinguishes as pronouns of laziness, they would have no special bearing on questions of reference; they would stand as mere abbreviations for their grammatical antecedents, and there would be no presumption that those antecedents were designations. Bound variables, if used in lieu only of such pronouns, would be substitutional rather than referential; they would be presumed only to admit expressions as substitutes and not objects as values.

However, matters do not remain thus. The pronoun or variable soon goes unequivocally referential when the relative clause is used in uneliminable positions, positions where it cannot be resolved back into a source sentence through predication. This happens, notably, when the substantivized relative clause 'things which . . .' is used as the subject term of a categorical sentence—thus preceded by 'every' or 'some'. Here there is no predication for us to equate to a source sentence of the relative clause. Nor, usually, can we expand the whole categorical into some great conjunction or alternation of singular sentences; for usually we have no exhaustive fund of designations at our disposal for the several things fulfilling the relative clause.

The pronoun or variable admits substitutions of constant singular terms even where these do not exhaust the relevant objects of reference. Such terms, as far as they go, are then properly seen as designating objects. This is how the pronoun or variable is primary and the name parasitic. Were it not for the irreducibly referential pronoun, or some idiom to the same effect, any distinction between designative words and others would be idle and arbitrary. Words would still be learned by conditioning to stimulation, and sentences would still be true and false, but a notion of objects would have no place.

Given the irreducibly referential uses of pronouns or variables, on the other hand, we naturally bring the pronouns of laziness in tow and treat them as referential too, except in some cases where, by defining them away, we can lop off some unwelcome ontological excrescence. Thus the *elle* of the French example is seen still as referential and *ma pauvre tante* as designative despite there being no relevant objects other than the aunt for *elle* to refer to. For there are other contexts in which *elle* is irreducibly referential, and contexts also in which the poor aunt is just one of the inexhaustibly many relevant values of a bound variable.

Designation by singular terms hinges thus on the pronoun or variable, which is basic to reference. The variable continues to be conspicuously firmer than the singular term, moreover, as an instrument of reference. Whether the term designates, whether its designatum exists, is commonly a casual question of fact and often a moot one; whereas the variable proceeds serenely on its smooth course of values, taking whatever there may be. What there may happen to be is stated or conjectured by the straightforward means of predicates and quantification. Even when a term does possess a designatum, there remain crucial differences in respect of reference between one occurrence of the term and another. There are occurrences *de re*, or purely referential, where the substitution of any other designator of the same object would leave the truth value of the containing sentence undisturbed, but there are also occurrences *de dicto*, where truth value can vary with the designator independently of the designatum. On the other hand the variable pursues its referential business with a reassuring constancy, in all positions where it can coherently be used at all. For the variable is strictly for reference, unencumbered with descriptive or identificatory offices.

When I was illustrating contexts where a relative clause could not be dissolved away into one of its source sentences, I cited the use of 'thing which . . .' or 'thing x such that . . .' after 'some' or 'every'. Here we have, of course, the springs of quantification. But there are further such contexts: there is the use of 'thing which . . .' or 'thing x such that' after 'the' (singular description), and there is its use pluralized after 'the class of all' (class abstraction). The familiar bound variable of quantification, of description, and of class abstraction is best viewed thus uniformly as the relative pronoun, the bound variable of the relative or 'such that' clause. Similarly for other, less familiar uses of the bound variable.

The reason for reviewing the relative clause as the home

The Variable and Its Place in Reference 169

ground of the bound variable is not just that the other uses are reducible to it; for reduction by contextual definition is easy in other directions as well, notably to quantification. The relative clause is fundamental rather in that it is simply the embodiment of the variable's work of rearrangement: the work of singling out and assembling various places in a sentence. Quantification imports quantity, description imports uniqueness, class abstraction imports classes, and all these matters are additional to the business of the variable.

Moreover the relative clause is more central to ordinary language than those other constructions. The importance of this point is not that ordinary speakers therefore need to move less far to master the variable. It is rather that a proper appreciation of the workings of ordinary language itself consists largely in an appreciation of how the relative clause works and what it accomplishes; and these matters are helpfully schematized and clarified by the 'such that' paraphrase with its bound variable. I am surprised that Strawson's work on 'essential grammar', occupying the second half of *Subject and Predicate*, does nothing with the relative clause, which for me would have been focal. It is the general way of making a general term out of a sentence.

Among the various contexts in which the relative clause resists dissolution into one of its source sentences, the quantificational ones are most central to logic. The others, moreover, are reducible by contextual definition to these. It has therefore been convenient in logic to fuse 'every' or 'some' and 'thing x such that' into a simple variable-binding prefix, a quantifier, and so to pass over the relative clause or 'such that' as such. In general logical practice the bound variable is thus first and foremost the variable of quantification. Hence, down the years, I have identified the objects of a theory with the values of its variables of quantification. This is contingent, I have stressed, on appropriate regimentation of the language: there must be only quantifiers, variables, truth functions, and atomic predicates. The standard applies to other languages only relative to one or another manual of translation, however arbitrary, into the regimented form. It hardly needs adding—though I have added it now and then—that there is nothing sacrosanct about the quantificational form as over against other forms that are conventionally intertranslatable with it; for an ontological standard phrased for the one form of language then carries over by translation to the others. If a theory is formulated in the framework of what I have called predicate-functor logic,[3] for instance, the objects of the theory are whatever fulfil any of its one-place predicates.

In focusing now on the relative clause rather than quantification os the locus of the bound variable, therefore, I am not shifting my old position. But I welcome this opportunity to argue for the fundamental status of the relative clause. I hope one effect may be that Strawson will find my identification of ontology with values of variables less strangely arbitrary than before. There is more to it than a fancy for a nice logic calculus. It lies at the hidden heart of ordinary language.[4]

Our ordinary language is intent on reference. First and foremost its objects are sensible bodies and sensible stuff. Such is its intentness on reference, however, that ordinary language presses its referential idioms far and wide, pursuing the most tenuous analogies. Strawson (p. 36) remarks on the process. An ironical affect of this referential expansionism, on the part of our ordinary language, is that referential talk in its outer reaches ceases to be felt as seriously referential. We say 'There is something about Lucy that fascinates me'; 'Lucy and Sally have only this in common.' In so saying we have no thought of recognizing these intangibles somehow as part of the furniture of our world, nor any thought of what sort of things they might be. Or again we look upon (A) and (B) above as mere stylistic variants, however ugly, of (a) and (b). Properties or propositions get talked of with never a thought of a principle of individuation. The referential force of our referential idioms thus grades off, and there is no boundary.

My point is not that ordinary language is slipshod, slipshod though it be. We must recognize this grading off for what it is, and recognize that a fenced ontology is just not implicit in ordinary language. The idea of a boundary between being and non-being is a philosophical idea, an idea of technical science in a broad sense. Scientists and philosophers seek a comprehen-

---

[3] *The Ways of Paradox and Other Essays*, enlarged edition, Harvard, 1976, pp. 300–3.
[4] See my speculations in *The Roots of Reference* (Open Court, 1974) on the ontogenesis of all this in ordinary language.

The Variable and Its Place in Reference 171

sive system of the world, and one that is oriented to reference even more squarely and utterly than ordinary language. Ontological concern is not a correction of lay thought and practice; it is foreign to the lay culture, though an outgrowth of it.

But continuities remain. The philosopher's concern with ontology penetrates ordinary discourse in varying degrees. To the extent that it does, the philosopher may try to fix the ontological assumptions underlying some piece of discourse and perhaps to contest them. This is where regimentation comes in: the imputation of ontological assumptions makes no sense except relative to an agreed translation into a notation that is explicit in the matter of reference. This operation of translation has two components. We paraphrase the discourse into the most explicitly referential of locutions; this is where the relative pronoun comes into focus, or, ultimately, the variable. And, second, we may charitably paraphrase some already rather explicitly referential constructions in such a way as to obviate the imputation; thus we might change (A) and (B) to (a) and (b). Freedom prevails; polemical force is nil, as I have long stressed, except as you call upon the author to do it himself. In the case of an isolated sentence this freedom is such that the ontological question tends to be uninteresting.

Even in the case of a large block of discourse the freedom can be great. As an example consider Strawson's suggestion (pp. 32 ff.) that predicates be viewed as designative, hence in effect as abstract singular terms naming properties. Only the copula then retains the office of what I would call a predicate. Contrary to what he supposed (p. 34), I recognize this as a legitimate alternative, quite compatible still with ordinary language (given a few precautions relating to Russell's paradox). Formally, as he sees, it would consist in admitting bound variables in so-called predicate positions. The line is not unfamiliar. My reason for not preferring it is one simply of ontological economy. Even if one foresees having for some purposes to quantify eventually over properties after all, or over classes anyway, I favour the strategy of holding to the economical line where we can. I distinguish predicates from abstract singular terms for no other reason.

But then I proceed to eliminate the singular terms themselves, by reparsing? This is quite another matter, having no effect on the ontology. An abstract singular term, naming say a class or property, gives way to a predicate of higher order that is satisfied uniquely by that class or property; the class or property is still in our universe of values of variables.

I must not close without some clarificatory remarks regarding this elimination of singular terms other than variables, for Strawson views it more dimly than it deserves. It is motivated by the reflection that the pronoun or variable is the vehicle of pure reference, while names, like predicates, serve to characterize the thing referred to. The elimination is wholly theoretical in intent: it exposes the basic apparatus of reference. Incidentally it simplifies the rules of the logic of quantification. It would be disastrous in practice, unless the terms were restored by contextual definition. Mathematics would be paralysed if we could not freely substitute complex terms for variables and equals for equals. The circuitous alternatives that are adequate in principle would be prohibitive in practice. If our actual language had had no singular terms but pronouns or variables, the invention of names and term-building functors would have been the first great mathematical breakthrough.

Strawson finds the elimination problematic even in theory, because he finds the recurrent use of a name indispensable in indicating that several references are to the same object (pp. 48, 51 f.). Answer: that purpose is served by recurrences of a variable, all bound by the same operator, or by use of an identity sign between variables.

Other misgivings over the dispensability of names are familiar from the literature. It has been felt that names ostensibly learned are needed to begin with. This is wrong; by ostension we learn far more predicates than names. The token-reflexive predicate 'here' is no less fundamental than 'this'. The distinction between token reflexives or indicator words and other expressions is independent of the distinction between names and predicates, and the corresponding enterprises of elimination are independent as well.

It is felt also that the names differ from predicates in their connotation of uniqueness, though predicates may just happen to apply uniquely. It is felt also that proper names lack connotation while predicates connote. Now these are traits of names that I simply transfer to the predicates, however unaccustomed the new setting. This is why I spoke of *reparsing*: the names can keep all their old traits except grammatical position.

Strawson's phrasing of my position may be helpful here: the view that

each name could be 'parsed as', or replaced by, a corresponding unitary predicate which did *not* covertly contain the name on one side of an identity sign (p. 48).

Perhaps I can make my position clearer by dropping his *'not'* and underlining his 'covertly'. The result is a fair description, seen from the point of view of the language to be revised. The occurrence of the name and identity sign become covert in that they disappear into a notationally atomic predicate. Shifting our viewpoint then to the language as thus revised, we view that predicate as irreducibly atomic but as inheriting various traits that had been traits of names. My verb 'reparse' was meant to encourage an appreciation of how superficially grammatical this move really is, despite being, as I think, philosophically and logically illuminating.

Strawson on Subject and Predicate

P. T. Geach

This essay is not meant as a scholarly résumé of all the various expressions of view Strawson has given us on this topic, but as what Frege called a critical elucidation; I shall use Strawson's work as the basis for discussion, but my main end is to throw fresh light on the substantive questions. I shall here concentrate on Strawson's recent monograph *Subject and Predicate in Logic and Grammar*.

Our first question must be what sort of distinction is marked by the terms 'subject' and 'predicate'. Is this a distinction of role, or one of category? In school grammar, some terms, e.g. 'noun' and 'verb', serve to assign words to grammatical categories, while others, e.g. 'subject' and 'object' and 'antecedent', describe the role a word is playing in a given sentence. This difference between two kinds of description applies to logical terms too; but unfortunately in logical terminology it is not so sharply and consistently drawn.

When we analyse a proposition (here as in other work I use this word to mean a linguistic item) into logical subject and logical predicate, we are distinguishing two roles played by expressions; but if we recognize an expression as a name, we are assigning it to a logical category, not describing its logical role in a proposition. A name can indeed be a logical subject in a sentence; but in recognizing a name as a name we are not thus far asserting that any and every sentence in which we can recognize the occurrence of this name admits of a subject-predicate analysis with the name as subject. The proposition:

(A) The first man who landed on the Moon was a Russian

may or may not be analysable as a predication with 'the Moon' as subject; I myself think it is so analysable, but a colleague at the University of Edinburgh said he was quite unable to see that (A) makes any predication whatsoever about the Moon. But however that may be, we can all agree that the name 'the

Moon' occurs here, and has its ordinary role of designating a certain heavenly body. So we ought not to use the terms 'name' and 'logical subject' indiscriminately: 'name' ought to mean a logical category, 'logical subject' ought to mean a term's role in a given proposition. It may be that names and names alone have the role of logical subjects in any proposition; again, it may be that for any term in a proposition that can be recognized as a name, there is *an* analysis of the proposition (of course not necessarily the only legitimate analysis) by which that name comes out as logical subject; I should myself defend both theses. But they are theses that need to be argued, and their truth should not even seem to be prejudged by a mere choice of terminology.

From this point of view, Strawson's terminology is not well chosen. For example, he writes as if 'designators', 'names', 'logical-subject-expressions', and 'subject-terms' were all different ways of describing the same bits of language (p. 4). He poses himself the question how the subject-terms are related to predicate-terms; but he does not clearly distinguish between our having to explicate a certain relation, for which 'subject *of*' and 'predicate *of*' would be the two correlative expressions, and our having to provide distinguishing notes to demarcate two mutually exclusive classes. We find Strawson both the question 'What distinguishes predicate-terms from subject-terms?' (p. 4), and also, as one answer to be considered for the question what this distinction amounts to, the thesis 'The predicate is true of (or false of) what the subject stands for.' But the question and answer are ill-matched. It is as though the question 'What is the relation of mother to son?' were confounded with the question 'What characteristic distinguishes mothers as a class from sons as a class?' Even though no mother is also a son, the two questions are entirely different. Strawson's use of the hyphenated phrase 'expression-in-a-role' appears to betray an uneasy teetering between category-distinctions and role-distinctions as the object of his inquiry.

To clear things up, let us agree henceforth to use 'logical subject' for marking out a term's role in a sentence, and 'name' for assigning a term to a logical category. We shall still be left with trouble over the term 'predicate'. We shall certainly need 'predicate' to mark out a logical role: the role of the term that a logical subject is subject *of*. But then we need some term for the logical category to which a term belongs if it *can* be a logical predicate. I have proposed, and used in some of my works, the term 'predicable' (though for mixed reasons, of tradition and euphony, I keep 'predicate' in 'predicate calculus', 'predicate variable', 'predicate letter', etc.). An expression may be recognizably one and the same predicable in two propositions even though in only one of them is it attached to a logical subject. In my example (A) there is no logical subject for 'landed on the Moon'; the pronoun 'who', grammatical subject of this grammatical predicate, is plainly no logical subject; nor is there *any* way of analysing (A) as 'F(*a*)', '*a*' being a logical subject, if 'F( )' is read as '( ) landed on the Moon'. But we have here the same unequivocal predicable as in 'Pushkin landed on the Moon'; in (A), however, this predicable is not actually a predicate, it has no logical subject and is not being predicated of anything.

Having got our feet out of the net, we may turn to the question whether it is correct to say 'There are compound and negative predicables, but not compound and negative names'; for this is how we shall have to reformulate the question Strawson discusses on pp. 6–9. On pp. 6–7 Strawson gives a formal argument to show that we ought to accept the quoted thesis, but he regards this as not really conclusive. All that can really be established this way, he thinks, is that we cannot have the logical procedures of negation, disjunction, and conjunction applying *both* to predicables *and* to names; that would indeed land us in contradictions; but we cannot tell from this whether it is on predicables or on names that these operations are legitimately performable.

In fact, however, our choice here is Hobson's choice. Negation, conjunction, and disjunction cannot be dispensed with as means of building up predicables out of predicables. The idea that we might analyse away this use of the operators by regarding them as attaching to entire propositions can be quickly refuted; we need only consider how complex predicables are combined with quantified phrases formed with 'all', 'some', or 'most'. 'Some (Most) men are both Q and R', and again 'All (Most) men are either Q or R', contain an irreducible conjunction or disjunction of predicables, not to be eliminated by any expansion that gives a conjunctive or disjunctive proposition. Given such complex predicables, Strawson's arguments show that we cannot *also* admit negative, conjunctive, and disjunctive names. Ordinary grammar might suggest that '*a* and *b*' and '*a* or *b*' may take the place of a simple name in a proposition, *salva congruitate* as medieval logicians say (that is, without destroying syntactical coherence); but the idea of using a hypothetical name-complex like 'if Smith then Jones' as a subject instead of a simple name is manifestly nonsensical, and the idea of so using a negated name like 'not Smith' is scarcely less manifestly so.

It is however very strange that any problem should be supposed to arise over the negation and conjunction of predicables (and with these once secured, disjunction is clearly admissible as well). Conjunction of predicables is used repeatedly in our thinking to build up complicated descriptions of things; I do not know how I'd begin to satisfy somebody who should helplessly say he does not see how all these details *fit together* into one description. It is equally obscure how anyone could feel negated predicables call for a 'justifying explanation', or what this could be like. Strawson tries to provide such a 'justifying explanation' of negated predicables, but apparently forgets the equally imaginary intellectual debt he has contracted about conjoined predicables. So from now on I concentrate on negation of predicables.

Whenever a predicable actually functions as a predicate, we can frame a yes-no question in which this predicable is attached to a subject; and the negative answer to this question may be regarded with equal logical right under either of two aspects: as predicating the negation of the predicable used in the affirmative answer, or as got by negating this answer taken as an entire proposition. So in the symbolism of predicate logic there is no need to distinguish two readings of '$\neg F(a)$'—as attaching the negative predicable '$\neg F(\ )$' to the subject 'a', and as negating the proposition '$F(a)$'.

' In the vernacular, sentence negation by a prenex operator like 'It is not the case that' or 'It is not so that' is rare and stylistically awkward; it is common only in the prose of logicians and philosophers. The natural negation e.g. of 'Socrates drank hemlock' is 'Socrates did not drink hemlock', and here we have visibly a negated predicable. To be sure, the complex syntax of vernaculars means that by blindly applying some simple mechanical rule we cannot write down the negation of any arbitrary predicable; we cannot for example say that if the predicable begins with the grammatical copula 'is', it can be negated by simply attaching 'not' to the copula, even though this procedure would often yield correct results. The negation of the predicable

—either is cynical or deceives himself

is of course not one of the following two:

—either is not cynical or deceives himself
—is not either cynical or deceives himself

but is to be got by negating the main operator within the predicable, 'either ... or ...':

—neither is cynical nor deceives himself.[1]

Again, the two sentences:

The Museum is open till October
The Museum is not open till October

are not contradictories, or at least there is a very natural reading of the second by which they are not: if we rephrase the first as:

All the time until October, the Museum is open

the second might correspondingly come out as

All the time until October, the Museum is *not* open

(whether because it is then shut, or because it has never yet been open). The contradictory is:

Not all the time until October is the Museum open.

As Frege remarked, we often negate a whole proposition by negating some part; but if we negate some part, it often needs

---

[1] My spelling this out may seem strange; but the possibility of error on this matter is not just notional. See V. F. van Neste, 'On Detecting Logical Predicates', *Philosophical Studies*, June 1975.

care and attention to tell whether we are thereby negating the whole. However, this gives no reason to doubt that a proposition allowing of subject-predicate analysis *is* negated by negating the predicate, if only we perform that operation correctly.

Not only do we in natural language most often negate a whole proposition by negating some part of it: we cannot even coherently describe some stage of understanding at which propositional negation is understood but predicate-negation is not. I here of course have in mind not an understanding of the logical terms of art 'propositional negation' and 'predicate-negation', but practical understanding of how to perform the operations so called. Frege compared a concept to a closed boundary-line on a surface; such a line determines an inside and an outside region of the surface, and neither is in any way *prior* to the other. Or again, sorting out the As that are F from those that are not F is indistinguishable from sorting out the As that are not F from those that are. We simply cannot grasp a concept without *ipso facto* grasping the contradictory concept; there is no question of later 'introducing' the contradictory, let alone 'justifying' its introduction.

How is it that Strawson fails to see all this? For one thing, I think he does not realize how tricky it may be to recognize contradictories in the vernacular. Perhaps Strawson most often straightway sees the 'not' in a sentence as negating the whole proposition; he may thus fail to realize Frege's point that 'not' has this effect by negating some part of the whole, and consequently also fails to see that he must take account, right at the outset, of negation as applied to predicables and other fragments of propositions. But I think this is only part of the story. We may discern in Strawson two bits of old logical lore: he inherits a view that contrariety, incompatibility, is more fundamental than plain negation and must be used to explain it; and he presents, in a much altered but still recognizable form, the tripartite analysis of predications, subject-copula-predicate, as opposed to the bipartite analysis into subject and predicate.

The first view has long tradition behind it in Oxford: we recall the disputes between Bosanquet and Neville Keynes (see Bosanquet's *Logic*, 2nd edition, vol. i, pp. 277–93). Strawson states the view by speaking of 'ranges': a concept will belong to a range of concepts such that if 'any particular (fairly and squarely) exemplifies one member of the concept-range, then there are other members (or at least one member) which that particular is thereby logically excluded from exemplifying' (p. 18): 'for any concept of the range, we know there are other concepts which are in logical competition with it throughout the field, i.e. no particular which exemplifies it can at the same time exemplify its competitors' (ibid.). In terms of this apparatus, Strawson thinks, we *could* 'define, for any concept, its complementary concept ... the concept which is not only incompatible with the original concept, but is also such that there is no logical room for a third concept incompatible with both' (p. 24). And this explanation would allow us to introduce negative predicables. A similar attempt to introduce negative names, capable of being logical subjects, would fail at the very first move; for names stand for particulars, and we cannot coherently assign particulars to ranges whose members are in logical competition for concepts. 'Indeed, we cannot find a single particular such that there is any other single particular which competes with it for concepts throughout the concept-ranges they both come within' (p. 18). 'The complementary particular of any given particular ... will have to exemplify all the concepts which the given particular does not exemplify. But since some of these are mutually incompatible, this is impossible. So no particular has a complementary' (p. 28).

To me it appears that this 'explanation' of contradictory opposition between predicables in terms of incompatibility or contrariety is radically misconceived. It is an attempt to explain what must already be understood before the explanation is given. That an object does not fall under a concept is already understandable from our grasping that very concept, and *therewith* the complementary concept; no thought of *other* concepts that are in 'logical competition' for the object need be brought in. If I say desperately 'My pen is *not* on my desk', or a detective says 'Mulally is *not* on the 5.30 from London', we do not do this because of bringing the pen, or Mulally, under some concept that is in 'logical competition' with these ascriptions of place that we reject; we just do not know where the devil the pen, or Mulally, may be—that is exactly the trouble. When my ancestors saw that a vessel was empty of beer or mead, they certainly did not do so by bringing the vessel under the recondite scientific concept *full of air*, which would exclude its containing any beer or mead. Strawson's view recalls the White Knight's question about the empty mousetrap and the empty beehive that he carried on the back of his horse: he could not accept this bare negation or emptiness without more ado, and wondered whether the bees kept the mice away, or the mice kept the bees away, from the homes for which, as you might say, they 'logically competed'.

I turn to Strawson's commitment to the logical copula. It is clear that he has such a commitment: he regards it as essential to a simple predicative sentence that it should contain, besides expressions for a concept and an object, something fulfilling the function of 'presenting particular and general concept as assigned to each other' (p. 22). In an *ad hoc* logical notation employed on pp. 25–8, Strawson uses the symbol 'ass' (sometimes negated by a line drawn over it) to play this role. (Strawson holds that relational concepts of any polyadicity require such a binding element too—p. 21 n.; cf. also his references to pairs, trios, etc. of particulars on p. 22. But he devises no notation for such cases; and I think I too may leave them aside.) It must surely be because Strawson thinks in terms of such a tripartite analysis, by which an expression for a concept needs a copula to join it to a subject and negation naturally attaches to this copula, that he says the odd things he does on p. 24 about negating a predicable; on the one hand, when we introduce the complement of a concept 'there is every practical reason why ... we should represent it linguistically in a way which displays its logical character, i.e. by affixing a negation sign to the expression specifying the original concept'; on the other hand, 'as a picture of any procedure we actually follow' he finds this 'not very realistic'; 'though with the help of the prefix "non-" we do form some negative terms which may figure in predicate-place, we do not form many such terms this way'. Here he must have in mind such a predicable as 'non-smoker' or 'non-conductive', with its grammatical need for a copula 'is' or 'is a' to join it to a subject; he is passing over such predicables as 'does not smoke' or 'does not conduct (electricity)', which have no such requirement. Negative predicables of this latter sort are of course abundant; Strawson's neglect of them is no doubt partly due to his reading the 'not' in them as negating *only* the whole proposition (I have already discussed this), but is also partly due to their not coming with a copula.

In opposition to this tripartite analysis, Frege stated, and I have defended, a bipartite analysis. On the Fregean view, a predicative expression needs no glue or bond to make it adhere to a subject. At some point we must have an expression that simply adheres to others without needing some further linguistic device to make it adhere; why not ascribe this character to predicables themselves, rather than postulate a copula? *Standum est in primo*! If there were a genuine problem how subject and predicate *can* adhere together, then only by mere fiat could we avoid raising the problem how the copula *can* adhere to both. And indeed it is only by fiat that Strawson does stop such a regress; he admits that on his analysis any sentence in which subject and predicate are joined by his copula 'ass' could be *replaced by* one in which the particular and concept here introduced are *explicitly* said to be related by the concept of *exemplification*, but he insists that we are not to *read* 'ass' as introducing this higher-level concept.

We need not indeed say anything so brutal about the poor copula as Frege did: that it means nothing at all. In many Greek sentences the copulative verb may be indifferently inserted or omitted: this I think suggests that we should regard it not as meaningless but as a trivial predicable-forming operator on predicables. There are other operators of the same category that are not trivial: '—*is* green' contrasts with '—*was* green', '—*looks* green', '—*became* green', etc. The 'is' operator is like adding zero or multiplying by one.

Strawson tells us that his understanding of the term 'concept' differs from Frege's, but I fear he fails to convey how he does understand the term. We are told (p. 21) that the word 'green' serves to specify the same concept in 'The door is green' and 'Green is a soothing colour'. (I need not discuss the third example 'The green door is locked'; for of course there is the paraphrase 'The door that is green is locked', so that visibly this occurrence is essentially the same as in 'The door is green'.) Now indeed 'Green is a colour' (let us forget about 'soothing'!) creates difficulty for any account Fregean in spirit. In that spirit, one would look for a paraphrase in which 'green' and 'colour' would occur only as fragments of the predicables '—is green' and '—is colour*ed*'; and I know of no really satisfactory answer to the problem. A moment's thought shows that 'Whatever is green is coloured' will not work, nor yet 'Necessarily, whatever is green is coloured'; try replacing 'coloured' by 'extended'. (I have elsewhere discussed the Thomistic style of analysis, which would run somewhat as follows:

> Any individual accident whereby a thing is green is also an individual accident whereby the thing is coloured.

This meets the formal requirement; but the notions expressed by 'individual accident' and by 'whereby', Aquinas's 'quo', are of course extremely problematic at best, and many would reject them as bogus.) But though there are difficulties for a Fregean, that does not entail success for Strawson in setting up his rival conception. Strawson indeed is not obliged to paraphrase away the nounlike occurrences of 'green' and 'colour', as a Fregean must; but he is still under obligation to tell us how these relate to the predicables '—is green' and '—is coloured'; for otherwise we don't know what he *means* by 'introducing a concept' or 'specifying a concept', which is supposedly done both by the predicable and by the corresponding namelike word. This obligation he has not discharged.

I remarked earlier that Strawson's use of the copula 'ass' is only *ad hoc*, provisional; and he appears in the end to wish to dispense with the copula. To use his own language: he thinks there is 'no doubt' that the 'grappling machinery' which binds subject and predicate together is located at the predicate end. 'The task is that of explaining why, when particular-specifying expression and concept-specifying expression are propositionally combined, the function of indicating propositional combination should be combined with that of concept-specifying rather than with that of particular-specifying' (p. 30). I shall give an extended quotation to show how Strawson copes with this task (p. 31):

The symbolism of propositional combination serves to show that we have a certain sort of combination of the particular-specifying expression and the concept-specifying expression, viz., a combination which yields truth under one set of conditions and falsity under another. The effect of negating the proposition is simply to reverse (or exchange) the connections between these truth-values and these conditions. Nothing is more natural than to indicate this effect by, as it were changing the sign of the propositional indicator, of whatever indicates that we have a truth-or-falsity-yielding combination. . . . So negation and the symbolism of propositional combination have a natural affinity for each other. But we have lately been engaged in demonstrating, among other things, the affinity of concept-specification and negation for each other. So here we have, as regards our basic class of subject-predicate sentences, a mediated or resultant affinity between the function of indicating propositional combination and the concept-specifying function; hence an explanation, or partial explanation of why predicates have the form of the verb. We might put it like this: the 'ass' function and negation are at home together; if negation can be absorbed into the predicate, conceived as that part of the combination which has the concept-specifying role, then the 'ass' function can be absorbed into it too.

I do not find here a clear distinction between groupings that are psychologically natural and easy, and groupings that are logically required and justified. Of course the distinction has to be drawn, and is not merely notional. Grammatically, in the phrases 'all men', 'some men', 'no men', the words 'all', 'some', 'no' are words by which the term 'men' seems to be qualified, so as to show which part of the class of men we are talking about: in Latin we have inflected adjectives agreeing with a noun—'omnes', 'aliqui', 'nulli'. Boole, notoriously, was deceived by this; he regarded even 'some' as an 'elective symbol', that is, one showing how to cull a class out of a class. 'No' on this view culls out the empty class of men. For logic such an association is useless; as Aquinas pointed out, and Frege too, the actual role of these signs is to show how a predicable in grammatical predicate position latches on to 'men' when we say men are all of them, some of them, none of them, F. So here it could be that the licence to shift negation from the copula to the concept-expression does not in the least *justify* the copula's being taken to go more closely with the concept-expression than with the subject, even though it may psychologically explain why we find such a fusion of roles natural.

Can we find a more satisfactory account of how negation goes with predicables as well as with propositions? We need one that will show us also how 'and' and 'or' can form conjunction or disjunction of predicables but never of names. In propositional calculus negation, 'and', and 'or' are all signs of truth-functions. Can we find something analogous to truth-functions in the domain of predicables? We can indeed. A predicable is not true or false *simpliciter*; but it is true or false *of* a given object, whether anybody actually makes a predication concerning that object or not. Taking some arbitrary object o as a parameter, we can construct truth-tables for predicables exactly like those for propositions; '⌐F( )' will be true *of* o just in case 'F( )' is false of o, and will be false of o just in case 'F( )' is true of o; 'F( ) G( )' will be true of o just in case each of the predicables 'F( )'. 'G( )', is true of o, and will otherwise be false of o; and so for other truth-functions. The predication of a truth-functionally complex predicable concerning a given thing is always equivalent to the corresponding truth-function of the simpler predications in which the constituent predicables are predicated of that thing. For example:

> John is (able to follow this argument only if (exceptionally talented in logic and not spoiled by bad early training))

is exactly equivalent to:

> (John is able to follow this argument) only if ((John is exceptionally talented in logic) and (John was not spoiled by a bad early training))

Strawson loses this clue of analogy between predicable and proposition early in the book (pp. 9–11). He first stumbles over an alleged linguistic impropriety: 'No one at all fastidious would allow "'swims' is true of Socrates" as tolerable English.' I do not wish to argue about that: at any rate, Strawson shows he quite understands the offensive expression, since he proceeds to give the *oratio obliqua* paraphrase:

> It is true of Socrates that he swims.

The relation between this and the *oratio recta* form that Strawson dislikes is of course exactly the same as the relation between 'It is true that Socrates swims' and '"Socrates swims" is true'. Tricky logical and semantical problems *can* arise about the relation between *oratio recta* and *oratio obliqua*, as Casimir Lewy has shown in his recent book *Meaning and Modality*; but these do not concern Strawson and need not concern us. And feelings about what is quite natural English are of very little importance in the philosophy of logic. There are, e.g. puzzles about the relation of quantification theory to sentences in the vernacular, e.g. about the relation between 'Some idiot is smoking' and:

For some x, x is an idiot and x is smoking;

but it is not germane to the philosophy of logic to observe that the 'x' here occurring thrice over cannot be consistently parsed in conventional grammatical categories, either as a count noun or as a proper noun or as a pronoun.

Strawson appears to suppose that 'It is true of Socrates that he swims' is obtained from 'It is true of Socrates that Socrates swims' via 'the permitted replacement, in the embedded that-clause, of noun or noun-phrase by pronoun'. This amounts to parsing the pronoun 'he' as what I call a pronoun of laziness, standing in for repetition of 'Socrates'. It is not *quite* clear that Strawson holds this; but anyhow it is worth while to show what would be wrong about holding it. If we consider the sentence

Something is true of Socrates and of Alcibiades likewise, namely that he swims

we see at once that 'he' is not standing in either for 'Socrates' or for 'Alcibiades': either attempt to replace 'he' by a proper name would be clearly wrong. The corresponding *oratio recta* is of course:

(The predicable) '—swims' is true of Socrates and of Alcibiades likewise.

When we go over to the *oratio obliqua* construction we have to supply a *dummy* subject 'he', to make the that-clause grammatical; but this does not then stand in for any one possible *logical* subject of the predicable rather than any other. We must give quite a different account of the sentence:

It is true of Socrates that Socrates swims

Here we are not really saying that the proposition in question stands in the relation *true of* to anything; rather, we are saying that it is true *simpliciter*, and moreover (an independent point) that it is about Socrates. As Nelson Goodman has shown, the notion of a proposition's being *about* something is exceedingly entangled and problematic; and we certainly need not possess even a rough criterion of which propositions are *about* Socrates and which are not, in order to know that'—swims' is *true of* Socrates if and only if Socrates swims.

Strawson goes on to remark that from 'Socrates swims' we may get:

It is true of *swimming* that Socrates does it.

(We may forget about the supposedly equivalent paraphrase:

It is true of *swimming* that Socrates swims.

It is simply a mistake to read 'does it' in this context as standing in for the verb 'swims': the same mistake as taking 'he' in:

It is true of Socrates that he swims

to be going proxy for the name 'Socrates'.) Strawson is clearly right in allowing such a paraphrase; and we may regard as quite unimportant the inflectional change from 'swims' to 'swimming'; that makes no more odds logically than the fact that in Latin or Polish 'Socrates' would need a case-modification in 'It is true of Socrates'.

This further paraphrase does indeed show that there is more than one logical analysis even of the simple 'Socrates swims'; but we need not be worried by that. If we consider such an example as:

It is true of *swimming* that Socrates does it and so does Alcibiades but Plato does not

we see that here we are bringing the concept of swimming under what Frege would call higher-level concepts. The concept *what Socrates does and Alcibiades does but Plato does not do* has its constituent notes (*Merkmalen*) *what Socrates does, what Alcibiades does, what Plato does not do*; the concepts of this level do not latch on to individuals directly, but only to concepts (expressed by such verbs of action as 'swims') under which individuals in turn fall. Confusion between concepts of different level is indeed, as Frege said, about the grossest that a thinker can commit; but the necessary distinction can be managed only if we have already mastered the distinction between individuals and the concepts they fall under. The analysis of 'Socrates swims' as equivalent to 'Swim—that's what Socrates does' cannot supersede the simpler analysis into subject and predicate, indeed depends upon it. And we must not confuse the logical role of 'what Socrates does', an expression for a second-level concept, with the logical role of the name 'Socrates'. We may negate 'what Socrates does' to 'what Socrates does not do', and we may form, as I said just now, such conjunctive higher-level predicables as 'what Socrates does and so does Alcibiades but Plato does not do'; it remains true that negation and conjunction are nonsensical as applied to names.

Sometimes these two analyses of 'Socrates swims' have been mixed up together. Frank Ramsey oddly thought that one and the same proposition could not admit of more than one logical analysis; he even said that if one proposition had as many as three distinct analyses, that would make it into an 'incomprehensible trinity'. Consequently, he supposed that the two constituents of 'Swim—that's what Socrates does' (or the like) must be the same (only in reverse order) as those of 'Socrates swims', and that it is arbitrary which of the pair we call subject, which predicate. But Frege said rightly that logic is crippled if we allow only one analysis of a given proposition. In his time Strawson has given a valuable expression of this Fregean point: he remarks that there is no such thing as *the* logical form of a bit of discourse: various logical forms can be recognized in the same argument or proposition, and these are not mutually exclusive like the Petrarchan and Shakespearean forms of sonnet (*Introduction to Logical Theory*, pp. 53 f.). More than one modern logician has followed Ramsey, and assimilates proper names to higher-level predicables, attached to predicables; the ingenuity shown in developing theories on this basis can only be called perverse. Strawson is right in not treating names as having a predicative role, but to my mind misguided in his attempted explanation. The matter cannot, I think, be explained in the sense of being given a *foundation*; it comes out in *all* our discourse, and a good understanding of it can be conveyed only dialectically, by removing errors and confusions, and for the rest talking around the matter in the hope that people will catch on.

What Would be a Substantial Theory of Truth?
David Wiggins

I

Any reasonably well-informed student of analytical philosophy, when asked what view of the problem of truth is to be associated with the name of P. F. Strawson, is likely to reply (correctly enough) that the philosopher who bears this name has done almost everything that can be done to demonstrate almost as thoroughly as it can be demonstrated just how difficult it is (how even more difficult it is than philosophers have been apt to suppose it is) to squeeze anything both *true* and *interestingly truistic* out of the supposed truisms of correspondence; and that the trouble with traditional correspondence theories was 'not primarily the tendency to substitute nonconventional relations for what [J. L. Austin supposed] was really a conventional relation': it was 'the misrepresentation of "correspondence between statement and fact" *as a relation of any kind between events or things or groups of things*'.[1] We can say if we like that a statement is true if there obtains or exists the particular situation, which, in the making of the statement, is stated to obtain; but this formulation abandons altogether the notion of an identified existing situation which it is a matter of a statement's identity that it refers to and with respect to which the question arises whether it is or isn't of a certain general type... [and] it drops all explicit allusion to conventional (semantical) relations between words and things... The semantical conventions help to determine what the statement is a statement to the effect that; whereas the statement's being true, if it is, is another matter altogether, viz. a matter of that situation's obtaining'.[2]

The student of the philosophy of the last thirty years will connect this relatively recent verdict with the claim that Strawson made in 1950 that 'if our task were to elucidate the

[1] 'Truth', *Proceedings of the Aristotelian Society*, suppl. volume xxiv, 1950.
[2] 'Truth: A Reconsideration of Austin's Views', *Philosophical Quarterly*, vol. 15, 1965.

nature of the [fact-stating, as opposed to command-giving] type of discourse, it would be futile to attempt to do it in terms of the word "fact", "statement", ["situation"], "true"; for these words contain the problem not its solution'.

Finally, one who was interested in the post-war development of formal as well as informal semantics might well be reminded here of the nearly parallel discovery that equal difficulty and/or bareness seem to afflict all attempts to make a philosophical doctrine of truth (even the doctrine that no revealing doctrine is needed) by generalization from the archetype ' "Snow is white" is true if and only if snow is white'.[3]

So much is very familiar, and almost as uncontroversial as anything can be in philosophy (which is not very close to uncontroversial). What it is rarer to encounter is an appreciation that there was another interest that Strawson identified in his 1950 article as of proper concern to the theory of truth—'the task of elucidating the nature of a certain type of communication (the empirically informative)', and elucidating it in such a way that a distinction will naturally result or supervene

---

[3] Cf. A. Tarski, 'The Concept of Truth in Formalized Languages' in *Logic, Semantics and Metamathematics* (Oxford, 1956), §§ 1–3. In more recent writings Strawson has treated such formulae as the 'situation' formula, or the formula 'a belief is true if and only if things are as one who holds that belief thereby holds them to be', as equivalent to what he rightly calls *schemata*, e.g. 'The statement or belief that p is true if and only if p'. (Cf. p. 276, 'Knowledge and Truth', *Indian Philosophical Quarterly*, vol. iii, no. 3, 1976.) Once we reflect that we understand the assertion of such a schema only by reference to the possiblity of speaking explicitly of supplanting its sentence letters by particular sentential values and of always obtaining thereby, in exchange for the schema, something *true* (or an axiom—but what is that except a sentence put forward as true?), we shall be tempted to deliberate a new version of the declaration I quoted from the 1950 article, now levelling against such formulations as the 'situation' formula the charge of *unmitigated circularity*. One cannot give a theory of truth simply in terms of truth. But that is all that a schematic account of truth can do, and all that is achieved by formulations (however *covertly* schematic) in terms of 'things being as one who holds the belief holds them to be' or 'situations obtaining'. (Indeed, so far as the use of schemata is concerned, theories of truth are surely in a singular or special difficulty.)

Admittedly, considered simply as an elucidation of truth (in the sense in which Frege and Wittgenstein used 'elucidation'), the 'situation' formula, as schematically construed, would not necessarily be useless *just* because it made covert use of the very concept that it sought to elucidate. (Only analyses in the strict sense are debarred from making all use of their analysandum. '($(x=y)$ & $(y=z)$) $\supset (x=z)$' is not an analysis of identity; but it can help to elucidate the notion.) What is objectionable is rather that the situation formula is shown up in the schematic interpretation, not only as using the concept of truth to elucidate truth, but also as using truth without involving truth with any concepts that are *established, genuinely collateral*, and *genuinely distinct from truth*. This is the real constraint on elucidation.

between this and, e.g. 'another kind of conventional communication (the imperative)', a mode of communication Strawson held to be just as badly served by the 'Correspondence Theory of Obedience' as the fact-stating was by the Correspondence Theory of Truth. The question was barely noticed, but it did not disappear. For, later in that decade, Michael Dummett appears to have been exercised by the same question (no matter how changed by translation to the new setting of a constructive theory of meaning) when he declared that what mattered most was to find some way to articulate the *point* of the concept of truth, and say what purpose was served by the distinction between truth and falsity. 'Classifications do not exist in the void, but are connected always with some interest which we have, so that to assign something to one class or another will have consequences connected with this interest ... At one time it was usual to say that we do not call ethical statements "true" or "false", and from this many consequences for ethics were held to flow. But the question is not whether these words are in practice applied to ethical statements, but whether, if they were so applied, the point of doing so would be the same as the point of applying them to statements of other kinds, and, if not, in what ways it would be different.'[4]

In spite of Dummett, those moral philosophers who occupied a non-communicating compartment continued to treat the question of the truth status of evaluative or deliberative statements as a matter to be decided by a stipulation (or by a ruling that the logic of evaluative sentences could be brought into the deductive fold by treating such sentences as as-if-capable-of-being-true). But Bernard Williams was led to treat the question of truth status as one of the central questions of the subject, and all of a piece with

[4] 'Truth', *Proceedings of the Aristotelian Society*, vol. lix, 1958–9. Cf. P. F. Strawson, *Indian Philosophical Quarterly*: 'The unassailable formula "It is true that p if and only if p" ... is no less hospitable to moral judgements and mathematical propositions than it is to records of common observation or history of propositions of natural science. At the very least this fact calls for explanation ... We should ... take [records of common observation or history or natural science] as a starting point, as the primary or basic cases of truth; and then seek to explain how we properly and intelligibly extend the notion of truth ...'. If Strawson had written, instead of the words 'Then seek to explain ...', the words 'and then seek to inquire *if* we can properly and intelligibly extend the notion of truth. ...', that would have been equally true to his intention (I surmise) and it would have greatly reduced the difference of emphasis between his view and Dummett's. (Strawson's actual emphasis is somewhat closer however to the view of the problem that I shall myself take.)

such issues as relativism *versus* absolutism, subjectivism *versus* objectivism, etc. When Williams noted that what he required in order to advance these matters was 'a substantial notion of truth',[5] I do not doubt that what he felt was needed was the very same thing that Strawson had envisaged in 1950.

Williams's principal purpose in 'Consistency and Realism' concerned the application to ethics of the question of realism and anti-realism, and it was more important for him to be able to allude to the need for a substantial theory of truth and the possibility that such a thing might be constructed than it was to embark upon this work. He did not lack suggestions about how a substantial theory of truth might be arrived at. But the beginnings that he actually essayed depended heavily on a contrast that he made by reference to the question whether or not sentences of a given category could or could not be said to purport to *match the world*;[6] and the trouble that one has with this is that, for purposes of determining the proper scope of 'true', there *is* perhaps no neutral or uncontroversial account of what the world is (no more than there is a neutral account of what a fact is). The difficulty is only a reflection of a much more general difficulty for which Strawson has prepared us: that any direct attempt on a 'substantial' theory of truth would appear to involve us in finding new or special ways of characterizing what it is ('in the world') for sentences of some sort to be true, ways that are independent and quite different from the ways in which the speakers of the language describe whatever they describe. But how is this possible? Surely the idea that the truth-condition of a sentence can be explained in terms intelligible quite independently of an understanding of the sentence itself—and intelligible independently of the actual conceptualizations of speakers of the sentence—is peculiarly suspect. Not

---

[5] 'The interesting question is what this notion is going to be like and what sort of account can be given of it', B. A. O. Williams, 'Consistency and Realism', *Proceedings of the Aristotelian Society*, suppl. vol. xl, 1966. See especially p. 202–3 in the reprint in *Problems of the Self* (Cambridge, 1973). Beside the reservations mentioned in the present essay, I have expressed other reservations about Williams's first step in this direction (the step taken via the conception of 'onus of match'). These may be found at p. 370 of 'Truth, Invention and the Meaning of Life', *Proceedings of the British Academy*, 1976–7. I would add to what I say there that Williams's analogy between deliberate judgement and imperatives was scarcely neutral with respect to the question of the truth or falsity status of deliberative judgements.

[6] Cf. § 32 of G. E. M. Anscombe, *Intention* (Blackwell, Oxford 1969).

What would be a Substantial Theory of Truth 193

even in the case of the most uncontroversially factual of sentences could one seriously or sensibly require it.[7]

I think that the right moral to draw from this apparent difficulty is that a substantial theory of truth will have to proceed not directly, but by a certain indirection that exempts it from presenting itself as a variant on the empty old 'situation' formula and exempts it also from posing as a more neutral or perhaps more analytical rival to those Tarskian or similar theories that exhaustively characterize the lexical and compositional resources of a language and thereby assign a homophone truth-condition to each of its sentences.[8]

How then should a substantial theory present itself? Here I think there is still something to be learned from the associations that are carried by the way that the word 'true' sounds outside philosophy. Consider the following passage written by the literary critic M. H. Abrams:

> We still need to face up to the full consequences of the realization that criticism is not a physical, or even a psychological, science. By setting out from and terminating in an appeal to the facts, any good aesthetic theory is, indeed, empirical in method. Its aim, however, is not to establish correlations between facts which will enable us to predict the future by reference to the past, but to establish principles enabling us to justify, order, and clarify our interpretation and appraisal of the aesthetic facts themselves. And as we shall see, these facts turn out to have the curious and scientifically reprehensible property of being conspicuously altered by the nature of the very principles which appeal to them for their support. Because many critical statements of

[7] Consider for instance past tense sentences and the dubious eliminability, for purposes of giving truth-conditions, of tenses and indexicals; and cf. Michael Dummett 'The Reality of the Past', *Proceedings of the Aristotelian Society*, **69**, 1968–9, John McDowell, 'On "The Reality of the Past"' in *Action and Interpretation*, ed. Hookway and Pettit (CUP, 1978), which gives particularly clear expression to the point I have made in the text.

For the lamentable effect upon moral philosophy (and upon such insights as those voiced by Emotivism) of the aspiration to proper or reductive analysis, see my 'Truth, Invention ...', p. 352, n. 1 and pp. 356–7.

The point made in the text is made very manifest by, *but is in no way dependent on*, the 'redundancy' conception of truth that is ascribed to Frege. See for instance pp. 271–2 of *Nachgelassene Schriften*, ed. Hermes (Felix Meiner, Hamburg, 1969) and 'The Thought', *Mind*, **65**, 1956; also F. P. Ramsey, 'Facts and Propositions', *Proceedings of the Aristotelian Society*, Supplementary Vol., 1927. For the ambiguity of 'redundancy' see P. F. Strawson, 'A Problem About Truth', in Pitcher (ed.), *Truth* (Prentice Hall, Englewood Cliffs, N.J., 1964), and also Dummett, 'Truth'.

[8] 'Homophone' (adjective) in the sense of sounding the same (by being the very same sentence), or in the loose and extended sense of employing the very same concepts.

facts are thus partially relative to the perspective of the theory within which they occur, *they are not 'true', in the strict scientific sense that they approach the ideal of being verifiable by any intelligent human being, no matter what his point of view.* Any hope, therefore, for the kind of basic agreement in criticism that we have learned to expect in the exact sciences is doomed to disappointment.

A good critical theory, nevertheless, has its own kind of validity. The criterion is not the scientific verifiability of its single propositions, but the scope, precision, and coherence of the insights that it yields into the properties of single works of art and the adequacy with which it accounts for diverse kinds of art.[9]

This passage will start a number of other questions or speculations—most notably about the extent to which science itself, with which Abrams contrasts criticism, lives up to the ideal that the passage suggested for science, or is contaminated by experimental phenomena having what Abrahams would call 'the curious and reprehensible property of being conspicuously altered by the nature of the very principles which appeal to them for support'. I quote it chiefly however for the sake of the reminder it provides of the pre-theoretical expectations we have of truth, and for the naturalness of the idea to which Abrams gives expression that the concept of truth has *marks* and that it is one such mark of the concept that sentences enjoying the property of truth approach the ideal of being *verifiable by any intelligent human being no matter what his point of view.*[10] But how is one to assay the claim that this is a mark of the concept? And how is one to ascertain what the other marks are?

The unsurprising suggestion that I seek to explore in this essay is that the development of a substantial theory of truth will consist first in the discovery of a principle for the enumeration of the marks of the truth concept and then in the refinement of that principle. But as regards the conditions under which any particular sentence holds true, the theory will add little and take away nothing—except in so far as it clarifies such general questions as what it is for a sentence to be good enough ('factual enough' in character) to be a candidate to have a truth-value.

[9] *The Mirror and the Lamp* (OUP, Oxford, 1953), p. 4. My italics.
[10] I use the expression 'marks of the concept' in the manner explained by Frege in 'On Concept and Object', pp. 51–2 in Geach and Black, *Translations from the Writings of Gottlob Frege* (Blackwell, 1952). A mark of the concept *true* is any property F such that: for any x, if x has the property True, then x has F.

11

What would be a Substantial Theory of Truth 195

One familiar problem in recent philosophy has often been described as the problem of characterizing meaning in terms of truth, assuming truth already understood. If this were a good description of that project, then a good description of my own would be the characterization of truth in terms of meaning (or the enumeration of the marks of the concept of truth) assuming that *meaning* is already understood. That makes the search for a substantial theory of truth the dual of the familiar project. But both projects require much more careful description. Properly conducted, neither of them can take quite so much for granted about the concept that the other is to investigate.

Frege claimed in *Grundgesetze der Arithmetik* I.32 that the sense of a sentence, or thought expressed by a sentence, is the sense or thought that certain conditions are fulfilled, these conditions being determined by the structure of the sentence and the several semantic contributions of the parts. To know the sense of a sentence is then to know under what conditions it is true. More formally put, with certain difficulties and obscurities a little clearer to view, the doctrine reads: (s means that p) if and only if (whether s is true or not depends on whether or not p, and depends only on that).

The refinements and improvements that have been visited upon Frege's formulation since the time when Michael Dummett's article on truth put the *Grundgesetze* dictum back into philosophical circulation[11] have been variously motivated. I shall recapitulate the most pertinent as briefly as possible under four heads.[12]

(i) It is no use to characterize the sense of a sentence as a function of the senses of its parts and the sense of a word as a

[11] Unluckily the *Grundgesetze* passage was not included in Geach and Black's *Translations*, and for a long time the only reference to it in the ordinary current literature were Dummett's op. cit. and David Schwayder's '=', *Mind*, 1956. Before Dummett's article, rather few philosophers knew of the Fregean origins of Wittgenstein's *Tractatus Logico Philosophicus* 4.024, or appreciated the general utility outside *Tractatus* scholarship of the Fregean insight.

[12] The important loci after Dummett are Donald Davidson, 'Truth and Meaning', *Synthese*, 7, 1967; 'Radical Interpretation', *Dialectica*, 27, 1973; 'Belief and the Basis of Meaning', *Synthese*, 27, 1974; Richard Grandy, 'Reference, Meaning and Belief', *Journal of Philosophy*, 70, 1973; Gareth Evans and John McDowell, 'Editorial Introduction' in *Truth and Meaning* (Oxford, 1970); John McDowell, 'Bivalence and Verificationism' in *Truth and Meaning*; John McDowell, 'On the Sense and Reference of a Proper Name', *Mind*, 86, 1977. My special debt to the last two items will be apparent to anyone who knows either.

function of the senses of all the sentences in which it figures by way of some stable contribution it makes therein, unless there is some way out of this circle. There would be a way out if we could first and independently characterize the senses of sentences in terms of truth-conditions. But, in any typical or interesting case of the problem, there will be infinitely many sentences. So that is the one thing that we cannot envisage someone's doing directly. Indirectly we can envisage his doing this by parsing sentences and then mating them with truth-conditions by reference to the meanings of their components. But, if that is to be envisaged as a possibility, then a general account of meaning that is done in terms of truth will need to formulate the general recipe or form in which the compositional and lexical resources of a language (constructions and words) can be enumerated, characterized by axioms of some suitable theory θ, and then put together in such a way that, for any arbitrary sentence built up from such and such linguistic elements, the relevant axioms of θ deliver a theorem that determines a truth-condition for the sentence. In adapting Tarski's general conception of formal theories of truth to this veritably Fregean end, Donald Davidson has filled an important lacuna in the *Grundgesetze* doctrine of sense.

(ii) Next it is necessary to clarify the *nature* of the interdependence on which the Fregean sense formula so heavily relies, between the truth or falsity of an indicative sentences and the obtaining or not obtaining of the condition that the theory θ assigns to s. The dependence we are interested in is not merely truth-functional.[13] Obviously the dependence is in fact semantical. But the idea of the semantical is the one idea that we cannot pray directly in aid here. Equally obviously, though, the dependence holds in virtue of that which any theory like θ of (i) above ought to aim to characterize. So it seems that, if all was well at (i), then we can say that the dependence is the kind of dependence that holds in virtue of that which a theory like θ is a theory of. Now θ was a theory of 'true_L'. And we were allowing ourselves the idea of truth. So it may seem that at this point we can say that a sentence s means$_L$ that p if and only if we have as a

---

[13] Cf. A. J. Ayer, 'Truth', *Revue Internationale de Philosophie*, 7, 1953; Donald Davidson, 'Truth and Meaning'; D. Wiggins, 'Sentence Sense, Word Sense and Difference of Word Sense' in *Semantics*, ed. D. D. Steinberg and L. A. Jacobovits (Cambridge, 1971).

theorem of some theory of 'true$_L$', given in the way specified at (i) above, ⌜True$_L$ s iff p⌝.[14] But here we have to be careful. To allow ourselves the notion of truth is one thing. To allow ourselves the intuitive notion of truth-*conditions* is another. Truth-conditions surely represent the abstraction of a certain semantically relevant feature of a sentence from the disorganized mass of linguistic and behavioural material that constitute, together with evaluations of various utterances of it as true or false, the data for our theory of human communication. What is the principle of that abstraction? I suppose that if we knew that there was only one theory that would generate a reliable non-accidentally true biconditional ⌜True$_L$ s iff p⌝ for each sentence s, then that would suggest that this was a small problem. But in fact there are infinitely many and they are distinct.[15]

(iii) What we shall rely on in order to select a suitable or designated theory θ from among all the true theories that equate or seek to capture ⌜s means in L that p⌝-type facts with biconditional facts of the form ⌜ ϕs iff p⌝—and what we shall rely on to refuse the name of theory *of truth* to theories that generate theorems of the form ⌜True$_L$ s iff p⌝ that are true all right but unfaithful guides to meaning—is something with which we are furnished by our actual understanding of truth. But evidently this something is as yet inexplicit in our understanding; and, where it carries the whole burden of explicating the specifically semantical character of the particular sort of interdependence in virtue of which we want content-specifying biconditionals to hold, the Fregean theory of meaning must surely do more to articulate or elucidate the notion of truth itself.[16] In this connection, it is worth remembering that this

---

[14] It is a difficulty that even a properly constrained axiomatic theory like θ will be capable of generating more than one equivalence of the form 'True $s \equiv p$' for a given s. Christopher Peacocke has proposed that we solve this difficulty by requiring of the meaning giving equivalences that they have a proof of a certain direct and canonical form. (Cf. *Truth and Meaning*, p. 188.)

[15] Cf. Evans and McDowell, 'Editorial Introduction' op. cit., p. xiv.

[16] Strawson made this point in his Inaugural Lecture, *Meaning and Truth* (Oxford, 1970), reprinted in *Logico Linguistic Papers* (Methuen, 1971); see also Christopher Peacocke: 'T-sentences [of the form "True $s \equiv p$"] contain the predicate "true"; so it is not unreasonable to claim that to verify the T-sentences we must be possessed of *some* access to the notion of truth independently of a recursion for a number of particular languages.... we can hardly avoid raising the question of the sense of [the predicate] "true in the language of population P" for variable P.' ('Truth Definitions and Actual Languages' in *Truth and Meaning*, p. 163.)

obligation was recognized explicitly by Tarski—no special friend of intensional notions—when he formulated his general conception of truth theories. He stipulated (in effect) that a theory could only be adequate as a theory of *truth* if it generated for every sentence of the language for which truth was to be defined an equivalence of the form ⌜x is true if and only if p⌝ in which the right hand side of the biconditional was *a translation* in the meta-language of the sentence mentioned on the left. This solution being scarcely open to a theorist of meaning and communication who wants to characterize ideas like meaning or translation in terms of truth, what was needed was a completely new idea:

In radical interpretation we cannot *assume* that a T-sentence [biconditional in the form ⌜True $s \equiv p$⌝] satisfies the translation criterion [of Tarski] ... [But] we have supplied an alternative criterion: this is that the totality of [a radical interpreter's] T-sentences [mating sentence s to be interpreted with interpretation p] should ... *optimally fit* evidence about sentences held true by native speakers. ... what Tarski [demanded] for each T-sentence can be indirectly elicited by a holistic constraint ... A T-sentence of an empirical theory of truth can be used to interpret a sentence, provided we also know that the T-sentence is entailed by some true theory that meets the formal and empirical constraints.' Donald Davidson, 'Radical Interpretation' (op. cit., 1973).

(iv) What then, once we carefully deprive ourselves of the notion of the semantical and of everything that we have not articulated explicitly about truth, must a theory θ be like if, for every L-sentence s, it is to be relied upon to furnish a derivation of ⌜True$_L$ $s \equiv p$⌝ if and only if s is suitable to be employed for saying that p? What is a theory's 'optimally fitting evidence about sentences held true by native speakers'? And what are the over-all 'empirical constraints' that are to be imposed on any theory with a colourable claim to offer a faithful reading of each sentence of the language that it sets out to interpret? A first approximation was Davidson's Principle of Charity: we have an optimal fit between a theory θ and evidence about sentences held true by native speakers if and only if the interpreter who used the biconditionals entailed by θ, and used them for purposes of ascribing beliefs to his subjects (wherever appropriate) on the basis of what they uttered, would end up ascribing to his subjects a larger number of beliefs that the interpreter himself held true than the interpreter would end up ascribing using a rival theory θ'. This idea was quickly seen to need adjustment,[17] however, because (quite apart from any complacency it evinced about the interpreter's own rationality) it paid insufficient regard to all the differences in beliefs one would *expect* between different communities who were exposed to different geographical environments, lived in different historical epochs or enjoyed different material conditions of life.

It is necessary to replace the idea of Charity with an idea that founds interpretation not in maximization but in *explanation* (generously conceived). And this is to say that something more anthropological seems to be needed. Let us then constrain the theory θ that provides sentence by sentence interpretations of the language L by the requirement that θ should combine with a plausible anthropology (an anthropology to be simultaneously developed) in such a way that *in concert* the two theories make the best total sense possible (not merely best linguistic sense possible) of the total life and conduct of L-speakers. Following Richard Grandy, who may have been the first to perceive the need for some such emendation of Charity, let us call this the Principle of Humanity. And let us gloss the Principle of Humanity with the requirement that the theory θ be such as to combine with a theory of contexts and a theory of speech acts or force[18] (further components of the anthropology, differentiating utterances both in respect of the outward aspects of a speech act that signal it as an assertion or a question or a command ..., and in respect of what is thereby held to be communicated) to the following effect: the anthropology that adopts the theory θ along with the best theories of context and force that it can find, and then deploys all of these *in concert* for purposes of the interpretation of utterances that are appropriate to be considered as expressive of beliefs, concerns, needs, wants, or whatever, (i) describes and

[17] See Richard Grandy, op. cit., and also John Wallace, 'A Query on Radical Translation' in *Journal of Philosophy*, 68, 1971.

[18] For theories of force and speech acts as they impinge on interpretation, and for other aspects of the formulation here, cf. John McDowell, 'Bivalence and Verificationism' in *Truth and Meaning*. The conception of a theory of force was introduced by Michael Dummett. See *Frege* (Duckworth, London, 1973), p. 416.

explains, in the light of what can impinge on L-speakers or is presented to their experience, the doxastic and affective reactions of L-speakers to their environment, and explains such reactions better than an anthropology with different theories of sense, force, and context; and (ii) makes intelligible, in the light of the doxastic and affective attitudes attributed to L-speakers by the total theory, the motivation and conduct of L-speakers—more intelligible than would an anthropology with different theories of sense, force and context. Finally, explanations are judged here, not so much by the successful predictions they generate (if these are plentiful and uniformly accurate, that is a bonus), but by the extent to which they enable us to grasp, or identify imaginatively with, a norm of rationality to which the thoughts and actions of L-speakers are seen as answerable.[19]

III

These emendations have taken us a long way from the Fregean starting-point. Truth still figures in the theory simply because we still think of θ as a suitably constrained theory that generates equivalences of the form $\ulcorner \text{True}_L s \text{ iff } p \urcorner$. But the process through which Tarski's 'translation' requirement was superseded by the idea of radical interpretation, and by general (not specifically *linguistic*) notions of understanding, explaining, and making sense, has progressively lightened the load that it carries there. By the end there are so many diverse collateral constraints on any θ that will provide the recipe to annex to an arbitrary sentence a content suitable for purposes of the interpretation of utterances of s, that we do not even need to stipulate that θ should be a theory of truth. Provided it generates a canonical equivalence of the form $\ulcorner (s \text{ has } \phi) \equiv p \urcorner$ for each sentence s, and provided that ϕ is some property of sentences and θ answers to all the anthropological requirements, then

---

[19] For more on explanation by reasons, and the asymmetry of explanation and prediction, see my 'Weakness of Will, Incommensurability, and the Objects of Deliberation and Desire' *Proceedings of the Aristotelian Society*, vol. lxxix, 1979. For the contention that we can only break out of the circle of belief and meaning if, in advance of any particular problem of radical interpretation, we know more than nothing, not only about the world (as Davidson emphasizes) but also about men in general; and for the relevant idea of human nature, see Longer Note 6.36 and the penultimate sections of Chapter Six of my *Sameness and Substance* (Blackwell, Oxford, 1979).

even a θ that does not mention truth can serve our anthropology as its theory of meaning component.[20]

And now the way is clear for a substantial theory of truth. Can we not say that truth just *is* what a theory like θ is a theory *of* and use the anthropological constraint as a principle to enumerate all the marks that truth would have to have in order to play the role of the property ϕ in a correct theory of interpretation?

This is almost the right strategy; but we must improve a little on this statement of it if we are to confront open-mindedly the questions that Dummett and Williams have raised about such propositions as the propositions of ethics. However plausible it is to say that the meaning of a geographical statement is given by its truth-conditions, we must neither assume nor even seem to assume that it is via *truth-* conditions that the meaning of a normative or evaluative utterance is given. Evaluative or normative utterances are certainly interpretable; but many philosophers doubt that they are true or false in any serious sense of 'true' or 'false'. The virtue of the construction recently described is that it precisely allows the word 'true' to drop out, with the effect that this question is no longer begged. (It is no longer begged against the more sophisticated non-cognitive positions. Against those positions which hold that evaluative and normative statements do not even have a serious claim to be reckoned as constative, more direct arguments are available.)

The right strategy, then, is first to use the anthropological constraint to generate as many marks as possible of the interpretation property ϕ, and then pause to compare what shortfall there may be between what the interpretation property demands and what marks the pre-theoretical notion of truth seems to demand, giving particular attention to those classes of sentences (if any) that are certainly interpretable, do have the marks of candidacy for possession of ϕ, but do not have all the

---

[20] Cf. p. 210, Donald Davidson, 'Truth and Meaning', *Synthese*, 1967, and John McDowell, 'On the Sense and Reference of a Proper Name', *Mind*, 1977. 'The fact that the [right hand side of biconditionals stating necessary and sufficient conditions for the property ϕ to attach to a sentence s] specified the content of sayings potentially effected by uttering the mentioned sentence [s] would guarantee that the theory with its theorems written that way was a true theory of truth. But it would be the guaranteeing fact, not the guaranteed fact, which suited the theory to serve as a theory of sense.'

marks of candidacy for possession of truth as pre-theoretically conceived.[21] For a sentence to be true is for it to have ϕ and possibly something more as well. But if truth at least implies possession of ϕ, and if all truth-conditions are at least ϕ conditions, then every mark of ϕ is a mark of truth—even if not the other way round.

Before attempting to implement this strategy, it will be useful to note certain points about the drafting of the anthropological constraint. It stands in need of improvement and amplification; and, even as a summary of what has been achieved by workers in this field, it may be defective. But, taking it in its present state and leaving unimproved also the amplifications we have offered, one will remark that there is nothing in the ideas we have used there—of an anthropology, of interpretation, or of a norm of rationality—that excludes the possibility that an interpreter might learn from his subjects. If he condescends to his subjects because of some colonial or methodological hang-up, this impediment to understanding has nothing to do with the constraint as it was drafted. Nor does the constraint impart any commitment to the existence of a unique best theory θ. It is consistent with a somewhat pessimistic assessment of the prospects for a completable unitary theory of human rationality, and emphasizes both the conditional and the dialectical or

---

[21] This was the strategy of sections VI–XI of my 'Truth, Invention...' cited in fn. 5, above, where the interpretation property ϕ was given the name 'assertibility' and truth as pretheoretically conceived was called 'regular truth'. The purpose of this was not to give the unfortunate impression that I really thought there was more than one species of truth but to *hold open* the same question whose existence has here (in the present paragraph and its two predecessors) discouraged the more direct strategy. It will not quite do to say perfectly generally with McDowell ('Bivalence and Verificationism') that 'the requirement of interaction [of a theory of sense] with a theory of force ensure that an acceptable theory of sense will remain acceptable if ["has ϕ"] is replaced by "[is] true"'. It will not do for the cases where the truth status of a class of interpretable sentences is questionable.

Having laid all these conditions upon the property ϕ in its interrelations with several other notions, and in its role within a theory of meaning, not only have we arranged matters so that it can *turn out*—as it evidently and obviously does for sentences like those of ordinary terrestrial geography—that truth fills the bill and satisfies all the conditions; we also have the beginnings of an idea of what might count against assigning to truth, at least as pre-theoretically conceived, this general role. This could happen if our pre-theoretical conceptions of truth were extremely strong (stronger than I think) and there were a surprising, demonstrable, and irremovable feature of truth that *unfitted* it to play the role one envisaged for ϕ. One could then, as Dummett once put it, dethrone truth.

trial-and-error character of the interpretative exercise. (So the determinacy or indeterminacy of interpretation is left as an open question.) And, while the account of what a theory of meaning is is consistent with the thesis that 'use exhaustively determines meaning', as Michael Dummett puts it in his paper 'The Philosophical Basis of Intuitionistic Logic'[22], that represents no feat of austerity. For the account does not undertake any of the clarifications that the meaning as use doctrine will require, and sets no limit upon the evidence that the interpreter who is *en route* to making belief ascription on the basis of utterances can count as evidence for use or call evidence for L-speakers' knowing the ϕ-conditions of a sentence s. Nor does it enter any stipulations about what sort of account of the world to which he has to see his subjects as responding the interpreter is allowed to bring to the task of interpretation. (For all that the constraint directly says, the interpreter can see his subjects as exploring the explanatory potential of an animistic conception of nature if that is the interpreter's own world view, or as investigating the ins and outs of Cantor's transfinite.) Finally, the account lends no support to the idea that θ should suggest a set of instructions for the practice of speaking L, or to the even more demanding idea that for any sentence s these instructions should be intelligible antecedently or independently of the content (p) of s itself. An account of meaning that is as hospitable, unpuritanical, and unpsychologistic as this may well deserve to be called a neo-Fregean account.

IV

It will be useful to recapitulate roughly, without details, one portion of the doctrine of II in an existentially quantified form:

There is a property ϕ such that, for any s,

---

[22] 'Grasping the meaning of a statement must in general consist of a capacity to use that statement in a certain way, or to respond to its use by others. Use exhaustively determines meaning.' Michael Dummett, 'The Philosophical Basis of Intuitionistic Logic', in *Bristol Logic Colloquium 1973* (North Holland), eds H. E. Rose and J. C. Shepherdson. Contrast Strawson's view in 'Scuton and Wright on Anti-Realism ...', *Proceedings of the Aristotelian Society*, vol. lxxvii, 1976, representing a standpoint that the account of meaning in the text may do something to reconcile with some qualified form of the meaning as use thesis.

{s means that p in L (or s has a content in L appropriate for the assertion that p)}
if and only if
{some θ canonically implies that [(s has ϕ) iff p], where θ is a theory of ϕ, and θ combines with an anthropology α to make better total sense of the shared life and conduct of L-speakers than any rival pair, $\langle \theta', \alpha' \rangle$ consisting of rival theory θ' plus rival anthropology α'}.

The relation between what was said in Section II and this recapitulation (which has not been drafted to manage the problems of distinct, equally good theories) is this: it represents the Ramsey sentence formed by existential generalization upon the place that would be occupied by the predicate 'true' in a rough summary of section II. And if Section II was right, then anyone who thinks that a certain language L is interpretable is theoretically committed to believe that there *is* some property of L-sentences that makes this Ramsey sentence true. What we are interested in first is the nature of the weakest property (or equal weakest properties) that will verify the open sentence standing within the scope of the initial clause 'there is a property ϕ such that...'. (This initial clause has as its scope the whole of the rest of the recapitulation.) I shall call this property by the title 'assertibility'. But I would emphasize that 'assertible' means no more here than the anthropological constraint makes it mean. The use is purely technical,[23] and it is eliminable.

For purposes of what follows, it will often be necessary for the reader to think of the two amplifications of 'making sense' suggested in Section II as transcribed here within the scope of the existential quantifier in the shape of constraints upon or further determinants of θ and ϕ. And it will be helpful to have in mind two further amplifications of Davidson-cum-McDowell provenance that were entailed or ought to have been entailed: (i) an interpreter who employs θ to interpret L-speakers projects upon L-speakers the minimum of inexplicable error or irrationality; (ii) the axioms of θ pull their weight singly and

---

[23] As it was also in 'Truth, Invention ...', cited in note 5 above. (For Ramsey sentences see F. P. Ramsey, 'Theories', in *Foundations of Mathematics and Other Logical Essays* (Routledge, London, 1931).

jointly in the project of ascribing an intelligible collection of propositional attitudes to L-speakers. ('Explicable', 'inexplicable', 'intelligible' may be glossed here as much as you rationally will in terms of *Verstehen*, projection, identification.) Belief will be the most important of these. There is much else that language does; but *par excellence* it is the vehicle for the communication and expression of belief. In so far as the idea of a norm of rationality requires the idea of information, and in so far as the discrimination of good from bad information has its rational culmination in belief, it is the idea of the communication of belief that organizes the interpreter's search for what speakers say; and it is the idea of reciprocal governance between what beliefs speakers can express and what speakers can discriminate and respond to in the particular environment impinging on them that provides us with a justification for using that environment itself as a partially independent clue to what it is that speakers believe and may, as they please, say or not say.

v

The first mark of assertibility (and so of truth) would appear to consist in assertibility's being *the primary dimension of assessment for sentences*, or that property which sentences have *normally* to be construed as aiming to enjoy. Suppose assertibility were not the primary dimension of assessment. Then there would be no general reason for it to be a *norm* for speakers to utter only sentences that they take for assertible sentences. (If this sounds odd, remember that 'assertible' is only our name for a sentence property that verifies the open sentence in the scope of the Ramseian quantifier.) *A fortiori* there would generally be nothing in the practice of L-speakers to sustain the idea that it was a norm for speakers of L to aim at assertibility (or truth) in their utterances. But, if there were no such norm, and if there were no rational expectation of there being any such norm, then interpretation would either be impossible (not only by the theorist of L-speakers, but also by L-speakers of L-speakers) or unjustifiable. Suppose that the utterance of a sentence had no systematic connection with the belief of the speaker, and that utterance gave no *prima-facie* ground for the interpreter to expect that a *belief* was being expressed. Then a vital link would be lost with that which can give an interpretation independent empirical support, namely what it *would* be rational for any man to believe, if he were placed as this subject is placed in this particular environment.

A second mark of the assertibility (and so of the truth) of a sentence s would appear to consist in *s's having a content such that with respect to this content there should be a tendency, under favourable conditions of investigation, for disagreement to diminish and for opinion to converge in agreement.* This is a weakening of something that Abrams claims. And the result of the weakening is a very slippery condition. What are favourable conditions of investigation? If the proviso is omitted, then what results is not even a plausible candidate for a mark of truth, let alone assertibility. But if it is inserted, then there is a problem of degradation of the requirement by very trivial forms of convergence, e.g. convergence resulting from changes in some subject-matter itself, or from convergence in the material conditions of life. As the airlines shrink the globe (as they put it), and as charter tourism makes every place more and more like every other place, there will no doubt result some convergence in opinions about what a bacon, lettuce, and tomato sandwich should taste like, or about the supposed right to three weeks' paid holiday *per annum*. But that is not what is meant. I should have liked to be able to say why this is too uninteresting a case of convergence even to satisfy the minimal demand that I have called the second mark of assertibility. But, rather than pause to attempt refinements that one might hope to be excused in the making of a maiden voyage on these ill-charted seas, let me say why assertibility will seem to need *something* like the second mark. It needs it because, unless there exists *some* such tendency towards agreement, there will be nothing to create the prospect that L-speakers need in order to continue, namely the prospect that making arguments and giving reasons should have non-random efficacy in persuasion. But, where argument has no non-random efficacy at all, there nothing protects L-speakers from the idea that there is simply nothing at issue in the question whether to accept or reject a given sentence. In which case it seems hard to see how speakers could regard either s or the negation of s as a fit expression for a belief of theirs, and hard to see how an interpreter could regard them as regarding it as one.

Again, interpretation requires that the interpreter who wants to determine what a speaker says by an utterance of the form Predicate + Term t should be able to see certain utterances of this sentence or its negation as prompted by some propositional attitude of the utterer's, viz. belief, that is both *en rapport* with the subject t and answerable in respect of ϕ or assertibility (that is the first dimension of assessment) to whether or not the bearer of the subject term really does have the property ascribed to it by the predicate. But the claim that the belief is so answerable cannot outlast the conviction that the strength and durability of the subject's disposition to hold that the entity has the property is conditional on the entity's *really* having it, and highly sensitive to the entity's proving not to have the property. M. F. Burnyeat has recently asked how the argument from illusion can be sustained by a principle that is logically equivalent to the wildly implausible principle 'If a thing is really F, then if it appears F to one observer, it doesn't appear *not*-F to any observer'.[24] My own answer to that question would be that the argument flourishes under the influence of a plausible but different principle that is insufficiently distinguished from those that support the argument from illusion: namely, 'If a thing is really F, then it will tend to appear F to any qualified observer—and its appearing *not*-F to anyone stands in need of explanation'. I think that an adequate account of convergence will clarify its relation to this principle (which implies that if there is no long-run tendency for observers to agree about whether item t is really F, then, unless the agreement is otherwise explicable, t is not really F). The adequate account will also need to exclude the debased species of convergence that we encounter where a whole chorus of agreement in the belief that p is explained, and explained without residue, by the desire for conformity or doxastic unison. For convergence to be interesting or relevant, an impressive number of those who concur in the judgement that p must be candidates to *know* or to *have found out for themselves* whether p or not. What then is knowledge? If p is to be truth, or that property which a semantic theory θ needs to be a theory of if it is to combine with an anthropology to make rational sense of L-speakers, and if (as I suppose) the combined

---

[24] 'Conflicting Appearances' in *Proceedings of the British Academy*, vol. lxiv, 1978–9.

theory needs the idea of knowledge, then ϕ must be a property that will render the following a truism: x's believing that p is x's knowing that p only if, where θ entails that s has the property ϕ if and only if p, and where s indeed *has* the property ϕ, an assertion of the sentence s figures indispensably within the text of the explanation why x preferred the belief that p to the belief that not-p.

I have admitted that there is something fugitive and unsatisfactory in the convergence requirement as I have left it. But I shall anticipate and guard against one dangerous misunderstanding of the position about ethics that would be consequential upon the completion of what is only begun here, if I seize the opportunity to point out that no plausible improved version of the foregoing deduction could possibly demonstrate that assertibility, as constrained by the anthropological requirement, was subject to the stronger and exceptionless requirement that is suggested by the quotation from Abrams. (If that were required by *truth*, then this would be a divergence of assertibility and truth.) Nor then shall we expect the same position in ethics that identifies our notion of assertibility with simple regular truth, and then calls itself 'cognitivism' or 'realism', to enter the philosophically suicidal claim that it is a consequence of cognitivism or moral realism that 'in some sense everybody *should* have the same moral beliefs ... [though] that *should* relates to a world in which we are cognitively more secure than is [in?] the actual world.... [M]oral pluralism is desirable not for liberal cum aesthetic reasons but for *epistemic* ones.'[25] There is nothing in the theory of interpretation, or in moral cognitivism as explicated by reference to the interpretation property ϕ, to support so single-focused a conception of the subject matter of morals.

Third putative mark: Assertibility is a property such that *every statement which lacks it lacks it independently of a speaker's means of recognizing it; and every statement which possesses it possesses it independently of a speaker's means of recognizing it*. The argument for

[25] See pp. 252-3 of *Ways of Meaning* by Mark de Breton Platts (Routledge & Kegan Paul, London, 1979). Contrast the much more plausible cognitivism (still in my opinion stronger, or less sceptical rather, than is evidentially warranted, but informed by a full recognition of the many real differences of perception and moral emphasis found in extant human societies) of Aurel Kolnai in 'Moral Consensus', *Proceedings of the Aristotelian Society*, 1969-70.

this, in so far as there is one, is similar to the argument for the second mark in turning upon the notion of belief. And, like the argument for the second case, it is at its best when seen as gaining initial favour for the conclusion that there must be central cases where assertibility has this property.

If finding a content for *s* involves linking it or its negation with a belief that the interpreter can envisage finding the right sort of grounds (either grounds that would count with the interpreter himself, or some intelligible deformation of them, circumstantially informed) to project upon his subjects, then some of the requirements on the determinability of belief, and on sentences' expressing something that is a matter for belief, must be translated into requirements upon assertibility itself.

We have many beliefs without knowing how we came by them. But of no genuine belief do we think that, *if* we were to scrutinize it afresh or for the first time, the question of its correctness would be simply arbitrary or dependent on the will of the maker of the judgement. The argument for this is very familiar.[26] Rather than repeat the argument, I shall illustrate it by an analogy with what Aristotle writes of animal movement:

There must be something which is unmoved outside an animal, supported against which the animal which is moved moves. For if that which supports the animal is always to be giving way (as when tortoises walk on mud or men on sand), then there will be no progression—that is no stepping forward, if the ground shifts, nor flying nor swimming, if the air or the sea should not offer some resistance. And that which offers resistance must be other than that which is moved, and wholly different from the whole of it and what is thus unmoved must be no part of what is moved. If not, it will not be moved.[27]

Mutatis mutandis the same applies to judgement and the determination of belief. Unless the content of the belief happens to be something which, from the nature of the case, it is up to me to decide at whim (say 'I'll touch that lamp post'), there must be

---

[26] See Bernard Williams, Problems of the Self IX, 'Deciding to Believe'; D. Wiggins, 'Freedom, Knowledge, Belief and Causality' in Vesey, ed., *Knowledge and Necessity* (London, Macmillan, 1971).

[27] *De Motu Animalium* 698^{b15-21}. For reading and interpretation, see M. L. C. Nussbaum, 'Aristotle's De Motu Animalium', (Harvard Ph.D. dissertation, 1973).

something potentially resistant, and outside the act of judgement itself, upon which the mind can gain purchase and *go forward* in judgement or denial. The assertibility of a judgement cannot consist (even in the case of pain, which might have been taken for a sort of counter-example to our third thesis) in the bare fact that the judgement is judged.

I think it will help to gain favour for the third mark as something genuinely forced upon the assertibility concept by the definition of a theory of meaning, if the statement of the requirement is contrasted with Dummett's characterization of a feature that he describes as a feature of the classical or realist notion of truth.[28] This is 'a feature which each mathematical statement either determinately possesses or determinately lacks, independently of our means of recognizing its truth value'. And Dummett says that, according to the intuitionist, 'this notion of truth cannot be the central notion for a theory of the meaning of mathematical statements'. It is important to notice here that Dummett speaks of the classical notion as requiring independence of *our* means of recognizing the property, where the *our* is presumably collective and may comprehend a whole culture or a whole race or species; whereas the requirement we are discussing only stipulates the independence of the property of assertibility from a native speaker's *own means of recognizing it*. In fact, I suspect that Dummett's intuitionist could accept the third mark (as I have characterized it) also as a mark of any conceivable assertibility predicate. Note also that, as we have drafted it, our anthropological requirement promises no particular support for the other classical idea that Dummett mentions, that in the case of every

---

[28] Op. cit. p. 16: 'The notion of truth, considered as a feature which each mathematical statement [1] either determinately possesses or determinately lacks, [2] possesses independently of our means of recognizing its truth-value, cannot be the central notion for a theory of the meaning of mathematical statements.' (My numeration.)

Note that there are at least two claims here. In so far as there is room to doubt that [2] does characterize the notion of truth corresponding to the English predicate 'true', the doubt is bound up with the drafting question I mention in the text. As for [1], someone convinced by Dummett of the questionability of bivalence or excluded middle, and convinced of this in connection with the English 'or' and the English 'true', would be entitled to distinguish claims [1] and [2], and then put Dummett's doubts to work in a critique of the usual *conception* of truth—doing this in an effort to get a plainer view of the *concept* itself, and of the meaning of the English word 'true'. Classical logicians do not have special or privileged access to that.

sentence either it or its negation has φ. There is nothing in the requirement of mutual interpretability of L-speakers and nothing in the phenomenology of belief that could require this. Nor is it even clear, as Daniel Isaacson has pointed out in a related connection, what could show that L-speakers definitely accepted the idea of bivalence.[29]

Fourth putative mark: Every assertible sentence is *assertible in virtue of something*. It is difficult to be persuaded that this adds very much—unless it serves to remind us of the fact that at least some interpretations of L-speakers (by L-speakers or by the theorist) must be by reference to L-speakers' responses to something to which interpreter and person interpreted have some measure of common (however indirect) access. But this is to say little. (Which means that to deny it would be to say far too much.) It will not even rule out the interpretation of L-speakers as conversing about sets of non-denumerable cardinality. This fourth requirement upon the assertibility concept does however summarize usefully the first three conditions. It records the intuitive consonance of property φ with the little that was reasonable in the correspondence theory of truth. And taking the fourth mark simply as a condensation of the first, second, and third, we are not tempted to confer some extra ontological commitment upon it.[30]

Fifth putative mark. Every assertible sentence is coassertible with every other assertible sentence. That is to say that *if s is assertible and s′ is assertible, then their conjunction is assertible*. Suppose s were interpreted in a way that made it fit for the expression of the belief that p, and s′ were interpreted in a way that made it fit for the expression of the belief that q. And suppose that the fifth mark were not a mark of assertibility. Then interpretation could not proceed on the assumption that the

[29] Daniel Isaacson, 'On Some Aspects of the Concept of Truth', D.Phil. thesis, Oxford, 1975.

[30] Perhaps there is a point in a fuller version:

If a sentence s is φ then s is φ in virtue of something; and what s is φ in virtue of is not something which any sentence inconsistent with s is φ in virtue of.

Giving 'in virtue of' a strict and constitutive interpretation, 'A is vermilion' is not then φ in virtue of A's being merely red. Thus the claim which the assertibility of s makes on belief (and the non-assertibility of s on non-belief) is assertibility in virtue of what counts constitutively against the assertibility of the negation of the sentence s. But the obscurities one can so easily find in this should not be permitted to embarrass the simpler formulation preferred in the text.

beliefs by reference to which s and s' were to be interpreted were themselves answerable to the principle that he who believes that p and also believes that q commits himself either to believe that (p & q) or to go back on the belief in one or other conjunct. It is not a universal or analytic principle that (If (x believes p) and (x believes q)) then (x believes that p & q). But it is a norm of rational belief that one is *committed* to conform one's beliefs to this requirement; and the interpretation of beliefs as beliefs has to see belief as *answerable* to it. A propositional attitude that could not be interpreted as in any way sensitive to the requirement could not be interpreted as what we mean by belief (though it could be interpreted as suspecting or fearing or wishing—or as some tendency of the primitive mentality, as yet imperfectly conformable to the reality principle, to make confident assertions).[31]

Here, as at earlier moments in this section, the reader may suspect a circularity, because the answerability of rational belief to the aggregation commitment can be traced back to the principle of non-contradiction; and a general statement of the law of non-contradiction requires the concept of *truth*. But, first, in so far as arguments of the sort I have rehearsed proceed through a step that essentially involves a propositional attitude of belief and in so far as this step cannot be omitted from *this* argument, they do not fail when judged by the proper standards for *elucidation*. And in the second place the Law of Non-Contradiction (which Frege called a Law of Truth) can itself be derived as a Law of Assertibility. I have not bothered with this

---

[31] Cf. fn. 3, above.

Mark Sainsbury once put it to me that I had not said enough to exclude *knowability* from counting as the property that verifies the Ramsey sentence at the beginning of section IV. I discussed this objection with Christopher Peacocke who pointed me in the direction of the following answer. If knowability is anything stronger than pure knowability *in principle*—where the complete parallelism with truth would be unsurprising—then it is not clear that it enjoys the fifth mark of assertibility. Peacocke himself made a similar point to Sainsbury's, but with respect to the property of a sentence s that is designated by the predicate 'the evidence now and in the future will increasingly support s in preference to rival hypotheses', suggesting to me that it was a mark of truth and not of this pretender that it should be that property *by reference to which convergence is to be explained wherever there is convergence*. The reader may wish to embrace this last as an extra mark of assertibility, and may prefer it over the attempts I have myself made in the discussion of the second mark of assertibility to give teeth to the requirement of convergence (viz. the candidacy for knowledge requirement, inserted there in response to Peacocke's pretender property).

because, like all the arguments for the Law of Non-Contradiction, the argument is circular. (Cf. Aristotle's discussion in *Metaphysics IV*.)

VI

The deduction of other marks of publicity, objectivity, convergence, etc. will require some considerable consolidation of the anthropological-cum-explanatory starting-point at the end of Section II, as well as the revision or refinement of the arguments just rehearsed. The next stage was to have been the comparison between assertibility as anthropologically constrained and truth as pre-theoretically conceived. But first it is necessary to make a general comment on the arguments that have been mustered at the first stage.

In each case the argument depended on a feature we should expect in a central case of interpretation (that is the case where it is relatively clear what it would be to make a direct test for interpretation via some propositional attitude that a sentence would be apt and suitable to express). But what about the other cases? Over and over again sentences are interpreted by speakers and theorists not directly but indirectly, by a process of extrapolation that it is the mission of the theory θ to license and systematize. Equally obviously, we should also expect that the speakers of the language will be constantly increasing its range and expressive power by a cantilevering process, building new and extended modes of expression on to old ones. Is it rational to expect that here, at the margin of innovation and discourse, all the supposed marks of property ϕ will be present invariably? The property ϕ is a property that supervenes upon utterances as an organized system secured upon a whole nexus of practices. Why cannot the weak be sustained by the strong or load-bearing elements? It is here that I shall be advised to expect a large difference between the possession of the property ϕ and the possession of the property truth. For even the five putative marks of assertibility that have been enumerated appear to fall short of being fully mandatory or absolutely essential to the possibility of all interpretation whatever. But for truth we shall require the presence of these marks, and then (someone may say) much more.

To this I reply that I doubt that many of the claims I have

entered about assertibility are overstated, because the objection overlooks the fact that, simultaneously with the extension of our modes of expression and in parallel with them, we have to have the criticism of old modes and the scrutiny of new ones. Criticism is not a contingent accompaniment of the process of the renewal of language. It is only within a system of practices which we can recognize as standing in the right relation to belief to be interpretation-sustaining that the property ϕ can supervene on utterances favourably assessed by reference to the first dimension of assessment; these practices will stand in the right relation to belief *only* if, by virtue of them, belief is (a) susceptible to criticism, (b) everywhere answerable to the charge that the content of some putative belief lacks the property whose marks it was the purpose of Section V to enumerate. There is no such thing, I maintain, as criticism that attacks the other pretensions of a certain sentence class (e.g. their objectivity) while leaving their significance immune to criticism. No would-be assertible sentence can escape the question whether it makes some however infinitesimal contribution to the load-bearing properties of the whole class of assertible sentences.

Here it may be helpful to take a familiar example. Take the locution 'must' and the opposing practical judgements 'Must V' and 'Must not V'. Unlike pairs such as 'good'/'bad', 'ought'/'ought not', 'obliged'/'obliged not' (i.e. the evaluations and appraisals on which practical judgements supervene),[32] 'Must V' and 'Must not V' are genuine contraries. Now consider the fifth supposed mark of assertibility. Nothing could seem more certain than that the fifth mark is a mark of *truth*. But, what if, contrary to the argument of section V, someone expressed doubt that it was a mark of ϕ (of assertibility, that is, as constrained by the simple requirement that interpretation should be possible)?

The claims of all true beliefs about how the world is are reconcilable, he will say. Everything true must be consistent with everything else that is true. That is the fifth mark of *truth*. But why suppose that all the claims of all rational concerns or even of all moral concerns (that the world *be* thus or so) will be

---

[32] For the distinction between evaluative and verdictive judgements see 'Truth, Invention ...', pp. 338–9; and, for the contrast between them in respect of certain problems of objectivity, ibidem, ss. VIII–X.

reconcilable? (Unless we suppose that the world was made for us.) When we try to judge that this is what we must do now, or that that is what we had better do, or that our life must now take one direction rather than another direction—all statements that are assertible and interpretable—we are not fitting truths (or even probabilities) into a pattern where a conflict or discrepancy proves that we have mistaken a falsehood for a truth.[33] If there is a disagreement over what is true in history or geography or science and two rational men have come to different conclusions, then we think it has to be theoretically possible to uncover some discrepancy in their respective views of the evidence. In empirical matters we suppose that, if two opposing answers to a *yes/no* question are equally good, then they might as well have been equally bad. But in matters of practice, the objector will say, it is not like that. And here the discrepancy comes to light between the properties of assertibility and of truth. One may have good undefeated reasons (reasons as good as the subject-matter can conceivably permit) to make a practical judgement, even though there are also good undefeated reasons to issue the denial of the judgement and pursue an alternative path. These sets of good undefeated reasons are good separately; but they cannot be conjoined to ground the conjunction of the two judgements that they separately support.

That is how it would seem. And here, in the problem of the universality of the fifth mark, is a way in which truth and assertibility certainly *could* come apart. But, if we now make the example still more concrete, then I think we may doubt whether practical judgements do in fact exemplify this apparent theoretical possibility. Consider for instance the situation of Dorothea in George Eliot's *Middlemarch* on the eve of Edward Casaubon's death.[34] The day before Casaubon dies he asks Dorothea to make a promise to fulfil his wishes, whatever they may be, after his death. She postpones the promise to the next day, contemplating with dread the task of continuing and completing after his death Casaubon's monumental but hopeless historical project, which is what she supposes his wishes

[33] Cf. Williams, 'Consistency and Realism'.
[34] The example was proposed by Peter Winch for discussion at a seminar on moral philosophy we gave jointly in the Lent Term of 1975.

will relate to. Should she make the promise or should she not? On the one side: 'Could she deny him? Could she say "I refuse to content this pining hunger"? It would be refusing to do for him dead what she was almost sure to do for him living.' 'She could not smite the soul that entreated hers.' On the other side: 'There is a deep difference between devotion to the living and an indefinite promise of devotion to the dead.' 'Was it right, even to soothe his grief—would it be possible even if she promised—to work as in a treadmill, fruitlessly?'

Such cases need to be taken seriously by a theory of moral truth, and it is not sensible to suppose that they will arise only (as George Eliot may have held) where men or women are alienated from themselves 'amidst the conditions of an imperfect social state, in which great feelings will often take the aspect of error, and great faith the aspect of illusion'. But I think that we can respect and comprehend the decisions that individuals make after weighing up incommensurables—and even applaud the way that they manage on the level of action—without necessarily exempting from all criticism the judgements they make if they say that this or that is what they literally *must* do. In fact it seems to be the worst way to take these cases seriously to bring the fifth mark of assertibility into question and say that the statement 'this is what I must do' is *true for me*, or *assertible for me* and leave it at that (open that is to all the well-known objections to Protagorean judgements that are exempt by their nature from criticism external to the act of judgement itself). Why, just because I had to choose between doing something or not doing it, did I have to choose between saying 'I must' and denying that.

There is powerful phenomenological support for cognitivism or realism in the experience of choosing between commensurable or incommensurable claims. Such support is worth as much as phenomenological support ever is worth (and will admit of some confirmation by the completion of our construction). The competing claims present themselves as objective and real, and continue to do so even after one or other of them wins. But we should not confuse this species of reality with that postulated by a much stronger and much more incredible cognitivism. The stronger cognitivism purports to provide positive assurance that there is always a realist answer, not merely to the question of the reality of the competing claims, but also to the question of which claim is the overall stronger claim.[35] That is an utterly different contention and equivalent to something that could not possibly flow from the characterization of the third mark of property ϕ. This is the contention that, for all s, either s is assertible or the negation of s is assertible. There is nothing in the theory of interpretation to make us believe this. And it is beginning to be notorious that there is little in the pre-theoretical notion of truth to assure us of the corresponding principle for truth. Someone can try saying that a sentence can only be true and substantially so if the subject matter it relates to is the sort of subject matter to validate the law of excluded middle. But the question is where he will muster an argument from to *justify* this restriction of 'true'.

VII

My provisional conclusion is that truth and assertibility coincide. Not only is truth the best candidate for the property ϕ determined by the interpretation requirement; it is the only candidate. I should counsel a realist to consider allowing the

---

[35] There are certain moral philosophical misconceptions that are certain to obscure the emergent alignment of the notion of assertibility, *qua* satisfier of the Ramsey sentence at the head of s. IV, and the pre-theoretical notion of truth.

It may be supposed that, in taking leave to doubt that we shall always be able to choose between *Must V* and *Not (must V)*, I am suggesting that we should resolve matters with the anodyne verdict *Permissible V and permissible not-V*. But this bland conclusion would be an absurd outcome of what I have been claiming (and not just because, if you could say that both V and *not-V* were permissible, then you could equally well say *Not-(must V)*). Where we have to decide how to act in the absence of any assurance of completeness, well, we *have* no assurance that there is a determinate answer to our question. If so we simply have to act without the benefit of such an answer.

This need not mean that there is just nothing we can say about the decision we are making. We can characterize the alternatives in terms of the virtues that they would exemplify. We can say what is good and what is bad about each course. On the level of evaluation, we can oppose one to the other and describe them as fully as we like without the slightest danger of contradiction.

Surely it is strange to disbelieve that there is an extra mundane God who made the world specially to suit us and then to rail against the incompleteness of the moral and practical ideas that remain to us if we disbelieve this. It is stranger still to seek to compensate for that incompleteness with various sorts of make-believe which would exempt our evaluative, normative and practical judgements from the answerability to internal criticism in the first dimension of assessment that precisely gives them their point. The remedy for the said incompleteness is not prescriptivism, but a reasonable and selective *scepticism*.

anthropological constraint as drafted to be the sole determinant of what he should mean by truth. If he were persuaded by this proposal then he would find that he had come to the point where he wanted to say that correspondence theorists and misguided empiricists have puffed up the notion of truth without any theoretical or pre-theoretical justification (except that which they had from a picture of reality that even physics now puts in doubt).[36]

Here I should predict that it will be felt that something has been left out. A characteristic preoccupation of the realist is the idea of the world as utterly independent of human conceptions of it.[37] One who was concerned with realism in this sense and wanted a notion of truth that would fix the whole content of his realism would be strongly motivated to enrich mere assertibility by constraints that have little or nothing to do with interpretation. In the case of the second mark, for instance, he might gloss the convergence it speaks of in Peircean fashion,[38] stipulating that for a sentence to be true in the serious and substantial sense is for it to express the opinion that is 'fated to be ultimately agreed by all who investigate', no matter how different their starting points, or how different their selection of facts, or how different their bent of mind. And he might well seek to adjust M. H. Abrams' characterization of truth to read 'Truth is what is verifiable by any intelligent being, no matter what his point of view.' If that were a sixth mark, then a seventh would be what resulted from strengthening the third mark by substituting for 'independent of a speaker's means of recognizing it' the phrase 'independent of our means of recognizing it'.

Now this is not a conception to be dismissed. It is undismissable. But, equally, the conception of truth that this realism

---

[36] In struggling through to this however simple conclusion (readily fortified by the distinction between the classical *conception* of truth, which sees truth as subject to the law of excluded middle, and the *concept* of truth which that classical conception aspired to be a conception of—a concept whose need for the law of excluded middle still appears to be an open question), I am conscious of owing much to the discussions at three courses of weekly reading classes devoted solely to Dummett's 'Truth' and held in New College each year between 1964 and 1966. I recall especially the oral contributions of Edward Hussey, John McDowell, and Ronald de Sousa.

[37] Cf. Bernard Williams, *Descartes* (Penguin, Harmondsworth, 1978).

[38] See the long quotation from Peirce's article 'How to make our ideas clear' given in 'Truth, Invention...', op. cit. p. 361; also that given by Williams in *Descartes*, p. 244.

invokes is not truth as it inheres or fails to inhere in the great generality of the significant sentence of a whole language. Relatively few of the predicates in a language—even in the most 'factual' portion of it—will pull their weight in theories of the causal order that come up to Peircean standards. Many predicates exist solely to denominate properties and thing-kinds of purely anthropocentric importance; and relatively few have a use that presupposes no relativity whatever to the perspective and concerns of speakers themselves. How many actual predicates possess a sense that is conditioned, corrected and regulated solely by interaction between scientific theory and features of reality that are perfectly indifferent to the point of view from which they are discerned?

Surely the contrast that this realist is in search of is not the contrast between mere assertibility and truth. It is the contrast between fully-fledged anthropocentric assertibility (ordinary workaday truth that is) and absolute truth, where absolute truth is truth that satisfies a demand for objectivity which is at once special and goes far beyond anything that could be required by the mere interpretability of language. Both absolute truth and assertibility as anthropologically constrained demand objectivity. But they demand it in different ways, and in widely differing degrees. Absolute truth demands it in a way that leads to a restriction of vocabulary so stringent as to raise altogether new questions about meaning. Truth that is not absolute requires the lower grade species of objectivity that is spelled out in the formulation of the first five marks of the assertibility concept. It is a matter of degree to what extent a species of discourse can satisfy either demand. But that does not entail that truth itself is a matter of degree. (If it is, then that is owed to some quite different consideration.)

Nothing that has been claimed here will entail that truths that are not absolute are merely relatively true. Absoluteness is not a modality of truth.

What then is ordinary truth, truth that is not absolute or Peircean? It is not a social construct,[39] though it supervenes

---

[39] Nor is it an anthropological construct, or a property that a whole culture can simply choose to invest a sentence with. Of course the Augustinian tag 'securus judicat orbis terrarum' (quoted aptly by Kolnai, op. cit., in a related connexion—the reference is to *Contra Epistolam Parmeniani* III. 24) is just wrong—because it doesn't matter what,

upon one. The only non-arbitrary way I can conceive of answering the question what it positively is to explore the constraints on any property ϕ that will play the role the assertibility property has to play in an ample, descriptively and conceptually replete, life-like, and well-observed theory of interpretation.

VIII

Strawson wrote in 1950:

> The only plausible candidate for the position of what (in the world) makes the statement true is the fact it states; but the fact it states is not something in the world. It is not an object; not even (as some have supposed) a complex object.... 'Fact' like 'true', 'states' and 'statement' is wedded to 'that' clauses; and there is nothing unholy about this union ... Facts are what statements (when true) state; they are not what statements are about.... Of course statements and facts fit. They were for each other. If you prize the statements off the world you prize the facts off it too; but the world would be none the poorer. (You don't also prize off the world what the statements are about—for this you would need a different kind of lever.)

But Strawson was right not to draw the conclusion that it would be impossible to elucidate the nature of fact-stating discourse. Just as nineteenth-century investigations of the foundations of geometry demonstrated that, without even giving sense to the idea of transcending the physical space that we inhabit, we can formulate questions about its over-all character (it cannot be Euclidean, for instance, if we find equilateral triangles which are not also similar triangles), so a substantial theory of truth has to find an indirect but internal way to understand truth and to elicit or educe, from the inside of our existing conceptual scheme and our existing modes of description and conceptual-

---

'without worrying', the world chooses to decide about the laws of motion, say, or the identity of the evening and morning stars. The whole world *can* be wrong about these things. But then nothing said by me or the authors I have cited entails that truth consists in a certain kind of agreement; or that, without worrying, the whole world can simply *decide* how things are or who is good and who is bad; or that any old intersubjectivity is objectivity. If I have implied anything at all about agreement, it is only that a certain minimum quantity of agreement in judgements among speakers is a precondition for a set of signs to constitute an interpreted language. And *that* is not to say that truth consists in a certain kind of agreement. Cf. Wittgenstein, *Philosophical Investigations*, ss. (Blackwell, Oxford, 1953, trans. Anscombe).

ization, the structural features of the concept. Indeed, once it is past the stage of defining itself against alternative conceptions of the topic, a substantial theory of truth which it is not an illusion of ours that we understand will not even *speak* of an inside and an outside of a conceptual scheme. Conceptual schemes cannot have insides and outsides.

Intentions as Judgements

David Pears

What are intentions? There are two answers that identify them with judgements, or, at least identify their formation with the making of judgements. One identifies the formation of an intention with the making of an unconditional value-judgement in favour of the project, while the other identifies it with the acquisition of the belief that one will carry out the project. In this essay I shall argue against both these identifications. If they are mistaken there must be many ways of doing this, but I shall confine myself to arguments which also suggest a positive answer to the question, what intentions are.

The positive answer is that they are dispositions. But I am not going to try to develop a defensible version of the disposition theory, which occupies the middle ground between the two judgement theories. There are well-known objections to it, but I shall try to show that the objections to its rivals are fatal, and so, if a simple argument by elimination is acceptable, some version of it must be defensible against the objections.

In the history of this subject, the theory that the formation of an intention is the making of an unconditional value-judgement has been found more attractive than the theory that it is the acquisition of the belief that one will carry out the project. I do not mean that many philosophers have actually adopted either theory, but that a number have moved towards them and that more have moved towards the valuational theory.

Hare holds that value-judgements imply self-addressed imperatives, assent to which necessarily involves the formation of appropriate intentions.[1] Davidson adopts a related view in 'How is weakness of the will possible?':[2] 'If an agent judges that it would be better for him to do x than to do y, and he believes

---

[1] R. M. Hare: *The Language of Morals*, pp. 19–21: Oxford 1952.
[2] D. Davidson: 'How is Weakness of the Will Possible?' p. 95, in *Moral Concepts*, ed. J. Feinberg: Oxford 1969.

himself to be free to do either x or y, then he will intentionally do x if he does either x or y intentionally.' His solution to the problem of akrasia implies that there is also a connection running the other way from doing x rather than y intentionally to the unconditional comparative value-judgement, that it would be better to do x than to do y: 'The akrates is characterized as holding that, all things considered, it would be better to do a than to do b, even though he does b rather than a, and with a reason. The logical difficulty has vanished because a judgement that a is better than b, all things considered, is a relational, or prima-facie, judgement, and so cannot conflict logically with any unconditional judgement.'[3] There would be no need to insist on this lack of conflict if the intentional action of the akrates were not connected with the unconditional judgement that b is better than a.

Evidently, these connections would be logical, but a philosopher who accepts them need not be identifying the formation of an intention with the making of an unconditional value-judgement. For they might be two distinct events even if each was necessarily accompanied by the other. The final step is taken by Davidson in his paper 'Intending'.[4] He identifies the formation of my intention to perform a ϕ action with the judgement that any ϕ action of mine would be desirable given the rest of what I believe about the immediate future. When I perform the action intentionally, the judgement that corresponds to, or is perhaps identical with it, is 'This action is desirable'.

The rival judgement theory has not proved so attractive. There are traces of it in G. F. Stout's 'Voluntary Action',[5] and Harman endorses a version of it in a recent article:[6] 'An intention is an idea of the future for which one has one sort of reason; a prediction is normally an idea for which one has another sort of reason. This is simply to say that an intention is an idea arrived at and maintained by practical reasoning, whereas a

---

[3] Ibid. p. 110.
[4] D. Davidson: 'Intending', University of N. Carolina Colloquium 1974, and in a slightly altered form in *Philosophy of History of Action* pp. 54–6, ed. Yivmiahu Yovel, D. Reidel 1978.
[5] In G. F. Stout: *Studies in Philosophy and Psychology*: London 1930.
[6] G. Harman: 'Practical Reasoning' p. 453, *Review of Metaphysics* Vol. 29, 1976.

prediction is normally an idea arrived at and maintained by theoretical reasoning.'

One reason why philosophers have been more attracted by the theory that intentions are unconditional value-judgements is that it is in a position to capture the effectiveness of intentions, whereas the rival theory, which identifies them with future factual beliefs, cannot secure that advantage for itself. Nobody thinks that all future factual beliefs are intentions, or that any, or more than a very few are effective. If we add the requirement that the belief be caused by the disposition to perform the action that would verify it, it will immediately appear more plausible to identify the intention with the disposition rather than with the belief. On the other side, Hare's account of making value-judgements actually is semi-dispositional, and perhaps Davidson's would have been, but for the difficulty of characterizing deviant causal chains.[7]

The source of this difference between the two judgement theories is not far to seek. If we draw a line representing the stepwise connections between an action and the desire and belief that caused it, the agent's belief that he will perform the action lies on a side-line. So a philosopher who begins by identifying the intention with the future factual belief caused in this way immediately finds it more plausible to locate the intention at the nodal point on the causal diagram. Where we locate an intention it must at least be possible to locate the basis of a similar-looking disposition.

This contrast in plausibility between the two judgement theories is compatible with the view that intentions imply future factual beliefs but do not imply unconditional value-judgements. (I shall defend the second part of this view in this essay and the first part of it in another essay.)[8] It may seem surprising that the more plausible of the two judgement theories should identify the formation of an intention with the making of a judgement that is not even implied by the sentence 'I intend to perform a ϕ action'. However, there are two reasons why this happens. First, intentions must be located on the main

[7] See Davidson: 'Freedom to Act' pp. 151-4 in *Freedom of Action*, ed. T. Honderich, London 1973.
[8] 'Intention and Belief' forthcoming in a Festschrift to D. Davidson, ed. Bruce Vermazen and Merrill Hintikka.

causal line from desire and belief to action. Second, it is not obvious that the sentence does not imply an unconditional value-judgement.

Does it? Before we try to answer this question, it is a good idea to remind ourselves that, even if it does, and even if there is also a logical connection running the other way, the making of the judgement and the formation of the intention may still be two distinct events. Suppose that a creature never acquired any future factual beliefs that were not connected with its intentions. It still would not follow that its formation of an intention ought to be identified with its acquisition of the connected future factual belief, and the most plausible causal diagram might show them as distinct events. The concomitant instantiation of two types is certainly not enough to prove the identity of the events instantiating the two types. There is also a constraint imposed by the flow of causation.

However, if there are intentions that are not accompanied by unconditional value-judgements, the case for identifying their formation with the making of the judgements will collapse. Let us test Davidson's version of this identification. Is it true that anyone who intends to perform a ϕ action judges that any ϕ action of his in the immediate future would be desirable given the rest of what he believes about the immediate future? This value-judgement is unconditional and implicitly comparative, and the field of comparison contains every alternative believed to be possible, including waiting to see how the immediate future actually develops.

It may seem obvious that someone can form an intention without making the corresponding value-judgement and without even having asked himself the question to which it would be an answer. But in such a case it is less obvious that the value-judgement would not express a thought that was essential to the formation of his intention. However, there certainly do appear to be cases of intentions formed merely as results of desires without the endorsement of any valuation. It is true that this appearance is often discounted by the argument that, if someone wants something, there must be some feature of what he wants that he finds desirable, and so even this source of intentions is valuational. But this is an argument of dubious validity. It is plausible to suppose that, when someone wants something, there will always be some feature of it that is desired by him. For example, it is the ϕ-ness of a ϕ action that is desired by him. But it does not follow that he finds ϕ-ness desirable in a valuational sense. Nor need it be true. Suppose that he had a perverse craving to eat coal. He might form an intention to eat some merely as a result of this desire without the endorsement of any valuation. It is irrelevant that he might value the indulgence of any desire, because it is also possible that he might not. All that is necessary is that he should have the desire, and the desire by itself cannot create a value for him.

If this reply to the argument is convincing, we are free to accept the appearances at face-value, and to take it that some intentions are formed merely as results of desires. This is the way in which many species of animal must form their intentions, or, at least, their analogues of intentions. Of course, if a creature responded only to present stimuli, there would be no case for ascribing intentions to it unless its response to one stimulus could be modified by the fact that it was going to respond in a particular way to another stimulus in the same field. Perhaps such short-lived dispositions would hardly count as intentions, but if it also had similar dispositions generated by past stimuli, the case for ascribing intentions to it would be stronger. We might still hesitate, but there would be no doubt that it had something very like intentions. It is plausible to argue that the same thing happens in us and that, when it does, intentions are unhesitatingly ascribed to us, perhaps because we are also capable of forming them in the valuational way. If this is right, the type-identification is blocked by examples of intentions located at a nodal point which has no connection with the making of value-judgements.

This result hardly affects the problem of akrasia. For even if intentions need not be based on valuations, it may be that they cannot flout them. It is a separate question, whether anyone who judges that any ϕ action of his in the immediate future would be desirable given the rest of what he believes about the immediate future necessarily intends to perform a ϕ action. Even this question does not touch all the problems of akrasia. It only asks whether the problem of akratic intentions is a problem of akratic valuational thought.

Before we deal with this problem, it is worth reminding

ourselves that practical reasoning from valuations would be intelligible even if intentions were not value-judgements. For actions are not value-judgements and yet they are deemed rational when and only when they accord with the agents' reasons. If rationality reaches beyond the line that separates the making of judgements from the doing of other things, intentions too may lie on the far side of the line.

But do they? Intuitions vary, but anyone who believes in the possibility of extreme akrasia has a strong reason for thinking that intentions cannot be value-judgements. In an extreme case of akrasia all the agent's considerations remain clearly in his mind all the time, and he forms the intention to do y rather than x in spite of his conditional judgement that, in relation to all the considerations known to him, x is better than y. Davidson's idea is that the identification of the intention to do y rather than x with the unconditional judgement that y is better than x allows us to exonerate the agent from the charge that he makes a logical mistake when he forms the intention. For his conditional judgement that x is better than y is logically compatible with his unconditional judgement that y is better than x.

However, it has often been objected that it is not easy to see what reason he could have for making this unconditional judgement. The obvious candidate, the value of y in relation to some available consideration, will not do, because the force of that reason has already been included and cancelled in his conditional judgement. He cannot be revoking that judgement, because, if he were, his action would not be akratic. He could be guessing that there are considerations, as yet unknown to him, which would lead him to revoke it, if they became known to him. But it would be quite unrealistic to suppose that it is typical of extreme cases of akrasia that the agent guesses that unknown considerations will let him off the hook.

Now when he makes no such guess, he cannot form his intention for a reason without self-deception, if forming it is making the unconditional value-judgement that y is better than x. Of course, he might deceive himself about the comparative value of y and x, but it is more difficult to make a judgement than to form an intention for a reason that is known to be overridden. For judgements tend to adjust to one another until consistency is achieved, but intentions and actions do not adjust so readily to judgements, because the will is more sensitive to other forces. It is true that the phenomenon of self-deception shows that judgements too are sensitive to other forces, but the will is more sensitive to them, because the formation and execution of an irrational intention tends to be more immediately rewarding than the making of an irrational judgement. It is, therefore, likely that in some cases of extreme akrasia the formation of the irrational intention will not be accompanied by the making of an irrational unconditional value-judgement. This certainly appears to happen and, if the explanation is convincing, there is no need to reject the appearance.

In such cases the cause of the formation of the irrational intention will be complex: it will include not only the valuational reason that is known to be overridden but also some auxiliary factor, and the most likely one is simply the desire to do y, which influences the will immediately in a way that is either totally rejected or only partially permitted by the conditional value-judgement. Naturally, the demand that the valuational reason be the sole, unaided cause of the formation of the irrational intention would take the case beyond the bounds of possibility.

If this account of extreme akrasia is convincing, it does not show that there is no necessary connection running from the making of an unconditional value-judgement to the formation of the corresponding intention, but it does strongly suggest that there is no such necessary connection. For there is often very little more irrationality in forming the intention to do y against the unconditional judgement that x is better than y than there would be in forming it against the conditional judgement that in relation to all considerations known to the agent x is better than y.

If this is right, it is understandable that the agent's intention-based attitude to the sentence 'I shall do it' is not directly caused by the making of an unconditional value-judgement. For though his attitude may not be as strong as belief, it must be an attitude that is as strong as is commonly attainable, and so it is likely to be caused by something that is a more reliable indication of action than the making of an unconditional value-judgement. This result, like the previous one, suggests that we should look for something else that occurs at the nodal point where intentions are formed.

When we do so, we face a familiar difficulty. If we describe what happens at the nodal point, we find that we are merely paraphrasing the statement that an intention is formed. On the other hand, if we try to get more details into our account, we find that we are mentioning things that occur at other points. Let us accept this predicament and treat the natural description of what happens at the nodal point as a clue to what happens elsewhere. It would be natural to say that a project is adopted and that the result is an intention that is definite and firm. This is circular, but it suggests two promising questions, 'How is it adopted?' and 'What is the effect of its adoption?'

One way of getting an answer to the first question would be to inquire why we might hesitate to ascribe intentions to a creature whose response to one stimulus could be modified by the fact that it was going to respond to another stimulus in a particular way. Some would hesitate for the Aristotelian reason that it made no value-judgements and merely had competing desires. Others would hesitate, because it did not form intentions, but, rather, they formed in it, if it had them at all, and they were not firm, but, at best, persistent.

These scruples about ascribing intentions are difficult to assess. Perhaps it does not matter that our intentions are not always the results of valuations, because they always could be, or that we do not always form them, because we always could form them. The real difficulty is that the creature might achieve mechanically what we achieve by reasoning from valuations. For its dispositions might be geared to living prudently, with occasional akratic lapses, just like us when we reason from valuations. There is a similar difficulty about the other suggested criterion. We certainly can form intentions intentionally, and when they remain with us we regard their firmness as something to which we can make an intentional contribution. Now we form and maintain our intentions not only in order to attain our deferred goals, which vary from case to case, but also occasionally for a further reason, which does not vary from case to case, the advantage of acquiring in advance, and being able to count on dispositions to perform particular actions.[9] But unfortunately, there could be a non-rational analogue of this further reason. Nature might have given the creature the capacity to feel the unpleasantness of indecision on a graduated scale that produced behaviour matching the intentions of a rational man in each predicament, so that it would never be caught like Buridan's ass and would respond to the occasional need to acquire a disposition before all the relevant stimuli had come in.

These difficulties may show that the two features are not necessary conditions of ascribing intentions, but they do not show that our ascriptions are not guided by them. Perhaps we need not be worried by the fact that they are not necessary conditions, because that can be explained in a way that leaves their importance undiminished. Nature has put such a large gap between the achievements of practical reason and the achievements of its analogue in non-reasoning animals that we have not been forced to choose between making our achievements criterial and making our method criterial.

It might be objected that it is circular to say that it must be possible to form intentions intentionally, even if this is not offered as a criterion. However, the circularity is harmless, because the fact, that it is always possible to form a secondary intention, is not being offered as a complete explication of the concept. It is a legitimate but small contribution to its explication to point out that forming an intention is something that people do, and so can form an intention to do.

But does it threaten an infinite regress? Harman thinks so, but argues that the regress is blocked by the fact that 'When one forms the intention to do A one intends to have the intention to do A, but these are not distinct intentions.... The intention to do A is in part the intention that one have that very intention. The intention to do A is the intention that, because of that very intention, it is guaranteed that one will do A.'[10]

This introduces two intentions which are claimed to be, or to be part of the intention to do A. One is the intention to have, and, therefore, earlier, to form the intention to do A. The other is the intention that, because of the intention to do A, it is guaranteed that one will do A. Each of those intentions may be

---
[9] A point emphasized by G. Harman, op. cit., s.2.
[10] Ibid. pp. 442–3.

part of the intention to do A, but if they are not identical with one another, they cannot both be identical with the intention to do A, and it cannot be argued that, because one of them is part of the intention to do A, the other must be too.

Is the intention to do A the intention that, because of that very intention, it is guaranteed that one will do A? Doubts might be felt about the strength of the guarantee and about the way in which it is included in the reflexive intention. The fact is that one intends only to make use of the guarantee, such as it is. So it might be better to reformulate the reflexive intention as 'the intention to do A as a result of that very intention'. It might still be doubted whether this intention is identical with the intention to do A, because 'intention to ...' is an opaque context. However, it is not implausible to credit agents with knowledge of such an essential part of the theory of intentions and acceptance of the identification.

If this is right, the intention to do A is essentially reflexive. but its reflexivity does not start an infinite regress. Many mental attitudes and performances are reflexive in this non-regressive and easily explicable way. If a person wishes that some event occur, and credits his wish with the magic power to bring about the event, he can say that he wishes that the event occur as a result of that very wish. If the second wish differed from the first, and this situation repeated itself at every stage in the specification of the contents of the resulting series of wishes, there would be an infinite regress. But the second wish does not differ from the first, and so there is no infinite regress.

If the reflexive intention to do A as the result of that very intention is identical with the intention to do A, it does not follow that the secondary intention to form the intention to do A is also identical with the intention to do A. That would require the identity of the reflexive intention and the secondary intention. But these two are evidently not identical with one another. It follows that we cannot identify both with the intention to do A. Nevertheless, the secondary intention might be part of the intention to do A.

Is it? If it is, then every intention involves a secondary intention to form that very intention and there really is an infinite regress, even if, as Harman argues, it is a harmless one. However, there is no reason to believe that every intention is necessarily shadowed by another in this way. It is true that after I have formed the intention to do A I will usually not regret it, and therefore, not revoke it, and this for whatever reason led me to form it. But this attitude cannot be represented as the intention to form the intention to do A, or even to have it, because I must form the intention to do A before I can have the attitude.

On the other hand, there is a secondary intention that I often form before I form the intention to do A. However, it is not the intention to form the intention to do A, but, rather, the intention to form some intention in the predicament that I see ahead of me. At this point I might be influenced by the reason that does not vary from case to case, the advantage of acquiring in advance a disposition to act in a determinate way. I might also be influenced by this reason in another type of case: I know that I can do A in one of two ways, but I have not chosen between them, and so, though I intend to do A, I still have to form another, subsidiary intention, and I can intend to form it not only for whatever reason led me to form the intention to do A but also for the invariant reason. These are two common kinds of secondary intention. There is also a third, uncommon case, in which I do form the intention to form the intention to do A. This is the case in which I want to do A but have to do something to myself in order to 'screw my courage to the sticking point' of forming the intention to do A, or, if I have already formed it, maintaining it.

Only secondary intentions of the last of these three kinds could threaten an infinite regress. However, like the other two kinds, they are not ever-present shadows of primary intentions but substantial additions to the history of the agent which occur only in special circumstances. Therefore, they do not start an infinite regress in all cases, but only a finite one in some cases.

It might be objected that this way of blocking the regress fails to take account of the essential reflexiveness of intentions. For if the intention to do A is the intention to do A as a result of that very intention, the formation of the intention to do A must be part of the agent's plan, and, if it is part of his plan, he must form the intention to form the intention to do A. So there is still a threat of an infinite regress of intentions, primary, secondary, tertiary, etc., and Harman's way of blocking it may seem to be our only resource: the higher-order intentions must already be included in the primary intention.

This goes against the apparent fact that, if I do form a secondary intention before I form the intention to do A, it will seldom and only in special circumstances be the intention to form, or maintain the intention to do A. How can this fact be reconciled with the nesting of intentions that seems to follow from their essential reflexiveness?

The nesting of intentions can be seen most clearly in the unusual kind of case in which wishful thinking is believed to be effective. A sick man wishes to get better, and believes that, if he believes that he will get better, he will. If he also believes that he can induce the belief, perhaps by hypnotic suggestion, he will intend to get better. But it looks as if he now need not bother to induce the belief, because having the intention he already has the belief. So Harman writes about a similar case, 'The belief is not distinct from the intention to go to heaven ... since [Pascal] forms his belief with that intention and the intention already involves the belief.'[11]

This is an unusual case, but Pascal's belief is certainly not incoherent. He believed that he would go to heaven because of that very belief, and perhaps he did. Nor is there any incoherence in a plan which includes the formation of the intention to achieve its own goal. If the sick man adopts his more economical plan, he will form the intention to get better because he believes that his intention-based belief, that he will get better, will make him better. It is true that, when he has formed the intention to get better, he will have already taken the first step towards carrying it out, and plans are seldom so labour-saving. But the possibility of this kind of plan is an acceptable consequence of the unusual structure of the example.

The example shows how this kind of nesting of intentions works. The man's formation of the intention to get better is part of his plan for getting better. In ordinary cases, when an agent adopts a plan, he forms the intention to implement each part of it. So it might seem that in this unusual case, he must form the secondary intention to form the intention to do A. However, that does not follow. For when he adopts this plan, he will say to

[11] Ibid. pp. 454–5.

himself, 'I shall get better as a result of the belief based on this very intention.' So he will realize that he has already implemented the first part of the plan, and therefore, cannot form the intention to implement it. True, at some earlier point in his deliberations he may form a secondary intention. But that possibility is not peculiar to this unusual kind of case, and it may be treated in the same way as in ordinary cases: there is no need for a secondary intention, and, if there is a secondary intention, it is unlikely to be the intention to form the intention to do A.

Can we now transfer this result to the ordinary case and use it against the argument that, if the intention to do A is the intention to do A as a result of that very intention, the formation of the intention to do A must be part of the agent's plan, and, if it is part of his plan, he must form the intention to form the intention to do A?

It would seem so. Intentions are effective and reflexive. Therefore in any ordinary case the formation of the agent's intention may be regarded as part of his plan. True, it is an omnipresent part, and so it does not need to be mentioned in the specification of his plan. Nevertheless, it is part of his plan, and this suggests that he might have to form the intention to form it. However, this suggestion is as misleading as it was in the unusual case. For the formation of his intention to do A is not his way of getting himself to do A.[12] It could be his way of getting himself to do A only if he had already formed the intention to do A and used it as a device for 'screwing his courage to the sticking point' of actually doing A. But his intention to do A cannot play that role. On the contrary, when he has formed it, he will realize that he has already implemented the first part of his plan. It is, of course, the limiting case of a part of a plan, but even if it had been a substantial part of his plan, like the belief in the unusual example, there is no way of showing that it necessarily involves the secondary intention to form the intention to do A. It comes too late for that.

If this is right, the essential reflexiveness of intentions does not threaten an infinite regress which would have to be shown

---

[12] Harman says that it is. Ibid. pp. 440–1.

to be harmless. There is, therefore, no need to suppose that every primary intention contains a secondary intention as part of itself, and so on.

The other promising question suggested by the description of what happens at the nodal point was 'What are the effects of the adoption of a project?' It has already been shown that, though first-order intentions promote their own execution and their peculiar kind of effectiveness is advantageous to the species, I do not form a first-order intention in order to get myself to carry it out. The same is true of the other effect. I do not form a first-order intention in order to acquire the belief that I shall carry it out, but only, perhaps, in order to acquire some belief about what I shall do.

If we concentrate on examples of single actions, intentions seem extraordinarily elusive and evanescent, and an ontological reduction, like Davidson's, strikes us as not too unnatural. It seems that, if an intention is important, it must be identical with something that explains the action, perhaps with the last step in practical reasoning from valuations. However, if we take into consideration examples of linked sequences of actions, we can see that intentions are also important in another way. They put the agent and sometimes others in a position to act and plan on, and make inferences from the assumption that he will perform a particular action. It does not follow that intentions are not value-judgements, but it does follow that the nodal point at which they are located may be pulled further down the causal line by the requirement that the assumption be as firm as is commonly possible.

We may suppose that in the agent's mind the assumption is a belief. (This needs to be qualified, but the qualifications would not affect my present argument.)[13] Now it is sometimes argued that the reason why I cannot intend to do what I believe to be impossible is that 'I intend to do A' implies 'I believe that I shall do A'. Davidson treats the connection as a cancellable implicature rather than an implication,[14] but even if it is an implication, there is another, independent reason why I cannot intend to do what I believe to be impossible. Quite apart from believed possibility in relation to my capacities and

[13] See my 'Intention and Belief'.
[14] D. Davidson, 'Intending', p. 58.

circumstances, I must believe that my project is intrinsically possible. So even if intending carried no implication of future factual belief, I would still have to believe that all the parts of my project were physically and logically compatible with one another. The things that I now intend to do must be compatible conjuncts. This is equally true of the things that I now hope to do, however sceptical I may be of complete success, but not true of the things that I now want to do, unless I am using the verb 'to want' in an additive way.

We need to be able to count on our own and other people's future actions. The theory that intentions are future factual beliefs is an exaggerated tribute to the importance of this aspect of intending. I have tried to explain why it is less plausible than the rival ontological reduction to value-judgements. I shall now try to show that it has no plausibility whatsoever.

The source of its weakness is located by Grice in his lecture 'Intention and Uncertainty'. If an intention were a future factual belief it would be absurd to regard it as the cause of the action. But nobody regards it as absurd. On the contrary, it is arguable that the content of the agent's belief when he intends to do A is that he will do A because he intends to do it. Of course, not all future factual beliefs could be identified with intentions, and it is necessary to pick out those that are caused by a desire to perform the action. However, that does not remove the absurdity, because it still represents intentions as pieces of 'arbitrarily licensed wishful thinking'.[15]

One way to appreciate the absurdity is to contrast the special case in which the sick man supposes that his intention-based belief will make him better with the ordinary case in which he does not suppose that it will make him better. In the special case he accepts the theory that belief in the effect will actually produce it. In the ordinary case he has no such theory. Consequently, in the ordinary case it would be absurd to suppose that belief in the effect would actually produce it. But we all suppose that intentions often produce the desired effects. Therefore intentions cannot be future factual beliefs. The intention must lie on the main causal line to the action, but the belief lies on a side-line.

[15] See H. P. Grice: 'Intention and Uncertainty' p. 268, *Proceedings of the British Academy* Vol. lvii 1971.

If this is right, the theory that intentions are future factual beliefs must be wrong. If my earlier arguments against the rival judgement theory are also right, the way is open to a consideration of the theory that intentions are dispositions, with a strong presumption that it must be possible to defend it against the well-known objections.

Prima-facie Obligations

John R. Searle[1]

In one of his earliest articles[2] Strawson offers a brief but powerful criticism of the notion of a prima-facie obligation. In spite of his criticism this notion continues to be commonly used in discussions of moral philosophy. I believe that the notion as it has been used by a series of authors from Ross to Hintikka is confused, and these confusions underlie several other philosophical mistakes, some of them contained in various criticisms of my derivation of 'ought' from 'is'.[3] My aim in this article is not to discuss Strawson's views, but to continue a line of argument that he began.

I

The first thing to notice about the notion of a prima-facie obligation (or duty) is that it is not a term in ordinary discourse, moral or otherwise, but is a technical term introduced by philosophers in discussing problems of moral philosophy. As such, one might hope to find some fairly clear explanation of the notion, but the discussions I have seen of this notion are extremely confused. Some, though by no means all of the confusion is due to Ross, who first introduced the distinction between prima-facie duties (and obligations) and some other kind of duties (and obligations).[4] I shall not spend much space

---

[1] This article was first written in 1975 for inclusion in the present volume, but in the meantime a portion of it has appeared in *Practical Reasoning*, ed. Joseph Raz (Oxford Readings in Philosophy, 1979).

[2] Strawson, P. F., 'Ethical Intuitionism' in Sellars and Hospers (eds.), *Readings in Ethical Theory*, 1952, pp. 250–9.

[3] Searle, John R., 'How to Derive "Ought" from "Is"', *Philosophical Review*, Jan. 1964, pp. 43–58.

[4] Ross, W. D., *The Right and the Good*, pp. 19 ff, Oxford, 1930. Ross speaks mostly of *prima facie* duties rather than obligations. I shall speak mostly of obligations because it seems to be a more accurate characterization of many of the cases in question. For example the 'obligation to keep a promise' seems to me more accurate than 'the duty to keep a promise' because duties in general are relative to some specific status or position that one occupies, e.g. one's duties as a father, or as a teacher.

on Ross's account, because it does not seem to me that it can be made consistent internally. But when any new technical term is introduced in philosophy without explicit definition, there are at least two questions one must ask of it; Ross answered these questions and his answers have influenced his successors. The two questions are, what motivates the introduction of the term in the first place, and what other terms is it opposed to? Ross's answer to the first question is reasonably clear:

> If, as almost all moralists except Kant are agreed, and as most plain men think, it is sometimes right to tell a lie or break a promise, it must be maintained that there is a difference between *prima facie* duty and actual or absolute duty. When we think ourselves justified in breaking, and indeed morally obliged to break, a promise in order to relieve someone's distress, we do not for a moment cease to recognize a *prima facie* duty to keep our promise, and this leads us to feel, not indeed shame or repentance, but certainly compunction, for behaving as we do; we recognize further, that it is our duty to make up somehow to the promisee for the breaking of the promise.[5]

The picture that Ross has is this: In real life situations one often has conflicting duties, obligations, etc. For example, I may have an obligation to Smith to attend his party (because, let us say I promised to come) and also an obligation to stay and help Jones (because, let us say, he is bleeding to death and crying for my help). In such a case I am justified in breaking the promise. In such a case the obligation to keep the promise, says Ross, is only a prima-facie obligation. For future reference let us call situations of this sort, where there is a conflict of reasons of a generally 'moral' kind *conflict situations*, and this particular example *the conflict situation*. The notion of prima-facie duty or obligation in Ross's account is introduced to characterize certain features of conflict situations.

But Ross's answer to the second question is much less clear. He begins[6] by opposing prima-facie duty to 'duty *sans phrase*' or 'duty proper'. Later, in the passage quoted above he opposes prima-facie duty to 'actual or absolute duty'. This multiplicity of opposing terms is inherited by his followers. Thus Hintikka[7]

---
[5] *Ibid.*, p. 28.
[6] *Ibid.*, p. 19.
[7] Hintikka, J., 'Deontic Logic and its Philosophical Morals' in *Models for Modalities*, D. Reidel & Co., 1969, pp. 184–214.

opposes prima-facie obligations to 'actual', 'absolute', and 'over-all' obligations, treating all of these as equivalent, at least for purposes of making the contrast. But this multiplicity of contrasting terms ought to arouse our suspicions. They are by no means equivalent, and there are in fact at least two quite different distinctions lurking in the notion of a prima-facie obligation, and these in turn provide two different and inconsistent descriptions of the conflict situation.

The first distinction: prima-facie vs. actual obligations:
According to one version of the notion of prima-facie obligations, which we might call Ross's official view, to say that

(1) X has a prima-facie obligation to do A.

does not entail

(2) X has an obligation to do A,

because it is consistent with

(3) X does not really have any obligation at all to do A, he only *seems* to have that obligation.

On this account prima-facie obligations are contrasted with actual or real ones and the correct way to describe the conflict situation is to say that

(4) I have no obligation at all to keep my promise. I do indeed *seem* to have an obligation, because promise keeping, as Ross says, has a 'tendency to be our duty', but when all the facts are known it turns out that I have an obligation to help Jones, but none whatever to go to Smith's party.

I shall later argue that this is a false description of the conflict situation. It is, however, the one which Ross explicitly endorses and which his theory commits him to holding. An immediate difficulty with it is that on this view the promise in the conflict situation ends up counting for nothing. It is exactly as if I had never made a promise at all. Ross is uncomfortable with this result, because it is hard to make it consistent with his original remarks about conflict situations quoted above. If there is no real or actual obligation at all, then what is it exactly that I 'do not for a moment cease to recognize'? And why should I feel any 'compunction' or 'make up' anything to the promisee if I have no real or actual obligation to him? Ross's remarks about tendencies are clearly not sufficient to obviate this inconsistency. To say, as he does, that promise-keeping has a 'tendency' to be our duty is like saying glass windows have a tendency to break when struck. If I strike this window and it does not break, it is just as unbroken as if I had never struck it at all. Similarly if all that promises do is generate tendencies to be duties, then the fact that in this case I have no duty at all to keep the promise renders the conflict situation exactly as if I had never made a promise in the first place, for in this case the 'tendency' is inoperative. But this view is unacceptable because it makes it mysterious and inexplicable that I should have any 'compunction' about breaking the promise and that I should have 'a duty to make up to the promisee for the breaking of the promise'. If the promise does not create any actual obligations but only seems to ('prima facie') then I should be able to ignore it altogether once all the facts are known. This difficulty with Ross's conception of prima-facie obligations leads to a second conception of prima-facie obligations which is implicit in Ross and explicit in other authors such as Hintikka.

The second distinction: prima-facie vs. absolute obligations:
According to this second version of the notion of prima-facie obligations which Ross denies that he holds, but which I believe some features of his account presuppose, to say that

(1) X has a prima-facie obligation to do A

does indeed entail

(2) X has an obligation to do A

but only because

(5) Prima-facie obligations are a species or kind of obligations. They are inherently subject to being overruled or overridden by other obligations (and other reasons for acting in conflict situations). An obligation that overrides them is called an absolute obligation. Relative to a given situation, a prima-facie obligation can become an absolute obligation if it overrides all other obligations.

Ross explicitly denies that he thinks of prima-facie obligations as a kind of obligation (p. 20), but unless we suppose that in some sense prima-facie obligations are a kind of obligation it is very hard to make sense of his account. For example he actually provides a list of the principal types of prima-facie duties (p. 21 ff.); also, he provides an analogy between the way different prima-facie obligations produce a resultant obligation and the way different forces operating on a body produce a resultant velocity (pp. 28–9). Unless we think of prima-facie obligations as a kind of actual obligations, like actual forces operating on a body, there is no point to the analogy. But, most importantly, his description of conflict situations, with all his talk of our 'compunctions', etc. for promises broken, makes no sense unless we ascribe some actual status to the prima-facie obligations, that is, unless we think of them as a kind of obligation. Ross apart, I am here primarily concerned to argue that there are in fact two different contrasts contained in the notion of prima-facie obligations. Whether or not Ross held the second, other philosophers certainly have.

According to the second contrast the proper way to describe the conflict situation is:

(6) In the conflict situation there actually are two inconsistent obligations. However, one is of a lower status than the other. It is only a prima-facie obligation and it is overruled by the other, which is an absolute obligation. The prima-facie obligation, however, does not cease to exist, it is simply a member of a class of obligations, the prima-facie class, which are less compelling than the absolute class.

II

The foregoing is an attempt to bring some sort of order into the discussions about, and those discussions which use, the notion of prima-facie obligations.

Its result, however, is that there are two quite distinct notions and they are not consistent, that is, if 'obligation' is supposed to be univocal, then the two contrasts provide inconsistent descriptions of the conflict situation, for on the first version there is no obligation at all to keep the promise and on the second version there is. Is there any way out of this inconsistency? and more generally is there any merit in these distinctions and their attendant terminology? I think the views embodied in both contrasts are mistaken—though there is more truth in the second than in the first—and we would do well in philosophy to abandon the terminology of prima-facie obligations and duties as it embodies confusions.

What is the correct way to describe the status of the obligations in conflict situations? The first point to emphasize is that most moral conflicts in real life are cases where there are genuinely valid reasons for doing one thing and at the same time reasons for not doing that thing but doing something inconsistent with it. In the case of conflicting obligations of the sort that we described above one is under an obligation to do one thing (go to the party) and at the same time one is under an obligation to do something inconsistent with it (stay and help the bleeding Jones). That is, using obvious abbreviations,[8] the basic terms of the conflict situation are

(7) (Op&Oq)& −poss(p&q).

In extreme cases I may have an obligation to do one thing and another independent obligation not to do that very same thing:

(8) Op&O−p

I would argue that where the possibility in question in 7 is logical possibility, that is, where q entails −p, 8 follows from 7. But whether or not that is a correct view of entailed obligations, both 7 and 8 describe the form of common conflict situations in real life: one has two obligations which are such that it is impossible to fulfil both. The states of affairs described by 7 and 8 are not only logically possible, they are what the study of

[8] Here and throughout I follow the practice of most deontic logicians in allowing the deontic operator to have propositional variables in its scope. But of course this is very unrealistic. Most, e.g. obligations are requirements on *people* that they perform certain *actions*. And this is not at all the same as a subjectless requirement that something be the case. 'Jones is under an obligation to leave the house' does not mean the same as 'It is obligatory that Jones leave the house', for I can satisfy the latter by physically throwing Jones out, but only Jones can satisfy the former. I ask the scrupulous reader to forgive the use of the barbarous 'Op', which should be read, e.g. as 'the person referred to in proposition p is under an obligation to do the act mentioned in p', and not as e.g. 'It is obligatory that p be the case.'

moral conflict, logically speaking, is all about. In some systems of deontic logic it is denied that 7 and 8 are logically possible; and it is even claimed that $Op \supset -O-p$ is a law of deontic logic. But this simply prevents such systems from having any interesting application to real life. The reason for claiming that Op implies $-O-p$ is presumably that it is awkward to construct a semantic model for a deontic calculus which allows 7 and 8, but that should not be surprising since the notion of a genuine moral conflict is a notion of a situation where there is no possible world which satisfies all one's obligations (duties, etc.).

Many philosophers—and not just Ross—have tried to deny that 7 and 8 correctly represent the structure of conflict situations, but there is no way that these denials can account for certain obvious features of moral conflicts, as we shall shortly see. Now, because 7 and 8 give the logical structure of conflict situations it is important to note that the negation of Op is not $O-p$, but rather $-Op$; that is the negation of 'X is under an obligation to do A' is 'It is not the case that X is under an obligation to do A' and not 'X is under an obligation not to do A' since one can be under independent obligations both to do and not to do A.

Now when one is in a situation of the sort represented by 7 and 8, one cannot act so as to satisfy both obligations. One obligation has to *override* another if one is to satisfy either. Often in real life it will be obvious how to resolve the conflict, and in the example we gave above the obligation to attend the party is quite trivial relative to the obligation to help Jones. But in the hard cases one may simply not be able to decide what to do on rational grounds alone. Reflection on the relative weights of our obligations (and commitments and duties and other sorts of reasons) may not be sufficient to provide a rational answer to 'What ought we to do, all things considered?'

This account of the conflict situation will provide a basis for seeing what is wrong with the two previous accounts. On the first account, 7 and 8 do not really represent conflict situations, because one of the obligations does not really exist at all, it is only 'prima-facie' and not real and hence there really is no such obligation. There are so many things wrong with this account that one hardly knows where to begin to criticize it, but here are three obvious objections to it. First, if taken seriously, it has the consequence of denying the obvious fact about human experience that there really are moral conflicts. According to it one element in the conflict is not really there at all. Second it becomes impossible on this account to describe the situation in which one obligation overrides another. In order for one obligation to override another, or to be more important than another, or to take precedence over another, the other has to be there in the first place, otherwise there is nothing to override. It is a paradoxical feature of this account that it denies the crucial feature of conflict situations—conflicting obligations where one overrides another—which gave rise to the doctrine in the first place. Third, the thesis denies such obvious conceptual truths as that promises create obligations. What its adherents are forced to claim is that promises create prima-facie obligations, but on this version all that can mean is that promises *seem to* create obligations or, on Ross's version, they *tend* to create obligations, but in cases where the obligations they seem or tend to create are overridden by other obligations they do not create any obligations at all. It is, I think, not surprising that no adherent of this view has ever given an adequate analysis of promising. I conclude that the first version of prima-facie obligations must be abandoned. It is simply a mistake to conclude from the features of the conflict situation that the obligation to keep the promise does not exist, that is not a real obligation.

But what about the second version? It at least has the merit of granting that conflicting obligations can actually exist and continue to exist even when one overrides another. Furthermore, it has the merit of recognizing the distinction between a weaker and a stronger obligation in cases like the conflict situation; but such cases hardly give any grip to the view that there are two distinct *classes* of obligations, prima-facie and absolute, because what is absolute in one situation may be prima-facie in another. For example, my obligation to help Jones may be overridden by my obligation to prevent an explosion which will otherwise destroy the whole city. That is, if the prima-facie versus absolute distinction is construed in terms of relative moral strengths then whether or not an obligation was prima-facie or absolute would depend on the particular conflict situation under consideration and we would not be able to specify two separate classes of obligations independently of specifying different conflict situations. To make this point clear we need to distinguish between particular statements of obligation such as

(9)   Brown is under an obligation to do A because he promised to do A

and general statements of obligations such as

(10)   All promises create obligations on the promissor.

The question we are now asking is can we make any sense of the distinction between prima-facie and absolute obligations construed as species of obligations where 'prima-facie' and 'absolute' are supposed to be prefixed to 'obligation(s)' in sentences of the kind exemplified by 9 and 10. In the particular cases, such as 9, we will not be able to get two independent classes of obligations because, if the criterion is overridingness, then the obligation in 9 may be absolute relative to one conflict situation and prima-facie relative to another. If on the other hand we think of the prima-facie absolute distinction as applying to general statements of obligation such as 10, then we would get the result that all types of obligations (or at least all minus one) are prima-facie. This is because any obligation is subject to being overridden by special considerations in particular circumstances. That is, given the reasonable assumptions that any two general obligations can conflict in particular (actual or possible) conflict situations and that overridingness is a transitive relation, then there could mathematically speaking be at most one absolute general obligation, because there could be at most one obligation such that it overrides all others and no others override it. In neither case, the particular or the general, do we get a useful classification of obligations into two kinds, prima-facie and absolute. Furthermore, actual conflict situations can be readily and accurately described without introducing this muddled terminology. The correct account of the way obligations relate to conflict situations is the following. Obligations (and similarly with duties, responsibilities, commitments, etc.) provide reasons for acting. Obligations for various purposes may be divided into or categorized as legal, financial, social, moral, parental, etc. and the classes are not in general exclusive. Often in particular situations our obligations are in conflict with each other and with moral as well as other sorts of reasons for acting. Sometimes it will be clear how to resolve the conflict, but sometimes it will not.

The terminology of 'prima-facie obligations' has survived in philosophy not in spite of but because of its ambiguity. Many philosophers are inclined to say that in conflict situations, the weaker obligations do not exist at all. But the obvious falsity of this position is an embarrassment, and the embarrassment is masked by saying it is only a 'prima-facie obligation'.

Is there any sense at all to the distinction between prima-facie obligation and something else, whatever it might be? As so often in philosophy, there is a genuine and valid distinction to be marked even though the terminology is a source of confusion. Consider the differences and similarities between the members of the following list

(a) Jones has an obligation to do A
(b) Jones has a duty to do A
(c) It would be a good thing if Jones did A
(d) Jones ought, other things being equal, to do A
(e) Jones ought to do A
(f) All things considered, Jones ought to do A.

No two members of this list are synonymous though they are obviously related in certain ways. Deontic logic has been a source of confusion here because various nonsynonymous members of this list have been offered as readings for the deontic operator O sometimes even in the same work. Now the correct insight that underlies the muddled jargon of prima-facie is simply this: Because (a) entails (d) but not(f), the assertion of (a) is consistent with the denial of (f) and indeed with the assertion of

(g) All things considered, Jones ought not to do A.

In characteristic conflict situations, statements of the form (a) and (g) are both true. That is what is meant by saying that the obligations to do A is overridden by some more important consideration. The truth, then, that underlies the prima-facie jargon is that in conflict situations one can both have an actual (real, valid, honest-to-john) obligation and yet one ought not, all things considered, do what one is under an obligation to do. The reason people have felt uncomfortable about this is that it sounds odd to say (a) *simpliciter* in cases where (g) is true, and this has led to the twin mistakes of supposing that (a) is not an actual but only a prima-facie obligation, or of supposing that it is a member of a special species of low grade obligations (prima-facie vs. absolute). But the reason for the oddness of saying (a) *simpliciter* derives from the principles of conversation and not from the semantics of 'obligation'. On the principle that one should give the maximum amount of relevant information, it would be misleading to say (a) *simpliciter* if one knew that (g) was true. Because (a) entails (d), that is, because obligations give reasons for action and 'ought' expresses reasons for action, one's saying (a) can be an indirect way of saying (e) or even (f). One can indirectly tell someone that he ought to do something by telling him that he has reason for doing it. But to use Grice's term, that is a matter of implicature and not of entailment. (a) does not entail (f) and it is not inconsistent with (g). So there is a third distinction underlying the traditional terminology, and it is indeed a valid distinction, between what one has an obligation to do what one ought to do all things considered. But this distinction is marked quite clearly in ordinary language and does not require the introduction of the term prima-facie to mark it.

But how would one formalize any such a distinction as this? The answer I think is quite obvious. If one is to have a symbolism that accounts for conflict situations, one will need (at least) two deontic operators to express the distinctions between (a) and (b) on the one hand and (f) on the other.[9] Let us introduce $O_1, O_2, \ldots O_n$ for the different obligations and duties that may be asserted to exist in statements of form (a) and (b). Let us use O^* for the deontic notion in (f). Then the conjunction of (a), (b), and (g) would be symbolized

(11) $O_1 p \& O_2 p \& O^* - p.$

And the conjunction (a) and

---

[9] A similar distinction is made by H. Castaneda, 'On the Semantics of Ought-to-do' in Davidson and Harman (eds.), *Semantics of Natural Language*, Reidel, 1972.

(h) Jones has an obligation not to do A

would be symbolized

(12) $O_1 p \,\&\, O_2 {-} p$

and these remove even the appearance of a logical inconsistency in the description of the conflict situation, because neither

(13) $O_1 p \supset {-} O_2 {-} p$

nor

(14) $O_1 p \supset {-} O^* {-} p$

are valid, unlike

(15) $O^* p \supset {-} O^* {-} p$

which is valid. 13 denies falsely that there can be inconsistent obligations, and 14 denies falsely that what one is under an obligation to do can be inconsistent with what one ought to do all things considered. 15 asserts truly that if one ought to do some particular thing, all things considered, then it is not the case that, all things considered, one ought not to do that very thing.

The results of our investigation so far may be summarized as follows: There are three possible ways to construe the alleged distinction between prima-facie and some other kinds of obligation, as the distinction is supposed to apply to conflict situations:

The first is the distinction between what are really obligations and what only seem to be obligations but are not in fact. This provides a mistaken description of the conflict situation.

The second is the distinction between two kinds or species of obligations, and this also provides a mistaken description.

The third is not a distinction of kinds of obligations, but a distinction between different kinds of deontic statements. It is a distinction between statements asserting the existence of obligations, duties, and other such reasons for acting and statements asserting what one ought to do all things considered. This third distinction enables us to give a correct description of the conflict situation; because it enables us to describe the fact that one may have inconsistent obligations and the fact that what one ought to do all things considered may be inconsistent with one or more of one's obligations, without either denying the existence of any of one's obligations of dividing them up into categories of absolute and prima-facie.

III

In two articles, 'Deontic Logic and its Philosophical Morals',[10] and 'Some Main Problems of Deontic Logic',[11] Jaakko Hintikka has attempted to analyse the notion of a prima-facie obligation in terms of formal features of his system of deontic logic. As the account in the second article is taken verbatim from the first I will confine my references to the first.

Hintikka distinguishes between

(11) $O(p \supset q)$

and

(12) $p \supset Oq$.

Concerning this distinction he makes two claims: first that the distinction between 11 and 12 expresses the distinction between prima-facie obligations (11) and absolute obligations (12) and secondly that an understanding of this distinction will expose what he alleges is a fallacy in my derivation of 'ought' from 'is'. I believe he is mistaken on both counts. The distinction between 11 and 12 has no relevance to the alleged distinction between prime-facie obligations and absolute obligations and it has no bearing on the derivation of 'ought' from 'is'.

The distinction of form between 11 and 12 is commonly remarked in philosophy in a variety of contexts. These forms are exemplified by the distinction between a conditional probability and the probability of a conditional, also by the distinction between a conditional speech act and the corresponding speech act of the conditional (between 'if p then $F(q)$' and 'F(if p then q)') and also by the distinction between conditional necessity and the necessity of a conditional (between $p \supset Lq$ and $L(p \supset q)$). In its deontic form the distinction is between the obligation to fulfil a conditional and a conditional obliga-

---

[10] See fn. 6, above.
[11] 'Some Main Problems of Deontic Logic', in *Deontic Logic Introductory and Systematic Readings*, ed. Risto Hilpinen (Dordrecht, 1971), pp. 59–104.

Prima-facie *Obligations* 251

tion. Why does Hintikka suppose that this familiar distinction casts any light at all on the alleged distinction between prima-facie and absolute obligations? It is not at all initially plausible to suppose that these distinctions discussed in the previous section can be explicated in terms of the distinction between 11 and 12, for it amounts to saying that the alleged distinction between prima-facie and absolute obligations is really a distinction between two kinds of absolute obligations, the absolute obligation to fulfil a conditional and the conditional absolute obligation. That is, if O is univocal in 11 and 12, it is just as absolute in one case as it is in the other; it simply has a different scope in the two cases. Why should this difference of scope explain either what Ross or Hintikka himself might have had in mind in their discussions of prima-facie obligations? This question becomes especially pressing when one reflects that 11 attaches no obligation to q, even on the assumption that p. That is, neither 'O(p ⊃ q)' nor 'O(p ⊃ q) & p' entail 'Oq' in any sense of 'O' that has been suggested.

Hintikka's answer to these questions is at best sketchy. First he imagines a conflict situation of the sort I described above, where a man's obligations to keep his promise is overridden by an obligation to see his father, who has fallen ill (p. 203):

Our distinction between 11 and 12 [my numbers] enables us to see precisely what has gone wrong in such a case. It is obviously and clearly true, even in the case of a promise overruled, that *in a deontically perfect world* such a promise cannot be given without keeping it. In such a world p cannot be realized without bringing it about that q. Even if the act of promising does not give rise to an actual duty to keep the promise (e.g. because of other duties), it nonetheless remains true that in this sense giving a promise commits one to keeping it.

The sense of commitment involved here is clearly 11. Thus it may be said that we need sense 11 to account for the possibility that a perfectly genuine commitment (e.g. a valid promise) may be overruled by other obligations, while 12 is needed to do justice to the conceptual fact that it sometimes does result in *actual* duties. (p. 203)

But this passage gives no support whatever to the view that 11 rather than 12 captures the notion of a prima-facie obligation on any of the three interpretations of this notion, because the notion of a deontically perfect world, a world where 'a promise cannot be given without keeping it' applies to 11 and

12 equally. That is, in such a world if 11 is true and p is true then q must be true as well. But similarly if 12 is true and p is true then q must be true as well. The fact that 11 is such that in a deontically perfect world if it is true then 'p cannot be realized without bringing it about that q' does not serve to distinguish it from 12 as far as elucidating the notion of prima-facie obligations is concerned, since exactly the same condition holds for 12. Hintikka's argument then produces no reason at all for accepting 11 rather than 12 as elucidating the notion of prima-facie obligation, it only seems to him to do so because he has already concluded that 12 is not even a candidate for the role. And the reason that he has already excluded 12 is clear from the rest of his text: 12, given p entails Oq by *modus ponens*. But Oq is such that in Hintikka's system it cannot be overridden, 'O' means 'acutal or absolute' obligation. And since prima-facie obligations by definition can be overridden, 12 cannot be a candidate for a statement of prima-facie obligations. 11 therefore is the only candidate that comes to hand if he is to have prima-facie obligations in his system at all. Now it is of course open to him to define his deontic operators as he likes and he can certainly define O in such a way that $Op \supset -O-p$ is valid in his system and this excludes Op from being overridden by conflicting obligations, but this terminological point provides no argument at all for saying that 11 rather than 12 is the *form* of prima-facie obligation statements, because it gives no reason at all for saying that the property of overridingness has anything at all to do with one *form* (11) rather than the other (12). What Hintikka would need to do to establish his claim is to show that the property of overridingness or non-overridingness of obligations—if one may so speak—is essentially a matter of the operator scope of certain sentences, but his argument fails to show this.

But showing his claims to be unjustified is not the same as showing they are false, a task to which I now turn. Let us consider the consequences of treating one of Ross's statements of prima-facie obligation as being of the form 11, as proposed by Hintikka. It is not at all easy to do this because the statements in question in Ross are not conditional in form to start with; whereas both of Hintikka's candidates for prima-facie and absolute obligation statements are conditional. In order to give

Prima-facie *Obligations* 253

his theory a fair run for its money let us transform one of Ross's examples into the conditional and try it out à la Hintikka. Consider

(13) If one makes a promise one is under an obligation to do the thing promised.

According to Hintikka this is of the form 11. That is, it should be read as

(14) One is under an absolute obligation to bring it about that (if one makes a promise to do A then one does A)

But since by contraposition 11 is equivalent to

(15) $O(-q \supset -p)$

then 14 is equivalent to

(16) One is under an absolute obligation to bring it about that (if one does not do A then one does not promise to do A).

And since in the conflict cases we have been considering the prima-facie obligation to do A is overridden by the absolute obligation not to do A then the extra premiss

(17) $O\text{-}q$
One is under an absolute obligation not to do A

entails

(18) $O\text{-}p$

One is under an absolute obligation not to promise to do A.

Thus on Hintikka's reading of Ross's prima-facie obligations to keep a promise, in the conflict situation there is an absolute obligation never to have made the promise in the first place. Hintikka recognizes this consequence but he fails to see that it is a *reductio ad absurdum* of his analysis. It is a *reductio ad absurdum* because Ross's notion of a prima-facie obligation was introduced to account for cases where one's 'morally' *neutral* act of promising creates an obligation which is overridden by some more important consideration. It is not part of Ross's notion that in such cases the act of promising is absolutely prohibited, i.e. that there is an absolute obligation never to have made the promise in the first place. There are indeed other readings of the deontic operator where 18 is true, e.g.

(19) It would have been a good thing if one had not made the promise in the first place.

But that reading is not open to Hintikka because his analysis requires O to be read as absolute or actual obligation in order to define prima-facie obligations in terms of the contrast between 11 and 12.

If it is not immediately obvious that we have produced a *reductio ad absurdum* of his analysis, there is a very simple argument that will demonstrate it. Just as the obligation to keep a promise can be overridden by some superior moral consideration, so the obligation not to make a promise which is overridden by some superior moral consideration can itself be overridden by some superior moral consideration. Thus, the obligation not to make an overridden promise can at best be prima-facie though it is a consequence of Hintikka's system that it must be absolute. Consider a conflict situation in which I have to *make* a promise to do something in order to save a man's life. Suppose further I later discover that I ought not to *keep* the promise because of some overriding moral reason. In such a case I ought all things considered to have made the promise and I ought all things considered to have broken it. Precisely the same sort of consideration that led both Ross and Hintikka to describe the obligation to keep the promise in conflict situations as only prima-facie would also force Hintikka to regard the obligation not to make such a promise as only prima-facie. But such a case would produce a straightforward inconsistency in Hintikka's system. For on his reading we have Op, $O(p \supset q)$, and $O-q$ as premisses. From which we can derive Op & $O-p$.

This inconsistency is not the only thing wrong with Hintikka's account. His 'explicit reconstruction' of the distinction between prima-facie and absolute obligations inherits the inconsistency of his general account', but it has some additional weaknesses:

In order to obtain an explicit reconstruction of the distinction prima-facie obligation vs. absolute obligation, let us consider some set of normative principles whose conjunction is n (the sentences formulating these principles may be of the form Oq, but they may also exemplify such more complex forms as 11 and 12). Let us also assume that we have as our factual premises a set of descriptive statements whose conjunction is p. Then we shall say that on the basis of the set of norms n, q is a prima facie obligation if and only if

(19) $O((n \& p) \supset q)$

is valid, i.e. if and only if q is a deontic consequence of (n & p). Likewise there is by definition an actual obligation that q if and only if

(20) $(n \& p) \supset Oq)$

is valid, i.e. if and only if Oq is a logical consequence of (n & p).

And later

If n does not contain any normative notion, there is a prima-facie obligation that q if and only if q follows logically from the non normative premiss (n & p).

These definitions are faced with an extraordinary number of objections, of which I will confine myself to the three most obvious.

1. It is hard to see how these definitions have any application since they require that any obligation statement, prima-facie or absolute be stated relative to some set of premises to which they are related either as logical consequence or deontic consequence. But obligation statements are not in general so stated relative to some sets of premises. Consider Ross's favourite, the prima-facie obligation to keep one's promises. What are the premises from which Ross—or anyone else—is supposed to have derived this? It is perhaps not surprising that Hintikka doesn't give us any examples of how this formal apparatus is supposed to apply to actual English sentences, because the definitions do not apply to the examples they were designed to elucidate. Given a set of general obligation statements we might use them to derive particular statements of obligation, but that is no help because it still leaves open the status of the general obligations, and this leads to the second objection.

2. Suppose that Hintikka can answer the questions posed in objection 1. Suppose that for every obligation statement q, whether prima-facie or absolute he can specify some n and some p such that the conjunction of n and p either strictly or deontically implies q. But remember n is a conjunction of

normative statements. These statements he tells us may be of the form Ot or they may be of the more complex forms 11 and 12, but in any case they will contain the deontic operator O since they are normative statements. But now what is the status of these statements containing O? Are they prima-facie or absolute? In either case we will soon have a vicious infinite regress because on the definitions for any statement Ot which occurs in n, whether that statement is prima-facie or absolute, there must be some further set of premisses n' and p' to which Ot is related either as logical of deontic consequence; and n' in turn must contain some prior normative statement Ot' which will in turn be a consequence of some prior p'' and n'', which must in turn contain some prior Ot'' ... and so on *ad infinitum*. In short, defining prima-facie and absolute obligations in such a way that each is expressed as the consequence of a conditional whose antecedent expresses another (prima-facie or absolute) obligation automatically leads to an infinite regress. Or are we supposed to think Hintikka has some other type of obligation in mind, neither prima-facie nor absolute? Or has the reading of O as obligation now been abandoned altogether? Hintikka doesn't tell us the answer to any of these obvious questions.

3. In the final paragraph quoted above Hintikka allows for a class of prima-facie obligations which are derived from non normative premisses. Would these allow him to escape from the infinite regress threatened above? It is an extraordinary consequence of this last definition that in these cases, where one has non-normative premisses, one has a prima-facie obligation to do something if and only if one has a set of premisses from which it follows that one is going to do it anyhow. For example, suppose Q is the proposition that I will eat beans tomorrow. On the absence of any normative premisses I will have a prima-facie obligation to eat beans tomorrow if and only if I have a set of premisses from which I can deduce that I will eat beans tomorrow. Since I presumably know the premisses and can make the deductions, I have prima-facie obligations to do all and only the things I know I am going to do anyway. How easy the moral life becomes.

These objections can be summarized as follows. The definitions have no application to the cases they were designed to elucidate, in order to give them any application we get either an infinite regress (objection 2) or an obvious absurdity (objection 3).

IV

I now turn to a discussion of Hintikka's objections to my derivation of 'ought' from 'is'. Oversimplifying my argument somewhat he says its structure is

(23) $$\frac{p, \text{ p commits one to q}}{Oq}$$

But he alleges that the second premiss is ambiguous between its reading as a prima-facie commitment (obligation) and as an absolute commitment, on his analysis between in short

(24) $$\frac{p, O(p \supset q)}{Oq}$$

and

(25) $$\frac{p, p \supset Oq}{Oq}$$

He then presents me with a dilemma: either I accept 24 or 25. If 24, then though the second premiss may be analytic, as I do indeed claim my second premiss is, the conclusion does not follow. If I accept 25 then though the conclusion follows the second premiss cannot by analytic and it is normative instead. The only way to make it analytic would be to pack so much evaluative content into the first premiss as to make the first premiss normative. Ignoring a digression that he makes about the *ceteris paribus* conditions the options are

(24) Invalid

(25a) $$\frac{p \quad \text{(factual)}}{p \supset Oq \quad \text{(normative)}}$$
$$Oq$$

(25a) $$\frac{p \quad \text{(normative)}}{p \supset Oq \quad \text{(factual)}}$$
$$Oq$$

Thus, he says either the argument is invalid, or it must employ at least one normative premiss. Do we need to accept this conclusion? I think not. We have already seen reasons to reject his analysis of prima-facie obligations as valid for any of the three notions we considered in the first part of this paper. We do indeed want to keep in our derivation the principle that the obligation to keep a promise is inherently overridable. But as we have seen in order to do that we do not need—and indeed it would not be correct—to treat the statement that if one makes a promise one is under an obligation to keep it as of the form O(p ⊃ q). So, 24 is not an option that we need seriously consider. My derivation of 'ought' from 'is' rests on the principle that it is a conceptual truth, deriving from the meaning of the word 'promise', that if one makes a promise one undertakes an obligation to do the thing promised. The nearest equivalent to that statement that Hintikka produces in his symbolism is p ⊃ Oq, the second premiss of 25. Now why does Hintikka suppose that such a formulation cannot be a conceptual or analytic truth but must be 'normative' in a way which also prevents it from being analytic or conceptual? It is important to notice that he does not advance the view of many commentators that no hypothetical with a descriptive antecedent and a normative consequent could ever be analytic. He does not, that is, rest his claim on the old view of 'the naturalistic fallacy'; he has a different argument. Here it is.

This reconstruction is based on the assumption that the notion of obligation involved in one's obligation to keep one's promises is an absolute (actual) obligation. If we adopt this position, then it becomes dubious whether the second premiss . . . . is really analytical, as Searle claims. At first blush it certainly appears an absolute (actual, overall) obligation to keep it. Saying this seems to overlook completely the possibility that the prima-facie obligation which is admittedly created by the promise should be overruled by some perfectly valid competing obligation.

But this passage only repeats the mistake we noted earlier. Hintikka simply assumes that the syntactical form p ⊃ Oq must ascribe an obligation to q on the given premiss that p which is such that nothing whatever could override it. But he makes this assumption only because he has already defined his operator O in such a way that there can never be conflicting obligations, it can never be true both that Op and O−p. But the fact that his symbolism cannot describe straightforward cases of conflicting obligations is a weakness of his symbolism, not a weakness in my argument. There is nothing about the *scope* of the operator in p ⊃ Oq which either prevents me from using it in a formalization of my argument or which forces me to claim that the conclusion of the argument contains an obligation which cannot be overridden. On my argument it is both the case that

> if one makes a promise one undertakes an obligation (which is of the form p ⊃ Oq)

and

> The obligation to keep a promise is sometimes overridden by other obligations.

The fact that Hintikka defines an operator in such a way that he cannot formalize these two points consistently using his operator is really quite irrelevant to the structure of my argument. I conclude that Hintikka's objections to my derivation of 'ought' from 'is' are without any force.

To summarize our conclusions, we have seen two attempts, Ross's and Hintikka's, to give an account of prima-facie obligations. Neither is successful. The real distinction which underlies both attempts is that between what one is under an obligation to do, and what one ought to do all things considered. But that distinction is not a distinction between one kind of obligation (prima-facie) and some other kind.[12]

---

[12] I am grateful to Bruce Vermazen for his comments on this essay.

P. F. Strawson Replies

REPLY TO AYER AND BENNETT

Ayer and Bennett both write sympathetically on the place in our lives of that range of feelings, attitudes, and responses which, in 'Freedom and Resentment', I brought together under the heading of 'reactive attitudes'. Their views show a measure of agreement. They both hold that reactive attitudes and feelings carry implications of 'desert' (Ayer) or 'praise- or blameworthiness' (Bennett) on the part of those towards whom such attitudes or feelings are felt or manifested; and, further, that the applicability of the notion of desert, and hence the appropriateness of those feelings and attitudes, requires, on any relevant occasion, that the agent could have acted or decided to act otherwise than he did on that occasion. Let us call this last 'the requirement of freedom'. The thesis that all events, and hence all human actions, are causally determined constitutes a prima-facie threat to the belief that the requirement of freedom is ever fulfilled on any occasion, hence to belief in the existence of any occasion on which reactive attitudes are appropriate. Two ways of meeting this challenge are rejected by both authors. One is the utilitarianism of Schlick which equates the requirement of freedom with liability to be influenced in socially desirable ways by exposure to normal and legal-judicial pressures. The other is the denial of determinism associated with the mysterious libertarian position which represents certain actions—those for which we are rightly held responsible—as issuing from uncaused acts of will.

There is one further point, not of doctrine but of sentiment, on which Ayer and Bennett agree with each other (and with me). All three of us view, with varying degrees of distaste or dismay, the prospect of a state of affairs in which human reactive attitudes and feelings would be displaced by a general prevalence of the 'objective' attitude.

From this point their views diverge. At the end of his essay, Ayer argues as follows. Any attitude involving a belief which the holder of the attitude has no good reason to accept is irrational. The concept of desert is empty, whether or not the thesis of determinism is true; for in either case there is no conceivable circumstance in which the concept could have application. But the holding of a reactive attitude involves the belief that the concept does have application. Therefore all reactive attitudes are irrational. He combines this conclusion with the avowal that it might, indeed would, nevertheless be rational to favour the retention of these irrational attitudes, since human life would be sadly impoverished by their disappearance. He finds this combination of views uncomfortable; and concludes with a mild reproach to me for accepting this position with more complacency than he can feel himself.

But here he misreads me. This is not the position I accept. When I said that the surrender of reactive attitudes would bring us nearer to being 'purely rational creatures',[1] I did not mean that some irrational elements would disappear from our lives; for I am not committed to the view that reactive attitudes are irrational. I meant only that some affective elements, elements of feeling or emotion, would disappear, leaving us more exclusively *ratiocinative* creatures than before. More of this later.

There is a superficial difficulty in reconciling Ayer's concluding remarks with the position he adopts earlier concerning the requirement of freedom. When he considers the prima-facie threat to this requirement posed by the thesis of determinism, he remarks that many philosophers who are disposed to accept the truth of the thesis, at least as far as human action is concerned, nevertheless show no disposition to forswear reactive attitudes. They can, however, Ayer maintains, be acquitted of the charge of inconsistency. They can be acquitted of this charge, he says, because of the nature of the interpretation which, in practice, we put upon the requirement of freedom: in practice, we regard this requirement as satisfied, we say that the agent 'could have acted otherwise', if we lack the detailed scientific knowledge which would be necessary in order to represent his action as an instance of the operation of some workable scientific law.

But Ayer's determinists cannot, on his own view, be so lightly

[1] *Freedom and Resentment*, p. 13n.

let off. For, on that view, the only 'freedom' which would show reactive attitudes to be rationally grounded would be a 'freedom' which guaranteed application for the concept of desert. But that concept is empty, ungrounded. Whether determinism is true or false, there is no such freedom. So our determinists can be acquitted of inconsistency only at the cost of being held guilty of confusion. They are consistent in believing that, while the reign of causality is universal, our knowledge of causes is limited. They are confused in taking limitation of knowledge to ground imputations of desert.

Ayer's position at this point must, then, be seen not as an attempt to *justify* the proneness to reactive attitudes on the part of professed determinists, or to vindicate their rationality, but rather as an attempt to *explain* the proneness to such attitudes on the part of everyone in general. The explanation brings him close to Spinoza who held, precisely, that our proneness to such attitudes is causally dependent on our ignorance of the actual determining causes of action. That this is indeed Ayer's position too is strongly suggested by his hypothesis that if exact knowledge of the causes of human behaviour in general were actually available, or known to be available, reactive attitudes would in fact tend to wither away—unless some countervailing process of conditioning were employed to preserve them.

This hypothesis is difficult to assess. I begin with a point which tells, though not decisively, against it. I do not think it is true that our adoption of objective attitudes towards an agent is normally associated with an ability to represent his behaviour as exemplifying exact scientific law. In 'Freedom and Resentment' I distinguish two kinds of case of the adoption of such attitudes. The first is the case in which the agent is seen as excluded from ordinary adult inter-personal relationships and from the ordinary operation of moral demand by the fact of being, e.g., a child, a psychotic, or a psychopath. The second is the case in which, for one or another of a variety of reasons, we have recourse to objectivity of attitude in relation to the normal and the mature.[2] In neither case do we have at our command workable and exact scientific laws under which we can bring the behaviour of the agent. We have, at best, a rough picture of

---

[2] *Freedom and Resentment*, pp. 9–10.

how our subjects work; but so we have in the case of many in relation to whom we feel no inclination to suspend reactive attitudes. We *may* also have a general conviction that their behaviour is in fact subject to exact scientific law; but if we have this conviction in respect of anyone, we are likely to have it in respect of everyone.

I say this point is not decisive; for to show that the adoption of a certain attitude does not in fact depend on the fulfilment of a certain condition is not to show that if that condition were fulfilled, the adoption of the attitude would not follow. But though the point is not decisive, it has some weight. For it dispels the appearance of positive evidence for the hypothesis. And in the absence of positive evidence for a hypothesis which could never be put to a direct test, there seems to be no reason to accept it. It is best regarded as idle.

But why do I say that this hypothesis could never be put to a direct test? Is this not intolerable dogmatism? What we are concerned with is the causal explanation of human intentional action. It is admitted that we already have, at a certain level, a certain competence in this activity: we explain people's behaviour by reference to the particular circumstances in which they find themselves and to their characters or personalities; and we sometimes have some knowledge of the causal influences which form and modify the latter. But it must also be admitted that this kind of explanation falls far short of the standard which we set for exact or scientific knowledge of causes. We are, however, increasingly able to view ourselves, in the light of the physical and biological sciences, as genetically programmed mechanisms of immense complexity, mechanisms constantly modified by their own history and responding, in constantly modified ways, to sensory inputs with behavioural outputs. The knowledge which these sciences deliver, and promise, is, as far as it goes, exact knowledge. Why, then, should we not suppose that our present vague and inexact kind of knowledge of the causes of action might eventually be replaced by exact and scientifically adequate knowledge? If this supposition were fulfilled, Ayer's hypothesis could be put to the test. What right have I to declare that it could not be fulfilled? How can we fix *a priori* limits to the advance of science?

I am not, I think, guilty of anti-scientific arrogance or presumption in declaring the supposition in question to be fantasy. We should remember that we are concerned with human behaviour understood as consisting of intentional action: with such matters—to take an example of quite modest complexity—as deflecting a conversation when it is noticed that its direction is causing embarrassment to one of the participants. It is to such acts as these that reactive feelings are responses. It is no derogation of the exact sciences to say that the idea of establishing workable laws invoking general correlations between such combinations of thought, feeling and action on the one hand and phenomena describable in terms belonging to those sciences on the other is a practical absurdity.

Ayer may appear to avoid the difficulty by imagining what seems a more serious, as well as a more sinister, possibility: that we should all be subjected, and know we have been subjected, to a kind of Skinnerian conditioning by reference to which all our behaviour—or 'almost everything that anybody said or did'—could be accounted for. It does not seem to me, however, that this last condition could be satisfied in detail—in such a way as to yield exact and scientific laws covering almost everything we say or do—unless the patterns of human behaviour were simplified out of all recognition. And, setting aside this possibility, I think we can cheerfully acknowledge that conditioning by reinforcement and its contrary is, and always has been, in full operation upon us anyway; though not, mercifully, under the direction of omnipotent authority.

Bennett, in the first eleven sections of his essay, sets out and elaborates the essence of my position with such thorough and sympathetic understanding as to leave me little to say beyond recording my admiring appreciation. There is one point which perhaps requires more emphasis than he gives it. He justly remarks that what, in 'Freedom and Resentment', I called the pessimist's response to the thesis of determinism cannot be explained as solely the consequence of *superficial* conceptual muddles about the requirement of freedom. He produces a convincing deeper explanation of (section 10), in part historical, in part more generally natural, of why accountability, and the appropriateness of reactive feelings, should be thought, not only by libertarians but also by sceptics like Ayer, to require some ultimate, and ultimately unintelligible, kind of 'freedom'.

He does not dwell as much as he might on the oddity of this view. It is, of course, frequently in order to declare that some instance of an emotional reaction is inappropriate or even irrational. This is so, normally at least, when we can state in intelligible terms a necessary condition of appropriateness which is not, in the given case, fulfilled. Thus the emotion of fear is linked to the independent possibility of *harm* in a way which rightly makes us speak of the fear of insects known to be harmless as irrational. But the idea that an entire range of emotions which pervade our personal and social lives as thoroughly as those in question should be thus linked to a condition which cannot be coherently described has a degree of implausibility which it would be difficult to rival. One is, indeed, inclined to say that the incoherence of the alleged condition infects the thought that the appropriateness or rationality of the reactive attitude requires its fulfilment. Bennett himself is prepared, or half-prepared, to allow this thought some place, though not a dominant place, in 'our ordinary concept of accountability'. But there is a quite general ambiguity in the notion of 'our ordinary concept' of whatever it may be. Should the lineaments of such a concept be drawn exclusively from its use, from our ordinary *practice*, or should we add the reflective accretions, however confused, which, naturally or historically, gather round it? The distinction is hardly clear-cut; but where it can be made, I prefer the first alternative.

What I was above all concerned to stress was that our proneness to reactive attitudes is a natural fact, woven into the fabric of our lives, given with the fact of human society as we know it, neither calling for nor permitting a general 'rational' justification. We can see where the limits of our proneness to these attitudes tend to fall, we can understand why they tend to fall where they do and we can find room for the idea of criticism, of appropriateness and inappropriateness, in particular cases. That is all; and that is enough.

In the remaining sections of his essay, Bennett seeks, in various ways, to produce a tighter and more unified organisation of the phenomena we are concerned with than I achieved in 'Freedom and Resentment'. He begins by attempting a general definition of 'reactive attitudes', but confesses that he succeeds in identifying only a consequential property rather than an essence. It does not seem to me to matter if a strict definition is not to be had. Bennett agrees that reactive attitudes are blame- and praise-related attitudes which are most characteristically and centrally manifested in relation to those human actions or omissions which themselves manifest attitudes of goodwill, its absence or its opposite towards another person or other people. Given this characterization, we can recognize that the responses which fall under it, or very similar responses, may also be evoked by behaviour which does not, or does not strictly, fall within its scope. Bennett further finds that I give an inadequate account of the link between personal generalized (or principled) reactive attitudes, and seeks to strengthen it by relocating the notion of interpersonal relations. Reading him and re-reading myself, I am driven to think that he construes some of the phrases I used as having a greater definiteness than I intended them to have or, perhaps, than the case admits of. But I freely admit that 'acknowledgment of claims' is too weak a phrase; and I freely reaffirm the central importance of that sense of sympathy, and of a *common* humanity, which underlies not only my indignation on another's behalf but also my indignation on my own. Finally, Bennett is certainly right in saying that I was wrong so to use the word 'moral' as to exclude the self-reactive attitudes from its scope.

REPLY TO MACKIE AND HIDÉ ISHIGURO

The contributions of both Mackie and Hidé Ishiguro are concerned with the concept of a person. I take Mackie's arguments first.

I begin with a point which seems to be generally agreed. If someone has, and formulates to himself or herself, such a thought as 'I am feeling terrible', then his or her use of 'I' is guaranteed against two kinds of failure to which the uses of some other definite referring expressions are sometimes exposed: it is guaranteed against lack of reference, and it is guaranteed against mistaken or incorrect reference (i.e. against lack of coincidence between the intended reference and the reference conventionally carried, in the circumstances, by the expression used). This is so for the very simplest of reasons. Anyone who is capable of formulating such a thought will have mastered the ordinary practice of personal reference by the use of personal pronouns; and it is a rule of that practice that the first personal pronoun refers to whoever uses it. So the fact that we have, in the case imagined, a user, is sufficient to guarantee a reference, and the correct reference, for the use. It is not in the least necessary, in order for the guarantee to operate, that the user should know *who* he is. He might be in a state of amnesiac shock, so that all his personal memories have, for the time being, deserted him. He can still think '*Whoever I am*, I am feeling terrible', and be secure against both kinds of reference failure.

This security, moreover, does not in any way depend on his ascribing to himself only mental states, states of thought or feeling. If, as a result of mistaking a part of someone else's body for a part of his own, he thinks, 'And I'm bleeding profusely', when in fact he is not bleeding at all, then what he thinks is false, but—and because—the reference to himself is unshaken. Similarly with all first-person self-ascriptions, of whatever kind. Even someone wholly deluded as to his identity, who thinks, say, 'I wrote the *Tractatus*', does not fail to refer correctly to himself; and if he thinks, 'I, Ludwig Wittgenstein, wrote the *Tractatus*', the reference of 'I' stands where it did and he merely makes an additional error in placing 'Ludwig Wittgenstein' in apposition to it.

At the risk of being wearisome, I must repeat the point that the immunity of 'I' from reference-failure (of either kind) in the thought, or speech, of any human user of it, whatever his condition, is guaranteed by the role of the expression in the ordinary practice, well established among human beings, of reference to themselves and each other. Hence it follows that no case for the existence of any use of 'I' other than its use in reference to a human being (a thinking and corporeal language-user) is established simply by the fact of this feature. It does not follow that there neither is, nor could be, any other use of the expression; but if there is, or might be, such a use, the case for its existence or possibility will have to be argued on other grounds.

Mackie shares with Miss Anscombe the view that there is such another use, though they differ as to its nature. In so far as this view of theirs rests, as it appears partly to do in

Mackie's case and wholly in Miss Anscombe's, on a restricted observation of the first personal pronoun's immunity from reference-failure, it appears to be ill grounded. I must ask, then, what independent grounds Mackie may have for this view.

But first we must get clear as to what form the view takes in Mackie's case. The answer is quite complex. First, inviting us to attend to our consciousness of our current thoughts and feelings, Mackie suggests that in ascribing these to ourselves in thought, we employ a meaning-rule for 'I' which renders it roughly equivalent to 'the subject, whatever it may be, of these present experiences'. Let me recall, by way of example, the case of the shocked amnesiac who thinks, 'I don't remember who I am; but, whoever I am, I am feeling terrible.' Mackie would, at this stage, have us render the second part of this thought by 'Whatever being, *of whatever category*, I may be, I am feeling terrible'; and would, at this stage, allow a comparable indeterminacy, as regards the category of one's being, to enter all ordinary self-ascriptions of thoughts and feelings on the part of anyone. One might be a human being; or, again, one might not. Mackie here seems to credit the ordinary man with a surprising degree of speculative philosophical open-mindedness in his ordinary thinking. Perhaps he later came to think this implausible; for, at the end of the paper, he withdraws the suggestion that the categorially open concept of the subject is 'our ordinary concept' and stoutly asserts that our ordinary concept of the subject of experiences, of the referent of 'I' in self-ascriptions of thoughts and feelings, is the concept of a Cartesian Ego. He implies that this is only part of our ordinary concept, but should perhaps say, rather, that this is not the only concept we have, of a referent of 'I'. For in saying or thinking such things as 'I am bald', we can hardly take ourselves to be ascribing baldness to a Cartesian Ego. Perhaps in this case the referent is what we take our Cartesian Ego to take to be 'his' body. Then we shall need a third referent, the human being or person composed of the other two, to function as the subject of such ascriptions as 'I am writing', an activity which cannot be credited to either Ego or body alone. So 'I', in its ordinary uses, is, on this view, at least doubly, and perhaps triply, ambiguous.

This view of our ordinary concept(s) of ourselves, or of what we ordinarily mean by 'I', seems to me quite implausible. When we say such things as 'I closed my eyes and (I) thought of you' or 'When I sit in that chair, I feel deliciously relaxed', we do not, I suggest, for a moment suppose that we are switching the reference of 'I' between its first occurrence in each sentence and its second. We are ordinarily content to operate with a concept of ourselves and other people as beings who are both corporeal and conscious; and it is to such beings that we ordinarily employ the personal pronouns to refer.

It is not, however, essential for Mackie to present the substance of his position as a thesis about our ordinary unreflective concept of the referents of personal pronouns. It is open to him to present it, rather, as a thesis about a concept which is forced upon us when we reflect upon certain possibilities or what we take to be such. The types of putative possibility which Mackie considers are two. The first is that of performing certain imaginative exercises which Vendler calls 'feats of transference'; the second is that of the existence of a disembodied consciousness enjoying experience which is somehow continuous with that of a human being who has died. We cannot readily suppose either of these to *be* a possibility, Mackie suggests, without making use of the concept of a Cartesian Ego and taking such an Ego to be the referent of the 'I' we employ when we indulge in these imaginings or speculations on our own behalf or the 'he' or 'you' we employ when we include others in their scope. But we do indulge in such imaginings and speculations. Therefore it is reasonable to suppose that we do employ this concept in the course of these indulgences; and, if we do, our recognition of the fact will, or in consistency should, dispose us to revise our ordinary, unreflective concept of ourselves in a Cartesian direction. So, Mackie may maintain, our ordinary *reflective* concept of ourselves is in fact Cartesian; though further critical reflection may lead us to abandon this conception on the excellent ground that nothing answers to it.

As regards 'feats of transference', I have nothing essential to add to the admirable treatment of the subject by Bernard Williams in his British Academy lecture, 'Imagination and the Self'.[1] He shows that, and how, it is possible to imagine being

---

[1] Reprinted in *Problems of the Self*, CUP.; see especially pp. 40-5.

Napoleon at Austerlitz or Hannibal at Cannae without any recourse to the Cartesian Ego; though he shows also how easy it is to become confused about the matter. Mackie explicitly allows his case to rest upon the supposed validity of the inference from 'I can imagine (myself) being at Cannae' to 'It is possible that I should have been at Cannae'. But there is no interpretation of the first sentence which is such that it both expresses a truth and licenses the inference. If there were, we should have to allow that the concept of a Cartesian Ego is at least coherent, even though lacking application. This conclusion Mackie is presumably prepared to accept.

The matter of disembodied consciousness is more complicated. I do not believe, any more than Mackie does, that the occurrence of such consciousness is a real, i.e. a natural, possibility. The question, therefore, is entirely devoid of practical interest. I have not, however, so far been able to find a *logical* absurdity or impossibility in the idea of the existence of states of consciousness, not themselves the conscious states of a human or any other corporeal being, which nevertheless have a similar kind of continuity with each other to that exhibited by the successive conscious states of a human being and which include quasi- or apparent memories of the past experience of a particular person who has died. Given this last provision, it is easy to see that the thoughts contained in such a series of states could include thoughts having the form of self-ascriptions, i.e. could include, as Mackie puts it, 'I'-thoughts, e.g. the thought, 'I seem to be disembodied.' (Compare the fact that, as things are, we can think 'I'-thoughts while quite unconscious of our bodies.)

If we suppose that we can coherently entertain such a possibility, i.e. that it is not logically excluded, what consequences follow? None, I think, that supports Mackie's case. It does not follow that our ordinary use of 'I' is governed by a meaning-rule which provides for anything but ordinary human reference. Nor does it follow that, in supposing the possibility realized, we must suppose the 'I' that figures in disembodied 'I'-thoughts to have a Cartesian reference. Rather, we should say—and for this special, supposed case I would agree with Miss Anscombe—that it has no reference at all; and that its *presence* in the supposed disembodied thoughts is to be explained by the supposition that those thoughts include apparent or quasi-memories of past experiences of an actual person, a human being who has died. Miss Anscombe's mistake lay in applying a thesis which holds for the peculiar supposed case in question to a certain range of uses of 'I' in the thought of human beings; and the origin of her mistake lay in a misunderstanding of the source of that immunity from reference-failure which necessarily characterizes the use of 'I' in the thought of any human being.

The case is not wholly without parallels to the case of those imaginings discussed by Vendler, Mackie, and Williams. If the supposition I have described is coherent, then anyone who is prepared to construe the notion of 'his' survival of bodily death in its terms may correctly regard it as a logical possibility. Let anyone, who will, take such comfort in the thought as he may.

Of course it has been no part of my intention to deny that the notion of a Cartesian Ego, or of something like it, has figured prominently in our Western culture. Since it is a natural enough illusion, it has no doubt figured prominently in others as well. If this were enough to establish the notion as part of our 'ordinary concept' of the referent of 'I', then philosophical argument on the point would not be required. But Mackie clearly does not regard it as enough; for he produces philosophical arguments. It is these arguments I have tried to meet.

The main emphasis of Hidé Ishiguro's essay falls on what might be called the social aspect of being a person. Put thus baldly, the thought of this aspect may seem relatively commonplace; but in fact she is able to draw from it, or to suggest, conclusions of great interest and importance.

Her enquiry is directed to the question: What is essential to being a person? or: What are the essential features of the concept of a person? She answers that persons are essentially beings which possess abilities and dispositions of certain kinds; which are self-conscious, capable of ascribing to themselves certain predicates or properties; and which are capable of entering into, and find themselves entering into, certain kinds of relationship, involving mutual communication, with each other, taking each other, thereby, to be creatures of the same kind as themselves. The most important and interesting point emerges in this last phrase. It can be otherwise expressed by saying that in order to *be* a person, one must see oneself and others *as* persons. One must *have* an operative concept of a person—such a concept as Miss Ishiguro describes—in order to *be* one. This is the point that I take her to be making in declaring the concept of a person to be 'indispensable'—to us persons. She suggests that, whatever unclarities attended my own declaration that the concept of a person is 'primitive', here is one good sense in which it may be said to be so; and, though I did not have such a point clearly in mind in writing *Individuals*, I think she is perfectly right.

Miss Ishiguro draws another important, if less striking, conclusion from her account. The only persons whom we human beings in fact encounter and enter into (personal) relations with are other human beings; and it is at least highly plausible to suppose that human beings form a natural kind, in the sense with which Putnam and others have made us familiar. But, even if this is so, it would be a mistake to think that the 'real essence' of personhood consists in the possession of whatever structural physical characteristics underly the possession by human beings of the characteristically personal range of abilities and dispositions. Whatever the facts of the matter may be, the concept of a person is such as not to exclude the possibility of persons of a quite different constitution from that of a standard human being. Miss Ishiguro's position seems to have the further consequence, which she does not explicitly draw, that the concept does not exclude the existence of a class of persons with whom human beings were debarred, perhaps by perceptual limitations, from mutual personal intercourse, but who were capable of such intercourse with each other. This last possibility, by its nature, lacks practical point for us; but the more general possibility may not.

Part of my own purpose, in declaring the concept of a person primitive, was, as Miss Ishiguro recognizes, to resist certain kinds of reduction of the concept. One is the Cartesian reduction, which represents the concept of a person as the concept of a unique kind of combination of an individual soul and an individual body. Few, even among those who, like Mackie, regard our 'ordinary', unreformed concept as Cartesian, would now be found to defend this reduction. But there is another apparently reductive view which is both more plausible and more popular. This is the view that the concept of a person is identical with that of a living human body. But if Miss Ishiguro is right in her second contention, then the view should at least be modified by the substitution of 'personal' for 'human'; and this substitution should make it clear that the concept of a personal body is secondary to, and derivative from, that of a person.

REPLY TO EVANS

Gareth Evans's essay sets me a practical as well as a theoretical problem. the line of argument is strong and subtle, the issues raised are many, complex, and deep. Any adequate and detailed response would be, for this volume, disproportionately long—at least as long as the essay itself. I shall, therefore, not attempt to comment *seriatim* on all the points which Evans makes. I shall move, rather, on a broad front; but I hope that, nevertheless, no major matter will be left untouched on.

We are to start, once more, with the notion of a being whose experience is purely auditory. We dispense, this time, with the master sound and its associated simplicities. We suppose our subject equipped with a capacious memory and extensive powers of generalization; and we suppose his auditory experience to be characterized by just such a kind and degree of complexity, richness, variety, order, and regularity as will best fit a certain 'hypothesis' or supposition. The hypothesis, which Evans regards with a tolerance strictly provisional, is this: that our subject views, or comes to view, the actual course of his auditory experience as explained by the combination of (1) the occurrence, independent of his experience of them, of particular sound-sequences which maintain or change their relative 'positions' in one or more quasi-spatial dimensions and (2) the change or maintenance of his own position relative to them. If this hypothesis is, within its own terms, coherent, then there is room in the subject's view of how things are for the idea of two qualitatively indistinguishable particular sound-sequences occurring simultaneously in different positions relative to the others which constitute, with them, the known sound-world; and also for his believing, at some time, that he is now hearing, after an interval, the later part of a particular sound-sequence of which he earlier heard an earlier part. Our subject, in fact, will have a working 'theory' of an objective world of sounds disposed in a quasi-space in which he himself follows an experiential route. It is this hypothesis which Evans confronts at the end of the second part of his essay, after making many telling and interesting points along the way, which, with only minor qualifications, I accept; and he devotes the rest of his essay to arguing that, given the limited materials at our subject's disposal, it is virtually, if not strictly, impossible to suppose him equipped with such a conception of an objective world. The hypothesis, as described above, is unacceptable. Or—to put the point in terms which guard against the danger of our subject's taking on, as Evans put it, 'a life of his own'—more must enter any conception of an objective world than is provided for by the thought of a purely auditory experience.

Evans has two main lines of argument for this negative conclusion. Before we inquire what they are, a preliminary point must be made. The hypothesis sketched above has two mutually dependent, but distinguishable, aspects. They might be called the aspect of objectivity and the aspect of spatiality. First the hypothesis looks to a conception of processes which occur (or, speaking generally, of objects which exist) independently of any experience of them, but of which some are, and, in suitable conditions, others would be, objects of perception for a subject. This is the aspect of objectivity.[1] Second, these processes (objects) are conceived of as ordered in a spatial or quasi-spatial manner which allows for the simultaneous occurrence (existence) of any number of distinct, but perhaps qualitatively indistinguishable, processes (objects) of the kind in question. This is the aspect of spatiality.[2] It will be seen that I have described the spatiality condition in such a way that it presupposes the satisfaction of the objectivity condition. The question I want to raise, at this preliminary stage, is whether Evans supposes that the satisfaction of the objectivity condition quite generally requires—in any kind of universe that we can conceive of—the satisfaction of the spatiality condition. His footnote 17 suggests, though weakly, that he does not; whereas the

---

[1] Strictly, of 'objectivity-cum-perceivability'; but let 'objectivity' cover the whole condition.

[2] I shall follow Evans in dropping the qualification, 'or quasi-spatiality'.

arguments of the last two sections of the essay suggest, rather strongly, that he does. I think the conflict, if there is one, can be resolved by taking him to hold that the only conception of an objective (perceivable) world which is sufficiently similar to our own to be of interest to us is a conception in which the two conditions—the objectivity condition and the spatiality condition—are to be seen as mutually dependent. I have no disagreement with him on this point; so I shall follow him in adopting the assumption of mutual dependence which dominates the last two parts of his essay.

My primary concern in what follows is not to defend the coherence of the original hypothesis of an auditory objective world. It is to raise certain questions, and to explore certain issues, suggested by Evans's arguments. If the Heroic hypothesis should seem in the end a little less vulnerable, this will be an incidental and secondary consequence.

As already remarked, Evans has two main lines of argument. One might be called the argument from the necessity of a causal ground (the Causal Ground Argument); the other, the argument from the necessity of 'simultaneous spatial concepts' (the Simultaneity Argument). The Causal Ground Argument may be roughly summarized as follows. If a subject is to have a conception of an objective world, a world of objects, spatially disposed, of which he enjoys sensible experience, but which themselves enjoy an existence genuinely independent of his experience of them, he must credit the perceptible objects of his world with sensory properties. But sensory properties are dispositional properties: they consist in the possession by objects of dispositions to produce in the appropriate subjects certain sensory experiences. As such, and as properties of genuinely independent objects, they require an abiding causal ground distinct from themselves. We human beings possess the concept of such a basis in the idea of space-occupying material substances, possessing properties which are not merely sensory, in that the concepts of these properties cannot be constructed out of material supplied by sensible experience alone. In general, no set of purely sense-given qualities and relations, however many sense-modalities were involved and however they were correlated in sense-experience, would suffice to yield the concept of an abiding base, or ground, for sensory properties. But our subject was supplied with no resources other than a highly restricted range of sense-qualities-and-relations. Unless we enrich his conceptual equipment in some way which is hard to imagine if we are to leave his experience as purely auditory, we must conclude that he lacks the resources for a conception of an objective world. (It should be emphasized that Evans recognizes a weaker conception of objectivity which would allow, e.g., a phenomenalist scheme to be a conception of an objective world; but he is interested only in the stronger conception which genuinely provides for *independently existing objects* of experience. In this I follow him throughout the succeeding arguments.)

The Simultaneity Argument is a kind of supplement to the Causal Ground Argument. It goes as follows. An essential element in the concept of an objective world of things in space is the idea of different things, or parts of things, existing *simultaneously* in spatial relations to each other. In visual experience we are often *simultaneously aware* of different things thus related; and we may then be said to make a 'direct' application of 'simultaneous spatial concepts'. Sometimes, e.g. in the dark, we find out about the simultaneous spatial relations in which things stand, not by simultaneous, but by sequential or serial, awareness of those things; we may then be said to make an indirect, or a less direct, application of simultaneous spatial concepts. It may be held that the blind have no way but that of sequential awareness of finding out about the spatial relations of coexisting things, so that they are never in a position, as the sighted are, to make a direct application of simultaneous spatial concepts. Nevertheless, on pain of holding—what no one believes—that the blind have no conception of an objective world at all, it must be supposed that they are equipped with the appropriate concepts and that they 'interpret' or 'synthesize' their sequential experience in terms of them. This is independently plausible in the case of the blind; but appears to have no independent plausibility in the case of the subject of a purely auditory experience, who similarly, and indeed far more certainly, lacks any opportunity for direct application of simultaneous spatial concepts.[3]

---

[3] Evans says I deny to my hero the possession of simultaneous spatial (or quasi-spatial) concepts. But of course I do not; I only deny him any sensory means of making a 'direct' application of such concepts.

I begin with a comment on the Simultaneity Argument. It is clear that Evans regards the possession and use of 'simultaneous spatial concepts' as a necessary condition of possessing a conception of an objective world. I think he is right to do so. I think it should be, but is not quite, equally clear that he does not regard the condition as sufficient. It is not quite clear; for he writes: 'Certainly any theory using simultaneous spatial concepts does genuinely embody the idea of an independently existing reality.'

Consider the notion of a purely visual experience. With minimal elaboration this notion will include that of the simultaneous presentation of spatially related elements. So the subject of such experience must, in the terms of the argument, be granted the possession and use of simultaneous spatial concepts. What is to prevent him, given an appropriate kind and degree of variety, complexity, and regularity in his visual experience, from elaborating a 'travel-based theory' of a world of independently existing, purely visual, objects on which he has a changing point of view and which extends beyond the limits of his observation at any moment? As far as the Simultaneity Argument goes, the answer must be: Nothing.

It seems to me legitimate to deduce, from Evans's general position, that he would hold the conception of an objective spatial world consisting of mere *visibilia* to be no more a possible conception than the conception of an objective spatial (or quasi-spatial) world consisting of mere *audibilia*. But why? The answer cannot lie in the subject's lack of simultaneous spatial concepts; for he possesses them. The answer must lie in the considerations adduced in the Causal Ground Argument. It is evidently time to turn to the latter. Of the Simultaneity Argument one can, meanwhile, say this: that it amounts to the assertion of a large implausibility in the supposition that a being whose experience was purely auditory could possess and use simultaneous spatial (or quasi-spatial) concepts and thereby satisfy one necessary condition of having a conception of an objective world.

We are to ask, then, whether the supposition of a subject of purely visual experience (call him 'Seer'), who takes his experience to be of an objective world of purely visual objects, is in fact vulnerable to the Causal Ground Argument. Evans will hold—we are presuming—that if such properties as those of colours and visually defined shapes are to be thought of as objective properties, then they must be recognized to be dispositional properties of objects which must in turn be conceived to have other, non-sensory, abiding properties to constitute them as space-occupiers and, indeed, to provide the causal ground of the dispositional sensory properties themselves.

A simple response to this position suggests itself. The position may indeed, at least on reflection, seem natural to *us*, living in the richly various world we know and possessed of the knowledge we do possess. Indeed we take our first unreflective steps towards the relative sophistication of this position as soon as we think of visual characteristics as—usually—characteristics *of* objects which we can encounter, identify, and find out about in other ways than by sight; as we notably do in the dark. But we must not let the natural tenor of our thinking in the world as we know it prejudice our sense of other possibilities. Given a sufficiently radical scaling down of a subject's sensory or experiential resources, there is no reason why the subject should not conceive of an objective world of things *constituted* of colour variously disposed in a space. (We have already seen the powerlessness of the Simultaneity Argument against such a conception.) The things so constituted would be thought of as simply causing, in a suitably positioned subject, the experience of seeing them; no more elaborate theory of the mechanism of perception would be either necessary or possible. It may be difficult for *us*, situated as we are, enjoying the range of perceptual experience that we enjoy and possessing the knowledge that we possess, to envisage such a conception. It is certainly impossible for us to embrace it as our own. But it by no means follows that such a conception is absolutely impossible, impossible in itself.

Evans's rejoinder to this simple response would presumably invoke his point that concepts of the genuinely objective must possess a theoretical character which is not provided for in the conception just described; for that conception, he would say, is 'directly and exclusively ... woven out of materials given in experience', which no genuine conception of the objective can be.

But this rejoinder demands closer examination. First, let it be conceded that no conception of an objective world can be 'woven' or 'constructed' out of sense-experiences alone. Such concepts as we have of types of 'sensation' peculiar to this or that sense-modality, and of the relations which sense-experiences, simply as such, can have to each other, are, and remain, just that—concepts of sense-experiences and their realtions. Now we human beings are subjects of sense-experience, but also take ourselves, in enjoying sense-experience, to be, usually or at least often, perceiving independently existing things in an objective, spatial world. We must therefore suppose that we are antecedently or 'innately' equipped with a disposition to react to sensory stimulation by forming and applying concepts which are not simply concepts of sense-experiences but which belong to the range of objective-spatial concepts: just such concepts, in fact, as we naïvely and naturally form of the mundane objects of our daily experience. But is not this, *mutatis mutandis*, precisely the supposition that was made in the case of our Seer? His concepts of *visibilia* reflect *his* antecedent disposition to form and apply concepts which are not simply concepts of sense-experiences no less than our mundane concepts of visible and tangible things reflect our antecedent disposition to do the same thing. If our mundane concepts of objects are 'theoretical' (i.e. not woven out of sense-experiences alone), his are no less so. It can be no objection that he enjoys sense-experiences of only one kind while we enjoy sense-experiences of several kinds; for it was held that the mere multiplication of types of sense-experience brings us no nearer to the conception of the objective. Neither can it be properly argued that objective visual properties *are* merely dispositional and hence, since Seer is debarred from conceiving visual properties as merely dispositional, he is debarred from conceiving them as objective. For this would be, at best, to judge the envisaged conception of the objective in the light of what reflection may seem to suggest about our own conception and hence to traverse the warning already given about conceptual parochialism.

I say 'what reflection may seem to suggest', for I think that yet closer examination shows Evans's position to have its own internal instability. Let us concentrate on the thesis that, at least in our own scheme, sensory properties in general, if they are to be thought of as objective properties of things and not merely properties of sense-experiences, must be acknowledged to be merely dispositional properties and hence to require an abiding categorical base of a different character from themselves. Then let us ask what the non-sensory properties of the abiding categorical base may be supposed to be. They cannot include, for example, shapes-as-seen or shapes-as-felt, nor roughness- nor smoothness- nor resistingness- nor softness-as-felt; for neither visual nor tactual-kinaesthetic experience can directly deliver us non-sensory properties, nor can non-sensory properties be constructed out of sensory properties. It seems that our search for the properties of the categorical base must finally lead us to the undeniably theoretical properties which physics assigns to the ultimate constituents of matter—perhaps force, mass, impenetrability, electric charge. But these properties themselves seem to be thoroughly dispositional in character, though the dispositions in question relate to the operations of objects upon each other rather then, directly, to their operations upon the human sensibility. If it seems true of the sensory properties in general that they all dissolve together, under reflective pressure, into dispositions, this seems even more certainly true of the 'physical' properties which are held to constitute their categorical base. Properties do not become less dispositional simply by becoming more theoretical. So if the argument is from dispositional properties conceived as objective to the need for a categorical base, then the categorical base is still to seek.

The story of how this apparent difficulty is resolved in our own human scheme of things is a complex one which I have told, by implication, elsewhere.[4] I cannot do more than hint at it here. Fundamentally, the question is whether we are to retain our hold on a direct realist view of perception, such as can plausibly be ascribed to unreflective common sense, or to embrace an exclusively representative theory. If we do retain our hold on the former, then we are released from the grip of the belief that sensory properties, conceived of as objective, must therefore be conceived of as merely dispositional, as requiring a categorical base of a different character from themselves. It

[4] See 'Perception and its Objects' in *Perception and Identity: Essays presented to A. J. Ayer*, Macmillan, 1979.

may be asked how, if we do retain our hold on the uncritical realism of common sense, we can simultaneously entertain, without contradiction, the scientific world-view—a view which, taken alone, is necessarily associated with a representative theory of perception and, if held with a consistent exclusiveness, inevitably runs into the difficulty just described. The answer lies in recognizing a certain irreducible relativity in our view of the world and in acknowledging our capacity to shift our standpoint from one position to another, while retaining our grasp of the identity of what we thus variously view from different standpoints. Self-consciousness on this point is what saves us from self-contradiction; though not, necessarily, from intellectual discomfort.

I have strayed from the immediate issue. Returning to it, we confront the question: if the scheme of objective *visibilia*—purely visual objects—can withstand the assault of the Causal Ground Argument, how does it fare with the scheme of objective *audibilia*? If Seer survives, must Hero perish? It is at this point that the weight of the Simultaneity Argument is felt; for Seer can, and Hero cannot, make a direct application of simultaneous spatial concepts.[5]

Now it was supposed that the blind were, in this respect, in the same case as Hero; and no one supposes the blind to lack a conception of an objective world of things in space. But there are profound differences between the blind and Hero; even if we suppose our blind subject to lack hearing, taste, and smell. For, first, the supposition that the blind subject has *only* sequential awareness of the spatial distribution of matter is itself a highly dubious supposition; second, the blind subject has rather complex modes of awareness of a particular body, namely his own; and, third, there is high, indeed overwhelming, initial plausibility in regarding the combination of tactual, kinaesthetic, and muscular sensation as critical in the formation of those concepts of things extended in space which we actually have. All these points deserve further elaboration, which I cannot give them here. But they amount to an admission that the case of the blind

[5] The example of Caliban—not, admittedly, a subject of high intelligence—shows how a conception of objective audibilia may flourish in an *independently* provided spatial environment:
>The isle is full of noises,
>Sounds and sweet airs that give delight and hurt not.

gives poor support, or none, to the case for Hero. In fact, the case for Hero seems, in the end, rather weak. We should have to imagine him antecedently disposed to react to auditory impressions of the right degree of complexity by the formation of concepts of *audibilia*, simultaneously disposed in a space or quasi-space, without possessing, what Seer possesses, the ability to make a direct application of simultaneous spatial concepts. And though such a supposition does not seem self-contradictory, its explicit statement may well make it seem unattractive.

But now I am running the risk, if I have not already incurred the reproach, of allowing Hero to 'take on a life of his own'. As Evans says, he is no more than a device to help us to explore some of the relations between some of the fundamental concepts of our scheme of things.

REPLY TO MCDOWELL

With much of McDowell's subtle and illuminating essay I am in agreement. In fact, I shall suggest that the apparent disagreement between us may be less, or less significant, than he seems to allow.

McDowell starts off by pointing out that theorists of formal semantics are not all cast in the same mould. Such a theorist need not be one who has to be persuaded by argument that 'appeal to the nature of linguistic behaviour' is necessary 'in order to underpin his interest in truth'. The notion of truth may enter only at the end, not at the beginning, of his reflections. He may begin, rather, by requiring of his theory of meaning for a given language that it should yield the content of any *act of saying* (or assertion) performed by the utterance of an indicative sentence of the language; and he may do so in the firm conviction that it is an essential feature of the concept of an act of saying that such acts are standardly communicative in intention. The further requirement on such a theory is that it should show the content expressible by the utterance of a sentence to be the upshot of the contributions made by its parts and their mode of combination. It is just because, or in so far as, a truth-theory—a theory which issues in a characterization of a truth-predicate for a given language—can be seen to satisfy these requirements that it holds attractions for anyone concerned to explain our linguistic abilities as parties to acts of linguistic communication, the abilities manifested in speech and in comprehension of speech.

Agreement on these points removes the need for argument on the main issue with which I was concerned in 'Meaning and Truth'. But some questions, as McDowell remarks, remain open. If our general philosophical curiosity about language is to be satisfied, we still need a general account of what saying is, or of what 'assertoric communication' is.[1] (McDowell appears to draw a distinction here, admitting the need for an account of assertoric communication, but apparently denying the need for an 'analysis' of saying. I do not fully understand this; first, because McDowell himself, as we shall see, appears to offer an analysis of saying; and, second, because, if it is an essential feature of the concept of saying that a case of saying is standardly a case of 'telling someone something' (i.e. an act of assertoric communication), then it seems that an account of the latter must be, or be an essential part of, an account of the former.

McDowell erects his theory of 'assertoric communication' on the basis of a broader concept of 'information-transmission', a concept realizable at a lower level than any at which self-consciousness or intention could be ascribed. Thus a creature may respond to a feature of its environment in a characteristic way and, by so doing, put another creature of the same kind in the very same information-state as it would have attained had it perceived that feature for itself. The response is part of the 'instinctive communicative repertoire' of such creatures: it 'represents' the feature in question; and its doing so is its having such-and-such an 'informational' content.

McDowell tentatively suggests that assertoric discourse as we know it may be seen as a descendant of this kind of instinctive communicative repertoire, having in common with its ancestor the power and function of information-transmission, but wholly foreign to its ancestor in being employed self-consciously and intentionally and, in fact, with the peculiarly characteristic aim of achieving mutual awareness of intention

---

[1] I follow McDowell in concentrating on this variety of speech-act, convinced, as he is, that assertion is primary and that, if it is well understood, other varieties present no major problems.

on the part of speaker and audience. The intention of which mutual awareness is achieved when communication is successful, however, is simply the intention *to say what is said*, i.e. to perform linguistically in a way which would be appropriate to transmitting such-and such a piece of information. No further analysis of the intention of which mutual awareness is secured in successful communication, hence no analysis in such terms as were suggested in 'Meaning and Truth', is either required or appropriate. And this is just as well, since that analysis is implausible.

It should be noted that McDowell is in fact here offering his own (partial) analysis of saying: to say that p is to perform linguistically in a way which would be appropriate to transmitting information that p; or to go through a linguistic routine whose primary function is to transmit such information; or, in his own words, 'to go through the motions of supplying an audience with knowledge of some circumstance'. On his own showing, the analysis, thus stated, is incomplete for the primary case where the saying is communicatively intended; since it omits the essential feature, essential, that is, for the case of fully-developed linguistic communication, of intended full overtness of intention. With this feature added, we have: to say that p is, in the primary case, to perform linguistically in a way which would be appropriate to transmitting information that p, with the intention that the intention so to perform should be recognized by the audience; that it should, in fact, be an object of full mutual awareness between speaker and audience.

It may be remarked that this characterization is ambiguous in a familiar way: in that the clause, 'which would be appropriate to transmitting information that p', might or might not be understood as specifying a character which the audience was intended to recognize as attaching to the linguistic performance in question. But surely the reading on which the clause in question *is* so understood should be preferred, at least for any case of an exercise of the communicative linguistic function as between mature language-users. And if this is so, certain consequences seem to follow as to the nature of the intention to *communicate*, when a linguistic and audience-directed performance of the saying kind is in fact accompanied (as it need not always be) by a genuine communicative intention. For only a very naïve, a far from mature, audience would be quite unaware of the possibility of honest mistake, or of intention to mislead or of sheer casualness or carelessness, on the part of a communicator; and only a very naïve communicator would be unaware of the audience's awareness of these possibilities. And if this is so, it seems hardly too much to say that it is a part, though normally a subdued or submerged part, of the genuine communicator's intention, that the audience's response to his performance should be governed by certain (normally subdued or submerged) assumptions regarding his (the communicator's) sincerity and reliability. And if this in turn is so, it seems that the position to which McDowell's analysis commits him is not, after all, so very different from that which was espoused in 'Meaning and Truth' and which he found implausible.

Not so very different, but, of course, different. And the difference is in McDowell's favour. For the position espoused in 'Meaning and Truth' does strongly suggest something that *is* implausible: viz. that the assertoric communicator who aims to inform (or to misinform) standardly intends that his audience should arrive at the knowledge (or belief) that p as a result of a process of calculation or inference of which one of the premises is supplied by the communicator's act of at least appearing to reveal his own belief that p by an utterance apt for the expression of such a belief. The trouble with this is not that it describes an absurd or impossible situation—for it (partially) describes a situation that sometimes occurs—but that, as a description of the normal case, it is quite unrealistic; whereas the strongly modified description which I find implicit in McDowell's position is not. Nevertheless a family resemblance between the two descriptions shines through their difference.

The difference noted may well be connected, though indirectly and inessentially, with another. It is remarkable how often attempts to elucidate the general nature of linguistic behaviour or, *pace* McDowell, of linguistic meaning, involve those who undertake them in speculative accounts of the *origins* of language, in the (only half-serious) construction of genetic models. Thus McDowell suggests that fully self-conscious linguistic behaviour somehow descends or evolves from the pre-self-conscious functioning of mechanisms of information-transmission; whereas Grice (and I, following him) imagined some perfectly self-conscious and successful attempts at pre-conventional communication (perhaps exploiting natural signs in a de-natured form) as laying the foundations for conventional, and hence linguistic or quasi-linguistic, systems of communication. I will not discuss the question, which type of story makes the emergence of language seem more of a miracle. A story of the second type would seem to give it more of the character of an *invention*—which may or may not be a merit of the story—but also to incline one more towards the above-mentioned implausibilities. Incline one only. There is no necessity about it, and the second type of story should not suffer discredit in consequence. In fact, when one considers the matter carefully, it seems that the difference between the two stories may be more apparent than real. As regards the evolutionary story, the whole mystery of the matter is contained in my phrase, 'somehow descends or evolves'; it is difficult to resist the thought of some deliberate exploitation, intended to be taken as such, of some naturally representative response— which thereby changes its status—as a necessary step in the descent.

The main drive of 'Meaning and Truth' was towards establishing the point that no general elucidation of the nature of language (of linguistic meaning or linguistic behaviour) is possible without reference to the concept of communication-intention, of audience-directed intentions on the part of speakers. What precisely is the correct account to give of the relevant concept of communication-intention is, though a difficult and important, yet a subordinate issue. On this subordinate issue I make a substantial, though modified, concession to McDowell. On the primary issue we are, as he says, in agreement.

There is, however, one other issue, raised by section 2 of McDowell's paper, on which I should like to comment, though it belongs to a quite different area of debate. He says of one who understands a given language, that his linguistic competence would be 'captured' or adequately 'described' by a theory which was such that anyone who knew the theory would be able to deduce the content and nature of what was said in an utterance of any sentence of the language from 'a suitable non-interpreting description, i.e. a description in terms of sounds or marks of that utterance'. He adds that 'it is hard to see what could have a better claim to count as a theory of meaning for a language' than a theory with these powers. But some have wanted, or have seemed to want, more. The theorist who produces a theory which satisfies McDowell's requirements must thereby represent structural features of the object-language by means of a certain semantic-syntactic structure which the theory is competent to handle. Now suppose it to be true that native speakers of the object language have, as it were, their own implicit understanding of the semantic-syntactic structure of the language, an understanding which, together with their lexical knowledge, underlies their linguistic competence, their ability to use and understand sentences of the language correctly. It does not appear to follow, from the fact that a semantic theory satisfied McDowell's requirements, that it would necessarily reflect the native understanding of the semantic-syntactic structure of the language concerned—if, indeed, there is such a thing as native understanding of structure which can be said to underlie native linguistic competence. But if there is such a thing, then it could properly be required, of a theory which claimed to 'capture' or adequately to 'describe' native linguistic competence, that it should mirror native understanding of structure. I think I differ from McDowell in regarding the question whether there is such a thing as, at least, open.

REPLY TO COHEN, QUINE AND GEACH

On the main points made by Cohen in his salutary essay on Proper Names I am most heartily in agreement with him. Of course the standard function of a proper name, *in use in any particular utterance*, is to designate or denote, in that utterance, a unique particular individual. But this function, as Cohen neatly puts it, is a feature of 'parole', not of 'langue'. One and the same name may, in different contexts of utterance, designate different particular individuals; and this, though the cases are otherwise different, is no more an indication of ambiguity in the name than the designatory versatility of 'I' is an indication of ambiguity in the first personal pronoun. So Cohen is right to insist on the 'linguistic' as opposed to the 'idiosyncratic' conception of proper names; and the popularity of the opposed position may perhaps be reckoned to a general reluctance, on the part of many philosophers of language, to allow contexual considerations their rightful place in semantics, i.e. in determining the truth-grounds of utterances or the identity of propositions expressed.

Cohen is right, too, it seems to me, in rejecting the dubious alliance of those who, while recognizing an indexical element in the standard usage of proper names, offer to explain this usage by invoking what is surely a secondary, descriptive, or predicative, use of these names as general terms having roughly, the kind of sense exemplified by such phrases as 'called "Smith" or 'bearer of the name "Smith" '. There is no reason to deny the existence of these uses; but equally no need to appeal to them to explain the primary designative or referential use from which they are derived.

But though Cohen officially rejects this explanation, it is perhaps possible to detect its lingering influence in the position he adopts on the question of the status of identity propositions coupling names. Given his general approach, one might have supposed that his view as to the semantic contribution made to an utterance by a proper name which, in that utterance, designates a particular individual, would be simply that and no more: i.e. that the name (non-connotatively) designates that particular individual. On this view, the truth-grounds of the utterance, *as far as the name is concerned*, turn simply on the denotation which the name actually has in that utterance, i.e. on the identity of the individual denoted. But from this it follows immediately that a statement in which the *same* individual is twice over designated, the two names being coupled by the identity-predicate, could not but be true; and that a statement in which two different individuals are designated by name, the two names being coupled by the identity-predicate, could not but be false. For, given the nature of the predicate in such a case (the identity-predicate), what fixes the truth-grounds of the statement fixes also its truth-value. So the non-contingency of such statements, which Cohen denies, is immediately guaranteed without appeal to the arguments which he criticizes.

We may, of course, feel the need of an explanation of how a man's knowledge-state may be changed when he is audience to such a statement; or of how he could understand what was said without already knowing it to be true or false, as the case may be. But, if we do, a little reflection on the conditions of command of a name as used—on our not very exacting requirements for knowing who or what is designated by a name as uttered on a particular occasion—should quickly ease our puzzlement.[1]

Cohen addresses himself to the question, what conditions determine which individual, if any, is designated by the use of a proper name on a particular occasion, in a particular utterance; or, as he puts it, how the context of a proper name's utterance determines its designation. I do not dispute the relevance of the factors he mentions. I only would re-emphasize the importance of the distinction, which seems to me implicit in his own position, between (1) the conditions which ensure that a proper name, as used in a particular utterance, designates, in that utterance, a particular individual and (2) the contribution which the name, as used, makes to the truth-grounds of that particular utterance. In other words, we must distinguish between the conditions of a name's making a particular semantic contribution to a particular utterance and the semantic contribution it makes.

Does Quine, or can he, accept the view that the standard function of a proper name in a particular utterance is as thus described: i.e. that of non-connotative identifying reference to a particular individual (object or person)? His paper does not yield a quite unequivocal answer. Its general tenor, certainly, is negative. The only purely referential terms, according to Quine, are the variables of quantification or their pronominal analogues in natural language. In so far as other singular terms may be allowed a referential role, it is only derivatively. For such other terms, in specifying their subject, carry information about it, 'serve to characterize the thing referred to', and hence differ, at most, only 'rhetorically' from the formally ampliative or predicative parts of a sentence. 'Were it not for pronouns or other devices to similar effect', Quine 'could make no sense of objective reference.' He would see 'no relevant distinction' between so-called names and 'other meaningful constituents of sentences.'

The position seems a little less unequivocal, however, when we turn to his remarks about the reparsing of names. How are

[1] See, for example, *Subject and Predicate in Logic and Grammar*, pp. 51–6.

we to understand the 'notationally atomic' predicate which replaces the name? If the predicate, in the context of a particular utterance is truly to inherit, as Quine suggests, the traits of uniqueness of application (*in context*) and non-connotativeness, then I think we must conclude, on pain of not understanding the role of the predicate at all, that its atomicity is *only* notational; that it is not 'irreducibly' atomic; that the name survives intact within the predicate, its purely referential function (in context) unthreatened and unmodified.

It is clear that Quine's theory of reference calls for a deeper effort of understanding. It seems that the purely referential function, as he understands it, must be distinguished not only from all indication of what an object referred to is like or how it is related to others, but also from all indication of what or which object it *is* that is being referred to. All the matter of description and identification is, as it were, the bloom or foliage of discourse and only the unadorned and undistinguishable stalks, which support this colourful show and are securely rooted in the common ground of 'whatever there may be', are irreducibly referential. These unadorned stalks are the quantifier-bound variables or pronouns—the 'tenable linguistic counterpart of the untenable old metaphysical notion of a bare particular'.

Here we have what I am tempted to call 'a vision of reference'. Like some other philosophical visions, it goes along with a revision of language; and, again like some other, though by no means all, philosophical visions, it has the appeal of a strong, bold, intransigeant simplicity. It presents a strong and simple theoretical structure, designed to make sense of our messy and convenient practice.

Appealing as this austere conception may be, it is not clear that it offers the best, i.e. the most realistic, way of making sense of our practices. We must consider what purposes those practices serve. It is a commonplace that the primary function of language is communication—and, especially, the communication of information or what purports to be such. Efficient communication takes account of the needs, capacities, and situation of its intended audience; and audiences do not in general take up their receptive role or station antecedently unequipped with any knowledge of their world and its objects. On the contrary, a typical audience, in virtue of his current situation, past experience and previous exposure to informative discourse, is already in possession of stores of knowledge about his world and about particular objects in his world. In particular, there will be included within the scope of his knowledge or present perception many particular objects each of which he somehow distinguishes from any other; of each of which, we may say, he has individually identifying knowledge.

I have often enough in the past spoken of the function of individually identifying reference. It is the function discharged by an expression which exhausts its semantic contribution to communication in indicating to an audience which particular object of those within the scope of the audience's identifying knowledge is being made, in that utterance, the subject of some predication. Here, if anywhere, we have, when all goes well, pure or direct objective reference. (The proper name achieves a just celebrity as a vehicle, though not the unique vehicle, of identifying reference.)

Quine lingers a little on the notion of identification, but, as we have seen, dismisses the distinction between the identificatory and the ampliative as merely rhetorical. 'The distinction between the identificatory and the ampliative is one thing, however, dim, and the distinction between reference and characterization is another.' He adduces my use of the concept of 'degree of identificatory force' as evidence that the notion of identification in general 'issues finally not in a distinction, but in a matter of degree'; but he omits to remark that I make use of this concept only in the context of an attempt to explain the extension of the notion of a *grammatical* subject (to embrace, e.g. indefinite descriptions). The function of pure, individually identifying reference (for short, 'direct reference') remains sharply distinguished from all others.

If this function is admitted at all, then it can be characterized semantically, or in terms of truth-conditions, as follows: when a direct reference is made, by some term, to a particular individual, in an utterance in which that term is coupled with a predicate, then what is said is true just in case *that individual* satisfies that predicate and false just in case it does not. Hence, if a term used to make such a reference carries any 'characterizing' or descriptive content, then that descriptive content does not enter into the truth-conditions of what is said, even though it contributes to determining what it is that is said. To call the difference between the function of this purely identificatory term and that of the ampliative or characterizing part of the sentence 'merely rhetorical' seems merely rhetorical.

Once this function of direct or pure individuality identifying reference is acknowledged for what it is, it must also be acknowledged that it stands on its own feet, owing nothing to the possibility of reference by way of quantifier-bound variables or pronouns. Quine points out, indeed, that terms of the kinds which, in some contexts, have this function may, in others, sometimes fail of reference, lacking a *designatum*; or that, when they have a *designatum*, they may sometimes occur *de dicto* rather than *de re*, their descriptive content then entering into the truth-conditions of what is said. Both points are good; but neither affects the status of the function of direct identifying reference. We must look deeper for the sources of reluctance to recognize this status, the sources of attachment to that 'vision of reference' which so signally elevates the variable. I suspect that the main source is to be found in the fact, commented on by Cohen in connection with proper names, that direct identifying reference to particulars (non-abstract objects) is thoroughly context-bound; and that the topic of such reference is one in which 'pragmatics' and semantics interpenetrate inextricably.

Where Quine speaks of the referential role of expressions, Geach speaks of their role as logical subjects; and is ready enough to recognize names, and perhaps only names, as performers of this role. In a simple subject-predicate proposition like 'Socrates swims', the object designated by the name 'Socrates' is represented as 'falling under the concept' expressed by 'swims'; or, to borrow another of Geach's terms, the activity of swimming is 'ascribed' to the individual, Socrates.

Geach agrees that expressions functioning as predicates can be negative or truth-functionally complex in form, whereas names, functioning as logical subjects, cannot; but he deplores the explanation which I offer of this fact. He also deplores, and attributes to me, the view that simple predications should be given a tripartite analysis into subject-copula-predicate, as opposed to the bipartite analysis into subject and predicate.

This attribution, however, is mistaken. It is true that I distinguish three functions performed in a simple predication:

that of specifying the object represented as falling under the concept; that of specifying the concept under which the object is represented as falling; and that of indicating the propositional or predicative mode of combination. But this description of functions is not a recipe for analysis. If someone says 'Socrates is brave' or 'Socrates swims', it is surely not incorrect, even if ponderous, to say of him that he specifies an individual, Socrates, that he specifies a quality or an activity (bravery or swimming) and that he *ascribes* the latter to the former; or, indeed, that he specifies an individual, specifies a concept, and *represents* the former *as falling under* the latter. But one is not committed, by this tripartite description of functions performed in the speech act, to a tripartite analysis of what is said. One of the points I sought to make, and explain, in the book which Geach refers to, is that both the second and the third of these functions are discharged by a *single* part of the utterance, viz. the predicate. Geach claims to find obscure the idea that a concept can be specified both by a predicative expression and by a noun or noun-phrase; but it is unacceptably paradoxical (even if Frege did not shrink from the paradox) to question the view that, e.g. the concept of swimming is specified by (Geach's phrase) 'the concept of swimming' or by the noun 'swimming'.

Geach offers his own informal explanation of the fact that predicates may be formally negative or truth-functionally composite, whereas names, functioning as logical subjects, may not. We simply cannot grasp a concept, he says, without *ipso facto* grasping its complementary concept: e.g. we cannot grasp the concept expressed by the predicable 'swims' or 'is brave' without grasping the concept which we express by the predicable 'does not swim' or 'is not brave'. Again, the ability to understand a number of atomic predications in which the same object is brought under different concepts entails grasp of the conjunctive concept under which that object may equivalently be brought in a single predication. These negative and conjunctive concepts are naturally expressed with the help of the truth-functional connectives. (With negation and conjunction of predicable secured, disjunctive, and hypothetical predicables are clearly admissible as well.) The idea that any parallel operation could be performed on names, functioning as logical subjects, is, on the other hand, 'manifestly nonsensical'.

It is not that I disagree with these observations; except that I would prefer 'demonstrably' to 'manifestly' as modifying 'nonsensical'. But I do think more can usefully be said. Geach himself remarks that the fundamental distinction we need to master is 'the distinction between individuals [i.e. particulars] and the concepts they fall under'. We do indeed. This distinction is fundamental to all experience of, and thought about, the world; let alone all talk about it. Therefore I thought to give as general an account as possible of the distinction between spatio-temporal particulars and general concepts, thereby fitting the facts which Geach remarks on into a wider framework. General concepts, as principles of wider or narrower discrimination among particulars, stand by their very nature in logical relations to each other; and I drew on this fact to show how, even if negative and conjunctive predicables were not already at our disposal, they could intelligibly be introduced. (I did not suggest that I was describing a procedure or thought-process that was actually followed.) As for negative or conjunctive or disjunctive names, functioning as subjects, there is no need to rest with an appeal to the 'manifest' absurdity of the idea of a negative or disjunctive particular; for it can be *demonstrated* that there could be no such things. Geach suggests that the logical matters with which he is concerned in his paper 'cannot be explained in the sense of being given a *foundation*'; rather, they 'come out' in all our discourse. But logical matters stand in connection with matters epistemological and metaphysical; and understanding may be enhanced by trying to make the connections clear.

REPLY TO WIGGINS, PEARS AND SEARLE

As the first step towards a substantial theory of truth, Wiggins seeks 'a principle for the enumeration of the marks of the truth concept', where a 'mark' of truth is a property which every truth possesses. His ingenious and fruitful suggestion is that such a principle may be found by considering the conditions that must be satisfied by an adequate interpretative theory, or theory of meaning, for a language. Such a theory will be adequate only if it matches the sentences of the language with interpretations of them in such a way as to give—in combination with an anthropological theory—the most satisfactorily explanatory account of the shared life and the beliefs and attitudes of actual speakers of the language, given their circumstances. A condition of being maximally explanatory is that the employment of theory in interpreting the utterances of speakers of the language should involve projecting upon those speakers 'the barest possible minimum of inexplicable error or irrationality'; it should issue in the ascription of a 'fully intelligible collection of propositional attitudes' to speakers of the language.

Given a theory satisfying these conditions, it seems clear that the interpreting sentences of our theory can be said to give truth-conditions for those sentences of the interpreted language utterances of which qualify as utterances having a truth-value. We shall have, in fact, as far as those sentences are concerned, an adequate truth-theory for the language. The mentioned qualification is intended to allow for the doubts felt by many philosophers as to whether certain utterances declarative in form, e.g. utterances of evaluative or normative sentences, really do qualify as utterances having a truth-value, are 'true or false in any serious sense of true or false'.

To this last question Wiggins returns at a later stage. Meanwhile, it seems that we should be able to pick up certain marks of truth—even though they may be marks of some other and broader property as well—from the conditions on our adequate interpretative theory. Given those conditions and given that language is, *par excellence*, 'the vehicle for the communication and expression of beliefs', it will be the *norm* for speakers of the language to utter sentences which they *believe* to have the property in question (i.e. truth, in the case of truth-valued sentences). This is the first mark of truth. Further, the conditions require that dispositions to believe should be answerable to evidence or grounds and hence that, in favourable conditions, there should be a tendency for beliefs to converge on truth. This second mark points to the third: viz. that possession or non-possession of the property is independent of the particular speaker's means of recognizing it. Possession of the property—and this is the fourth mark, which, Wiggins usefully suggests, condenses the first three and encapsulates what there is in the correspondence platitude—is in virtue of something to which there is, in principle, some measure of common access on the part of speakers and interpreters. Finally, Wiggins adds a fifth mark, viz. the possession of the property by the conjunction of any two assertions which possess it severally.

Wiggins is disposed to reject doubts about the possession of truth-values by moral or evaluative judgements. He espouses a moderate moral 'realism' or 'cognitivism' or 'objectivism'. To the objection that incompatible courses of action may seem to present themselves as equally mandatory he appears to answer that we may consistently recognize the objectivity of two irreconcilable moral *claims* or *concerns* without being obliged to say that either is *mandatory*, still less that both are. Thus conflict between moral realism and the fifth mark of truth is avoided. What of the second mark? How to reconcile moral realism with what appears to be the fact that informed and rational men can differ, at least in part, in their general moral outlook? Wiggins appears to see no difficulty here; he explicitly rejects the view that it is a consequence of cognitivism that 'in some sense everybody *should* have the same moral beliefs.' In what is confessedly an exploratory voyage it is perhaps too much to ask for a full explanation of this point. Nevertheless an explanation would have been welcome. Certainly a moral realism or cognitivism that uncensoriously accommodates some divergence of moral and evaluative standards seems more acceptable than one that does not.

More generally, the concept of truth which Wiggins endorses in section VII of his essay—anthropocentric truth or truth 'for the working day'—is the one we will do well to accept; for it consists with the species of realism to which we are naturally committed, however much we may be tempted, in some metaphysical moods or moments, to forswear it in favour either of a more austerely 'scientific' realism on the one hand or of some variety of anti-realism on the other.

Pears argues convincingly against identifying the formation of intentions with the making of judgements, whether judgements of value or factual beliefs about the future; and Searle clearly exposes some of the confusions attending the notion of prima-facie obligation. In neither case have I anything to add to, or subtract from, their arguments.

Select Bibliography

BOOKS

1952 *Introduction to Logical Theory* (Methuen, London), 266 pp. (reprinted 1964).
1959 *Individuals: An Essay in Descriptive Metaphysics* (Methuen, London), 255 pp. (reprinted 1964).
1966 *The Bounds of Sense* (Methuen, London), 296 pp.
1967 (ed.) *Philosophical Logic* (Series: Oxford Readings in Philosophy) (OUP), 177 pp.
1968 (ed.) *Studies in the Philosophy of Thought and Action* (OUP).
1971 *Logico-Linguistic Papers* (Methuen, London), 249 pp.
1974 *Freedom and Resentment and Other Essays* (Methuen, London), 214 pp.
1974 *Subject and Predicate in Logic and Grammar* (Methuen, London), viii and 144 pp.

ARTICLES

1948 'Necessary Propositions and Entailment Statements', *Mind*, 57, pp. 184–200.
1949 'Truth', *Analysis*, vol. ix, pp. 83–97.
1949 'Ethical Intuitionism', *Philosophy*, vol. xxiv, no. 88, pp. 23–33.
1950 'Truth', *Proceedings of the Aristotelian Society*, suppl. vol. xxiv (reprinted in *Logico-Linguistic Papers*).
1950 'On Referring', *Mind*, 59 (reprinted in *Logico-Linguistic Papers*).
1953 'Particular and General', *Proceedings of the Aristotelian Society* (1953/4) (reprinted in *Logico-Linguistic Papers*).
1954 'Wittgenstein's *Philosophical Investigations*', *Mind*, 63 (reprinted in *Freedom and Resentment and Other Essays*).
1954 'A Reply to Mr Sellars', *Philosophical Review*, 63, pp. 216–31.
1955 'A Logician's Landscape', *Philosophy*, vol. xxx, no. 14.
1956 'Construction and Analysis', in Ayer, A. J., et al., *The Revolution in Philosophy* (Macmillan, London), pp. 97–110.
1956 (with Grice, H. P.) 'In Defense of a Dogma', *Philosophical Review*, 65, pp. 141–58.
1956 'Singular Terms, Ontology and Identity', *Mind*, 65, pp. 433–54.

Select Bibliography

1957 'Propositions, Concepts and Logical Truths', *Philosophical Quarterly*, 7, pp. 15–25.

1957 (with Grice, H. P., and Pears, D. F.) 'Metaphysics', in Pears, D. F. (ed.), *The Nature of Metaphysics* (Macmillan, London), pp. 1–22.

1957 (Symposium with Lejewski, C.), 'Proper Names', *Proceedings of the Aristotelian Society*, suppl. vol. xxxi.

1961 'Singular Terms and Predication', *Journal of Philosophy*, 58, pp. 393–412 (reprinted in *Logico-Linguistic Papers*).

1961 'Perception and Identification', *Proceedings of the Aristotelian Society*, suppl. vol. xxxv (reprinted in *Freedom and Resentment and Other Essays*).

1961 'Social Morality and Individual Ideal', *Philosophy*, vol. xxxvi (reprinted in *Freedom and Resentment and Other Essays*).

1961 'Analysis, Science and Metaphysics', *La Philosophie Analytique* (1962) (reprinted in Rorty, R. (ed.) *The Linguistic Turn* (University of Chicago Press, Chicago, Ill.).

1961 'Philosophy: the Post-Linguistic Thaw', in *The British Imagination* (Cassell, London), pp. 168–74.

1962 'Freedom and Resentment', *Proceedings of the British Academy*, vol. xlviii (reprinted in *Freedom and Resentment and Other Essays*).

1963 'Carnap's Views on Constructed Systems vs. Natural Languages in Analytical Philosophy', in Schilpp, P. A. (ed.) (CUP and Open Court, La Salle), pp. 503–18.

1964 'A Problem about Truth: A Reply to Mr Warnock', in Pitcher, G. (ed.), *Truth* (Prentice Hall, Englewood Cliffs, N.J.) (reprinted in *Logico-Linguistic Papers*).

1964 'Identifying Reference and Truth Values', *Theoria*, vol. xxx (reprinted in *Logico-Linguistic Papers*).

1964 'Intention and Convention in Speech Acts', *Philosophical Review*, 73 (reprinted in *Logico-Linguistic Papers*).

1965 'Truth: A Reconsideration of Austin's Views', *Philosophical Quarterly*, vol. xv (reprinted in *Logico-Linguistic Papers*).

1966 'Aesthetic Appraisal and Works of Art', *Oxford Review*, 3 (reprinted in *Freedom and Resentment and Other Papers*).

1966 'Self, Mind and Body', *Common Factor*, 4 (reprinted in *Freedom and Resentment and Other Essays*).

1966 'Paradoxes, Posits and Propositions', *Philosophical Review*, 76.

1967 'Is Existence Never a Predicate?', *Ciritica*, vol. i (reprinted in *Freedom and Resentment and Other Essays*).

1968 'Bennett on Kant's Analytic', *Philosophical Review*, 77, pp. 332–9.

1969 'Body and Mind', in Mays, W., and Brown, S. C. (ed.),

Linguistic Analysis and Phenomenology (Macmillan, London, 1972), pp. 163–205 (symposium of the 'Philosophers into Europe' conference held under the joint auspices of the Royal Institute of Philosophy and the British Society for Phenomenology at the University of Southampton, September 1969).

1969 'Grammar and Philosophy', *Proceedings of the Aristotelian Society* (1969/70) (reprinted in *Logico-Linguistic Papers*).

1969 *Meaning and Truth* (Inaugural Lecture at the University of Oxford, November 1969) (OUP 1970).

1970 'The Asymmetry of Subjects and Predicates', in Kiefer, H. E., and Munitz, M. K. (ed.), *Language, Belief and Metaphysics* (vol. i of *Contemporary Philosophical Thought* (State University of New York Press)) (reprinted in *Logico-Linguistic Papers*).

1970 'Imagination and Perception', in Foster, L., and Swanson, W. (ed.), *Experience and Theory* (University of Massachusetts Press) (reprinted in *Freedom and Resentment and Other Essays*).

1970 'Categories', in Ward, O. P., and Pitcher, G. (ed.), *Ryle: A Collection of Critical Essays* (reprinted *Freedom and Resentment and Other Essays*).

1970 'Chisholm on Identity through Time', in Kiefer, H. E., and Munitz, M. K. (ed.), *Language, Belief and Metaphysics* (vol. i of *Contemporary Philosophical Thought* (State University of New York Press)) (reprinted in *Logico-Linguistic Papers*).

1970 'Phrase et Acte de Parole', *Langages*, 17.

1973 'Austin and "Locutionary Meaning"', in Berlin, I., *et al.*, *Essays on J. L. Austin* (Clarendon Press, Oxford).

1974 'On Understanding the Structure of One's Language', in *Freedom and Resentment and Other Essays*.

1974 'Causation in Perception', in *Freedom and Resentment and Other Essays*.

1974 'Positions for Quantifiers', in Munitz, M. K., and Unger, P. K. (ed.), *Semantics and Philosophy* (New York University Press).

1974 'Does Knowledge Have Foundations?', in *Conocimiento y Creencia* (Teorema, Universidad de Valencia).

1975 'Semantics, Logic and Ontology', Neue Hefte fur Philosophie, Heft 8: *Semantik und Ontologie*.

1976 'Entity and Identity', in Lewis, H. D. (ed.), *Contemporary British Philosophy*, Fourth Series (Allen and Unwin, London).

1976 'Scruton and Wright on Anti-Realism etc.', *Proceedings of the Aristotelian Society* (1976/7).

1976 'Knowledge and Truth', *Indian Philosophical Quarterly*, vol. iii, no. 3.

1979 'Universals', in *Studies in Metaphysics* (vol. iv of *Midwest Studies in Philosophy*).
1979 'May Bes and Might Have Beens', in Margalit, A. (ed.), *Meaning and Use* (Reidel; Dordrecht, Boston, and London).
1979 'Perception and its Objects', in Macdonald, G. F. (ed.), *Perception and Identity: Essays Presented to A. J. Ayer* (Macmillan, London).
1980 'Belief, Reference and Quantification', *Monist*, 62.

Index of Names

Abrams, M. H., 193f., 206, 218
Anscombe, G. E. M., 48–50, 51–3, 56f., 58, 60, 192n., 267f., 270f.
Aquinas, 184
Aristotle, 209, 213, 229
Austin, J. L., 189
Ayer, A. J., 196n., 260–4
Ayers, M. R., 100n.

Bennett, J., 82n., 98n., 112, 260, 264–6
Berkeley, 96f., 100
Berlin, Sir I., 102, 104
Boër, S. E., 149n.
Boole, 184
Bosanquet, B., 179
Brown, D. G., 17n.
Burge, T., 140n., 149ff., 159
Burnyeat, M. F., 207
Butler, Bishop, 10n.
Butler, J., 57, 58

Campbell, C. A., 17
Cantor, 203
Carnap, 81
Castaneda, H., 248n.
Cohen, L. J., 287–9, 292

Daniels, N., 98n.
Davidson, D., 17n., 120n., 121n., 160n., 195n., 196, 198, 200n., 201n., 204, 222f., 224, 225, 227, 235, 264–6
Descartes, 49, 58, 59ff., 62, 268ff., 272
Deutscher, M., 17n.
Devitt, M., 152n.
Dostoyevsky, 39
Dummett, M., 101f., 131–3, 141, 191, 193n., 195, 199n., 201ff., 210f., 218n.

Evans, G., 155n., 195n., 197n., 273–82

Fine, A., 71
Fraassen, Bas C. van, 67
Frege, 67, 140, 141, 174, 178f., 182f., 184, 187f., 190n., 193n., 194n., 195, 196f., 203, 212, 293

Geach, P., 118n., 236, 248, 285f.
Goodman, N., 187
Grandy, R., 195n., 199
Grice, H. P., 118n., 236, 248, 285f.

Hare, R. M., 222n., 224
Harman, G., 223, 230–3, 234n.
Henson, R. G., 26n.
Hintikka, J., 238, 239f., 241, 250–9
Hobart, R. E., 17, 19n., 33
Hobbes, 76
Hornsby, J., 149n.
Hospers, J., 19n., 29

Isaacson, D., 211
Ishiguro, H., 266, 271–3

James, W., 11

Kant, 25–8, 50, 58, 59, 77, 79ff., 87, 239
Katz, J. J., 140n., 153n.
Keynes, N., 179
Kolnai, A., 208n.
Kripke, S., 5, 48, 55, 63, 141, 145n., 147n., 163n.
Kuhn, 71

Leibniz, 69, 71–3
Lewis, C. I., 78n.
Lewis, D., 141, 156n.
Lewy, C., 185
Locke, 52, 72f., 99, 100n.
Locke, D., 85n.
Lotze, H., 107

Mackie, J. L., 98n., 266–71, 272

Martin, C. B., 17n.
McDowell, J., 193n., 195n., 197n., 199n., 201n., 202n., 204, 282–7
Mill, J. S., 96f., 107

Neste, V. F. van, 178n.
Nowell-Smith, P. H., 19n.
Nussbaum, M. L. C., 209n.

Pascal, 69, 233
Peacock, T. L., 11n.
Peacocke, C., 148n., 197n., 212n.
Pears, D., 296
Perry, J., 17n.
Peirce, C. S., 218f.
Platner, E., 107
Plato, 69
Platts, M. de Breton, 208n.
Poincaré, 107, 109
Putnam, H., 63, 70, 272

Quine, W. V., 67, 141, 289–92
Quinton, A. M., 98n.

Ramsey, F., 188, 193n., 204f., 212n., 217n.
Reid, T., 97, 100n.
Revesz, 108
Ricketts, T., 127n.
Ross, W. D., 238–45, 251, 252–5, 259
Russell, B., 63, 140, 163, 177

Sainsbury, M., 212n.
Schlick, M., 19–22, 24, 260
Schwayder, D., 195n.
Searle, J. R., 130, 296
Senden, von, 107n.
Shemyakin, F. N., 110n.
Skinner, 5, 264
Spinoza, 25–31, 262
Stout, G. F., 223
Strawson, P. F., 1–13, 14–47, 48, 50f., 58f., 60, 62–75, 76–116, 117–39, 140, 163, 164–73, 174–88, 189–92, 203n., 220, 238
Swinburne, R., 57, 58

Tarski, A., 122, 190n., 193, 196, 198, 200

Unger, P., 126

Vendler, Z., 48, 49, 51f., 54–7, 59f., 269, 271
Villey, P., 108f.

Wallace, J., 199n.
Wiggins, D., 148n., 294–6
Williams, B., 25f., 67f., 137n., 191f., 201, 209n., 215n., 218n.
Winch, P., 215n.
Wittgenstein, 70, 98f., 106, 132, 137n., 138n., 190n., 195n., 220n.

Yeats, W. B., 31, 39